HOWARD WILSON

"Ernest L. Boyer and his colleagues at the Carnegie Foundation for the Advancement of Teaching published essential works on higher education, and *Campus Life: In Search of Community* was certainly among them. This important report was valuable to me as a university president when it was originally published. So often I would hear from faculty, students, and staff: 'You have a problem and you must solve it.' The key, I learned, was to shift the matter to 'We have a problem and we must do something about it.' But that shift is possible only when there is a real sense of campus community, a sense of belonging on the part of everyone. This fine volume is a valuable guide in building and maintaining a campus community. The editors of this expanded edition have done an important service not only by making *Campus Life* available again but also by combining it with essays focused on Christian campuses. As David Brooks suggests in his splendid forward, leaders of all colleges and universities can gain insights on building community from those campuses, whether or not they are faith-based."

Thomas Ehrlich, president emeritus, Indiana University

"Nearly thirty years ago, Ernest Boyer issued a call for colleges and universities to be not just research and teaching centers but true learning communities. Today that need is as urgent as ever, and Christian colleges and universities are uniquely positioned to create the kind of vibrant communities that educate the soul as well as the mind. In this important volume, seasoned higher education professionals offer practical insights and examples of how such communities can thrive in today's challenging environment. This book will be valuable to readers interested in understanding what makes Christian colleges and universities so unique, as well as to educators seeking to develop such communities at their own institutions."

Rick Ostrander, vice president for research and scholarship, Council for Christian Colleges & Universities, Washington, DC

"This is a thoughtful, justice-oriented approach to thinking about some of the most difficult topics and challenges on college campuses today, as well as the obligations Christian colleges have to the world, their faculty and staff, and most of all, the students who attend them. A thorough and invaluable resource."

Donna Freitas, author of *The Happiness Effect and Sex and the Soul*

EXPANDED EDITION

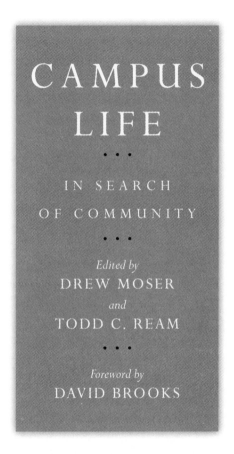

CAMPUS
LIFE

• • •

IN SEARCH
OF COMMUNITY

• • •

Edited by
DREW MOSER
and
TODD C. REAM

• • •

Foreword by
DAVID BROOKS

CARNEGIE FOUNDATION FOR THE
ADVANCEMENT OF TEACHING
with ERNEST L. BOYER

An imprint of InterVarsity Press
Downers Grove, Illinois

InterVarsity Press
P.O. Box 1400, Downers Grove, IL 60515-1426
ivpress.com
email@ivpress.com

InterVarsity Press® is the book-publishing division of InterVarsity Christian Fellowship/USA®, a movement of students and faculty active on campus at hundreds of universities, colleges, and schools of nursing in the United States of America, and a member movement of the International Fellowship of Evangelical Students. For information about local and regional activities, visit intervarsity.org.

All Scripture quotations, unless otherwise indicated, are taken from The Holy Bible, New International Version®, NIV®. Copyright © 1973, 1978, 1984, 2011 by Biblica, Inc.™ Used by permission of Zondervan. All rights reserved worldwide. www.zondervan.com. The "NIV" and "New International Version" are trademarks registered in the United States Patent and Trademark Office by Biblica, Inc.™

While any stories in this book are true, some names and identifying information may have been changed to protect the privacy of individuals.

Part Two from Campus Life *by Carnegie Foundation for the Advancement of Teaching © Wiley. Used with permission.*

The foreword, "The Cultural Value of Christian Higher Education" by David Brooks, was originally a speech at the CCCU's 40th Anniversary Gala, then published in CCCU Advance (Fall 2017). ©2017 by David Brooks. Used by permission.

Cover design: Cindy Kiple
Interior design: Daniel van Loon
Images: © Ryan Herron / E+ / Getty Images

ISBN 978-0-8308-5259-8 (print)
ISBN 978-0-8308-6523-9 (digital)

Printed in the United States of America ∞

InterVarsity Press is committed to ecological stewardship and to the conservation of natural resources in all our operations. This book was printed using sustainably sourced paper.

Library of Congress Cataloging-in-Publication Data
A catalog record for this book is available from the Library of Congress.

P	24	23	22	21	20	19	18	17	16	15	14	13	12	11	10	9	8	7	6	5	4	3	2	1
Y	39	38	37	36	35	34	33	32	31	30	29	28	27	26	25	24	23	22	21	20	19			

To the bright and hardworking

scholar-practitioners

who cultivate vibrant campus

communities all over the world,

we dedicate this work to you.

Your servant leadership is essential,

often unnoticed, and to be celebrated.

Drew Moser and Todd C. Ream

CONTENTS

PART TWO: *CAMPUS LIFE* BY THE CARNEGIE FOUNDATION FOR THE
ADVANCEMENT OF TEACHING (1990)

THE CULTURAL VALUE OF CHRISTIAN HIGHER EDUCATION

DAVID BROOKS

Whenever I'm at events, especially in a Christian community, I think about how odd it is that I got here. I grew up in Greenwich Village in the 1960s in a somewhat left-wing household. When I was five, my parents took me to a "be-in" in Central Park, which was where hippies would go just to be. One of the things they did was they set the garbage can on fire and threw their wallets into it to demonstrate their liberation from money and material things. I was five, and I saw a five-dollar bill in the fire, so I broke from the crowd, reached into it, grabbed the money, and ran away, which was my first step over to the right.

I grew up in a Jewish home but went to a church school, Grace Church School on Lower Broadway. I was part of the all-Jewish boys' choir at Grace. We were about 40 percent Jewish—it's Lower Manhattan, New York—and when we would sing the hymns, to square with our religion we wouldn't sing the word "Jesus." The volume would drop down and then it would come back up again. So that was unusual background to get here.

I've spent much of my life with secular morality. I think the most spiritual institution I would go into is Whole Foods. So it's odd, but God willed it in some way. Five years ago, I started writing a book on cognitive humility. I had a colleague at the *New York Times* named Anne Snyder who's a Wheaton grad, and she persuaded me it should be about moral and spiritual humility. The book changed a lot, and over the ensuing two years, Anne fed me so many books from her Wheaton College curriculum that I feel I deserve a Wheaton diploma by proxy. Writing the book and working in this sphere turned out to be more transformational than I could have imagined.

There are moments of writing that book, I remember, where I was expanding my knowledge of theology and God's work. I was coming to new understandings of history. There were moments when I was experiencing the lives of my characters, like Augustine's final conversation with his mom, Monica, who was the helicopter mom to beat all helicopter moms. But at the end of her life, she says to him, "You are the Christian I wanted you to be." They had a conversation of harmony after a life of conflict. They go beyond the material to the spiritual, talking about the life behind and the life to come. She's about to die and he has a word repeated over and over again: hushed. "As we spoke, the sound of the trees was hushed. The sound of the birds was hushed. The sound of the voices was hushed. The sound of our hearts was hushed." You get the sense of tranquility in falling into God's grace.

Since the book has come out, I've gone on a Christian college tour in the last couple of months. I went to chapel at Hope College. I met students at Calvin College, Union University, Whitworth University; a beautiful dinner at Gordon College; a choir performance by Nyack College students at St. Patrick's Cathedral; commencement at Westmont College; a retreat with Wheaton faculty members; and many others. I've come to love and appreciate the world of Christian colleges.

Some Christian institutions adopt an adversarial posture toward the mainstream culture, a "Benedict Option" of circling the wagons, because things seem to be going against them. From my vantage point, it's the complete opposite for Christian colleges. You guys are the avant-garde of twenty-first-century culture. You have what everybody else is desperate to have: a way of talking about and educating the human person in a way that integrates faith, emotion, and intellect. You have a recipe to nurture human beings who have a devoted heart, a courageous mind, and a purposeful soul. Almost no other set of institutions in American society has that, and everyone wants it. From my point of view, you're ahead of everybody else and have the potential to influence American culture in a way that could be magnificent. I visit many colleges a year. I teach at a great school, Yale University. These are wonderful places. My students are wonderful; I love them. But these, by and large, are not places that integrate the mind, the heart, and the spirit. These places nurture an overdeveloped self and an underdeveloped soul.

My students, as I say, are amazing. By the time they get to Yale, they've started four companies, solved three formerly fatal diseases, and majored in a lot of obscure sports. They have the ability to dominate classroom discussion while doing none of the reading. They do amazing community service. In class, they are vibrant and curious and wonderful to be around, but they've been raised in a culture that keeps them frantically busy putting out fires—the next deadline, the next test. Their friendships are never on fire, and they get neglected. Their souls are never on fire, and they get left behind. They've been raised in a culture that encourages them to pay attention to the résumé virtues of how to have a great career but leaves by the wayside long periods of time to think about the eulogy virtues: the things they'll say about you after you're dead.

They go through their school with the mixture of complete self-confidence and utter terror, afraid of a single false step off the achievement machine. Many of them are victims of conditional love. Their parents shine strong beams of love on them when they're doing what their parents approve, and the beam of love is withdrawn when they do something the parents disapprove. They have not been provided with a moral vocabulary, so the only vocabulary they have is a utilitarian one. They use economic concepts like "opportunity cost" in an attempt to understand their lives. They have not been taught words like *grace, sin, redemption,* and *virtue* that would enable them to get a handhold on what's going on inside.

They assume that the culture of expressive individualism is the eternal order of the universe and that meaning comes from being authentic to self. They have a combination of academic and career competitiveness and a lack of a moral and romantic vocabulary that has created a culture that is professional and not poetic, pragmatic and not romantic. The head is large, and the heart and soul are backstage.

Most universities have made this worse. Most universities have got out of the business of spiritual and character development, and they've adopted a research ideal. We've all benefited intellectually from this research orientation, but as Tony Kronman writes, this orientation "draws our attention away from the whole of our lives and requires that we focus on some small special aspect of it instead." It makes the idea of our lives as a whole seem less familiar and less compelling. It emphasizes instrumental reasoning over the other faculties of heart and soul. It teaches students how to do things but less why they should do them and less how to think about what is their highest and best life. To ask about the meaning of life is to appear unprofessional.

In a sense, what's happened is obscene. "Obscene," if taking that word literally, means it's something that covers over and eclipses the soul. The result of this is not shallowness, particularly. It's not decadence. It's hunger. My students are so hungry for spiritual knowledge. On book tour, I would go into rooms of CEOs or into these rooms of business conferences. These guys would be the most materialistic people you could imagine, and I'm coming in with this wahoo stuff about soul—I don't know how they're going to take this. Yet when I would start talking about this stuff, the audience locked in because they, too, are hungry. They're hungry because God made us restless until we rest in him. They are hungry because they have an unconscious boredom when they realize they have not achieved the highest level of their own fulfillment.

I think that God has given us four kinds of happiness. First, at the lowest level, material pleasure—good food, nice clothes. Second, ego and comparative happiness—winning status, being better than other people. Third, generativity—the pleasure you get from giving to others. Fourth, and the highest and the necessary kind of happiness, transcendence—an awareness of one's place in a cosmic order; a connection to a love that goes beyond the physical realm; a feeling of connection to unconditional truth, love, justice, goodness, beauty, and home. God calls us, and our nature demands, that we try to achieve level four. We're endowed with a moral imagination, and if it is not met, there's a longing; there's a loneliness; there's a hunger for life's meaning.

Many of our institutions, and especially our universities, don't do much to help our graduates achieve that transcendence. But for Christian universities and other religious institutions, this is bread and butter. This is the curriculum. This is the chapel service. This is the conversation students are having late at night. It's lived out. Now, you in this room, have the gospel. You have the example of Jesus Christ. You have the Beatitudes; the fire of the Holy Spirit; you believe in a personal God who is still redeeming the world. As Pope Francis demonstrated, when a single person acts like Jesus, the whole world is transfixed. Carrying the gospel is your central mission to your students and to those you serve beyond the campus walls, but that's not all you have. You have a way of being that is not all about self. You have a counterculture to the excessive individualism of our age. You offer an ideal more fulfilling and more true and higher than the ideal of individual autonomy.

You offer lessons in the art of commitment. When I go to Christian colleges, the students there strike me as especially adept at making commitments—sometimes too adept; they want to make all their commitments by age twenty-two. But they know how to commit, and they've been taught how to think about commitments. After I finished my book, I realized that the thing all my characters had was the capacity to make infinite commitments. All the characters in my book—some religious, some not—made a covenant. They made a promise, the kind of promise that Ruth made to Naomi: "Where you go, I will go. Where you lodge, I will lodge. Your people shall be my people and your God, my God. Where you die, I will die and there I will be buried."

For most of us, our inner nature is formed by that kind of covenant in which the good of the relationship takes place and precedence over the good of the individual. For all of us, religious or secular, life doesn't come from how well you keep your options open but how well you close them off and realize a higher freedom. Hannah Arendt wrote, "Without being bound to the fulfillment of our promises, we would never be able to keep our identities. We would be condemned to wander helplessly and without direction in the darkness of each person's lonely heart, caught in its contradictions and equivocalities."

I came to see that the fulfilled life involves four big commitments: to a spouse and the family; to a vocation; to a faith or philosophy; and to a community. Achieving levels three and four happiness requires those commitments to be solid and in good shape. We live in a society that is in conspiracy against commitment-making. My students are plagued by FOMO: Fear Of Missing Out. They don't want to close off any options. We live in a culture that puts a lot of emphasis on individual liberty and personal choice. We live in a society filled with de-commitment devices. The entire internet is commanding you to sample one thing after another. Tinder is luring students to sample one person after another. Our phones are always beckoning us to shift our attention. How do you make long commitments when you can't keep your attention on anything for more than thirty seconds?

Moreover, commitment-making is hard, especially for young people. One philosopher said it's like a vampire problem. Maybe you want to be a vampire; the problem is you don't know what it feels like to be a vampire. Vampire problems are the kinds where, when you make the decision, you're making a decision to become somebody else. It's very hard as your present self to know what it will feel like to be your future self. Getting married is a vampire decision. Your marriage will change you, but you don't know how. Having kids is certainly a vampire decision. They will change you. Going to med school is a vampire decision. Committing yourself to a faith is a vampire decision—God will change you.

It's cognitively a very hard problem, and many people are paralyzed at its face. You can't think your way through these problems. You can't do it by pure reason. In any commitment, love is at the core. A commitment is falling in love with something and then building a structure of behavior around it for those moments when the love falters. It arises at a deep sensation of certainty, a moral and spiritual sensation that something is right, that you've been called to something.

To understand a calling, to make a commitment, your mind and heart and soul have to be prepared. First, the emotions have to be educated. We're not necessarily born with wise emotions. At some level, we have to be taught what to feel, what to revere and what to love, what to detest and what to reject. We educate our emotions through having experiences and relationships. We educate them through religious practice. We educate them through culture and literature and the arts. *Middlemarch* educates the emotions about love and regret. There are symphonies that teach us about joy. There are Taylor Swift songs that teach us about sadness.

Second, we have to provide students with opportunities to fall in love with a person, a subject, an activity. This capacity for love is part of our nature, but to know what to love and to fall in love in life's busyness takes some encouragement. Love humbles you because you realize you're not in control of your own mind. You think obsessively about the person you love. It opens up the crust of life and reveals soft, tender flesh below so you enjoy more and you suffer more. It de-centers the self. You realize your core riches are not in yourself; they're in another. Love also teaches you how to endure. We've all had that first romantic passionate love, but when you educate a love, it's not reliant on that immediate, passionate first embrace. It longs and endures. It's what the philosopher Roger Scruton calls a second love. This long second love carries people through the tragedies and the blessings of life.

A commitment is about fusion. The author Louis de Bernières wrote in the book *Corelli's Mandolin* about a love that fused people together. One of his characters says, "Love itself is what is left over when being in love has burned away, and this is both an art and a fortunate accident. Your mother and I had it. We had roots that grew towards each other underground, and when all the pretty blossoms had fallen from our branches, we found that we were one tree and not two." To cultivate that facility is part of the mission for people who educate young people so they know what love is.

The second thing is to teach an appreciation of God's beauty and use beauty as a guidepost toward what is good and virtuous. Plato said in *Symposium*, "He who would proceed aright in this matter should begin in youth to visit beautiful forms." First, the outward forms, and from outward forms would become an appreciation that the beauty of the mind is higher than the beauty of the form. From that, it would become an appreciation of the beauty of laws and the beauty of existence and that he who follows the trail of beauty, Plato wrote, will come to see "a nature of wondrous beauty, a nature which in the first place is everlasting and not growing or decaying, a beauty absolute, separate, simple and everlasting, which without diminution and without increase or any change is imparted to ever growing and perishing beauties of all other things." Colleges can thrust objects of beauty before their students and hope for one in a thousand you will provoke one of those primordial experiences of wondering awe that can transform a life and point toward a vocation, a marriage, or a faith.

Third, secular colleges have got out of holding up exemplars of excellence. At Christian colleges, you have the ultimate exemplar: the life and example of Jesus. But there are other ideas to copy and to inspire, and the ideals of exemplars inflame a desire for excellence. We've ruined the word *eros*; in this culture, we associate it with sex, but for the Greeks, the word *eros* was a longing for the pure, a longing for excellence. In our culture, we don't even have a name for this longing. Dorothy Day called it loneliness. She wrote a book called *The Long Loneliness*, but she didn't mean solitude. By loneliness, she meant longing, longing for God. C. S. Lewis famously called it joy. Joy is not the fulfillment of desires. Joy is the longing itself. We've lost that vocabulary, as we've lost a lot of moral vocabulary. With it has gone some of the insufficient ideals. There was a guy named Robert Livingston in the nineteenth century who said that when people don't do good, it's often not because they're bad but they have been given an insufficient ideal. That is not true at Christian schools, but it's often true at other schools.

I've tried to express the things that help people find their commitments, find the things that make their lives valuable. Those are things like falling in love with something, being attracted aesthetically to beauty, and having this hunger for excellence. Those are all motivators. But to do a commitment through life and through decades, a commitment is not only motivated—it's disciplined. These are the other things colleges can offer their students: ways to discipline their longings.

The first thing a commitment is disciplined by is truth. Tim Keller said that truth without love is harshness, but love without truth is just sentimentality. The ability to look at something and study something honestly is a thing that has to be taught to young people. John Ruskin, the nineteenth-century art critic, said, "The more I think of it, I find this conclusion more impressed upon me, that the greatest thing a human soul ever does is to see something and tell what it saw in a plain way. Hundreds of people can talk for one who can think, but thousands can think for one who can see."

The second discipline is the deep commitment to the craft. When you undertake a craft, a doctor has to lay out the tools. The carpenter has certain practices. My practice is laying piles out on the floor as a writer. It is that craft of organizing the structure of a column or a book that is the discipline that keeps my life in structure and order. Of course, all religions have disciplines.

The final thing that discipline loves is community. None of us is capable of acting out our commitments alone. We all depend on redemptive assistance from outside. We're all uplifted by contact. We're all reinforced by the norms of the people we know and admire. We're all purified by the service to those around us. I have a friend named Rod Dreher who had a sister who lived in little town in northern Louisiana. She loved her town, and she was one of those people who touched lives. The town had maybe six hundred people in it, but when she died of cancer in her early forties, twelve hundred people showed up at the funeral. She had a practice in her life as part of her commitment to her community of going around on Christmas Eve and going to the one town cemetery. On each gravestone, she would place a lit candle. She died just before Christmas, and Rod was home with his family. He asked his mom on Christmas Eve, "Should we go out and place the candles on the gravestones?" His mom said, "You know, in some future year, I'll do it, but right now, with her death so fresh, it's just too much. I just can't do it." They were driving to another family gathering on Christmas Eve, and they drove by the cemetery; somebody else had placed a candle on every gravestone in her honor. That's community reinforcing community and disciplining the commitment to each other.

What I've tried to describe is this task of helping young people build the commitments, the foundations of their lives. A lot of the schools I go to do a great job at many other things, but integrating the faith, the spirit, the heart, and the soul with the mind is not one of them. When I go to Christian colleges, that's exactly what I see. That is the gift your institutions offer the wider culture. That gift is a gateway drug to the gift of the Almighty.

I'll close by reading one of my favorite prayers from one of my characters in my book, St. Augustine, his famous and beautiful prayer, "What Do I Love When I Love My God?"

> It is not physical beauty, nor temporal glory, nor the brightness of light so dear to earthly eyes, nor the sweet melodies of all kinds of songs, nor the gentle odor of flowers or ointments or perfumes, nor manna, nor honey, nor limbs welcoming the embraces of the flesh. It is not these things I love when I love my God. Yet there is a light I love, and a food, and a kind of embrace when I love my God. A light, voice, odor, food, embrace of my innerness, where my soul is floodlit by light which space cannot contain, where there is sound that time cannot seize, where there is perfume which no breeze disperses, where there is a taste for food no amount of eating can satisfy, where there is a bond of union that no satiety can part. That is what I love, when I love my God.

That is the highest ideal. Everyone, religious or not, is on a road to a holy place. You guys have the language. The rest of the world needs it. I hope you'll be out in the world leading the way.

A NOTE TO READERS

We designed this updated and expanded edition of *Campus Life* to be read in at least two contexts. First, we are hopeful this book can meet the needs of individuals interested in what they can contribute to the fabric of the communities they serve. However, by virtue of the nature of the topic and how we believe this book can be of greatest use, we have added several components that will allow this book to serve groups of campus leaders. Regardless, readers are encouraged to consider following an eight-step or eight-week reading plan. As a result, the way to do so is to proceed by reading the front matter for parts one and two, chapter one for parts one and two, and so on. For reading groups of campus leaders, we also provided a discussion guide designed to be used in relation to each one of those sections. Regardless of how one chooses to read this book, we hope what is offered is a window into both the timeless and timely qualities of the original and updated editions of *Campus Life*.

EDITORS'
ACKNOWLEDGMENTS

In more ways than we can count, this book is an expression of collective wisdom. That wisdom began thirty years ago when, under the leadership of Ernest L. Boyer, the Carnegie Foundation for the Advancement of Teaching published the original edition of this report. As detailed in the introduction, the genesis of that effort was the perception that some unique challenges were plaguing the fabric of the campus communities constituting American academe. To the credit of the authors of that original report, they generated a document that was both timely and, as we argue, timeless. We thus begin by offering our thanks to the Carnegie Foundation for its permission to republish the original edition of the report and, in turn, demonstrate those timeless qualities.

A slightly modified version of the insightful address David Brooks offered at the gala held in Washington, DC, on January 27, 2016, honoring the Council for Christian Colleges and Universities' fortieth anniversary serves as the foreword. We are thus both grateful to David and to the Council for Christian Colleges and Universities for permission to include it in this volume.

Much of the work included in the expanded edition of this volume was contributed by pairs of authors who serve as chief academic and chief student development officers at George Fox University, John Brown University, Messiah College, Vanguard University, Westmont College, and Wheaton College. They were selected by virtue of their own reputations as scholar-practitioners as well as the reputations their campuses have gained in relation to the qualities discussed in their respective contributions. After working in pairs for several months, initial drafts of their chapters were offered at the Council for Christian Colleges and Universities International Forum in Dallas, Texas (January 31–February 2, 2018). We are indeed grateful for their efforts and for their willingness to share their wisdom.

In many ways, Beck A. Taylor and his colleagues at Whitworth University have emerged as leaders in conversations concerning campus community. In particular, those efforts are reflected in the 2018 President's Colloquy on Civil Discourse. The events making up that colloquy can be viewed at the Whitworth University website.[1] Those efforts also garnered the attention of media outlets such as the *Chronicle of Higher Education*, whose interview with Beck can be viewed online.[2] We are grateful to Beck for his willingness to share the wisdom he learned through those efforts as the epilogue.

At Taylor University, we owe a considerable debt of gratitude to Kayla (Springer) Hunter, who recently graduated from the master of arts in higher education program and kept us organized in relation to this project in more ways than we can count. We are also blessed to serve as faculty members in that program. Students such as Kayla serve as tangible points of hope to us about the future of higher education. Colleagues such as Steve Bedi, Scott Gaier, Tim Herrmann, Heather Sandlin, Skip Trudeau, and Kelly Yordy support projects such as this one and care enough to help us refine our thinking about such critical topics.

We are truly grateful for the love and support our respective families offer. Our wives, Bekah Moser and Sara Ream, offer us more love than we can repay, but we are blessed with lifetimes to try. All too often, the work scholars conduct seems disconnected from the direct needs of their families. However, we are hopeful that the wisdom found in these pages contributes to the fabric of community our own children (Benjamin, Eloisa, Samuel, Stella, and William Moser / Addison and Ashley Ream) will find when they go to college.

Drew Moser and Todd C. Ream
Tenth Week in Ordinary Time 2018

---

[1] Beck A. Taylor, "President's Colloquy on Civil Discourse," Whitworth University, October 19, 2017, www.whitworth.edu/cms/administration/president-beck-a-taylor/colloquy-on-civil-discourse.

[2] Beck A. Taylor, interview by Eric Kelderman, "A Faith-Based Institution Invites Civil Discourse," *Chronicle of Higher Education*, February 9, 2018, www.chronicle.com/article/A-Faith-Based-Institution/242515.

PART ONE

• • •

CAMPUS LIFE

• • •

A RECURRING CHALLENGE OR OPPORTUNITY?

IN SEARCH OF RENEWAL (AGAIN)

DREW MOSER AND TODD C. REAM

In our current climate, it is difficult to imagine a public intellectual who transcends partisanship and polarization.[1] The names that come to mind tend to fall firmly into ideological camps, their popularity fueled by both support and disdain. In the 1980s and 1990s, Ernest L. Boyer (1928–1995) was a public intellectual on all matters of education, and was widely appreciated for his accessible wisdom and rhetorical flair. Democrats and Republicans, religious and nonreligious, all looked to him for guidance on the educational challenges of their day.

As a result, Boyer became a household name. His rise to prominence from chancellor of the State University of New York system (SUNY), to US Commissioner of Education under President Carter, to president of the Carnegie Foundation, is well known. In his latter and most popular role, Boyer led the production of an impressive slate of monumental reports on education, including *A Quest for Common Learning: The Aims of General Education;*[2] *High School: A Report on Secondary Education in America;*[3] *College: The Undergraduate Experience in America;*[4] *Campus Life: In Search of Community;*[5] *Scholarship Reconsidered: Priorities of the*

---

[1] This prologue is partially adapted from Drew Moser, "Ernest L. Boyer and the American Christian College: Historical Considerations," *Christian Higher Education* 13, no. 1 (2014): 29-42, www.tandf online.com/doi/abs/10.1080/15363759.2014.856650.

[2] Ernest L. Boyer and Arthur Levine, *A Quest for Common Learning: The Aims of General Education* (Princeton, NJ: Carnegie Foundation for the Advancement of Teaching, 1990).

[3] Ernest L. Boyer, *High School: A Report on Secondary Education in America* (New York: Harper & Row, 1985).

[4] Ernest L. Boyer, *College: The Undergraduate Experience in America* (Princeton, NJ: Carnegie Foundation for the Advancement of Teaching, 2009).

[5] The Carnegie Foundation for the Advancement of Teaching, *Campus Life: In Search of Community*, foreword by Ernest L. Boyer (San Francisco: Jossey-Bass, 1997).

Professoriate;[6] *Ready to Learn: A Mandate for the Nation;*[7] and *The Basic School: A Community of Learning.*[8]

Those that know the name Ernest Boyer are familiar with these roles and reports. What is lesser known is *why* and *how* he rose to prominence. To put it simply (but not simplistically), Boyer's formative experiences in Christian higher education shaped him into the effective educational leader of his day.

A CHRISTIAN COLLEGE BEGINNING

Before Boyer rose to national and international prominence, he first served as a student and then eventually as a faculty member and administrator with several Christian colleges. Born to industrious, successful business owners in Dayton, Ohio, Boyer observed the value of hard work and lifelong learning.[9] His greatest influence, his Grandfather William Boyer, was the founder and director of a Brethren in Christ–affiliated mission located in the heart of Dayton, Ohio.[10] The Reverend William Boyer ran the mission for over thirty years. The Dayton mission became young Ernest's second home. Together, his father's success and his grandfather's faithful service compelled Ernest to pursue excellence and service throughout his life.

He finished high school and received his two-year degree at Brethren in Christ Messiah College (1948), where he met his wife Kathryn (Kay) Tyson. He then attended Greenville College (IL), a Free Methodist institution. There he received his BA in 1950. After brief stints pastoring in Orlando, Florida, and pursuing graduate studies at Ohio State University, Boyer received a call from John Z. Martin, a senior administrator of the fledgling Brethren in Christ–affiliated Upland College in California.[11] Martin offered him a full-time salary to teach half-time at Upland College and pursue his PhD in audiology at the University of Southern California (USC). Upland College would also cover his tuition. Upon earning a PhD, he would become the school's academic dean.

---

[6]Ernest L. Boyer, *Scholarship Reconsidered: Priorities of the Professoriate* (San Francisco: Jossey-Bass, 1990).

[7]Ernest L. Boyer, *Ready to Learn: A Mandate for the Nation* (Princeton, NJ: Carnegie Foundation for the Advancement of Teaching, 1994).

[8]Ernest L. Boyer, *The Basic School: A Community for Learning* (Princeton, NJ: Carnegie Foundation for the Advancement of Teaching, 1995).

[9]Kay Boyer, interview by Richard Bonnabeau, 2003, Ernest L. Boyer Center archives, Box T02, Folder 02, Messiah College, Mechanicsburg, PA.

[10]Ernest L. Boyer, University of Utah commencement address, 1993, Ernest L. Boyer Center archives, Messiah College, Mechanicsburg, PA.

[11]John Z. Martin, interview by Merle Brubacher, 2004, Ernest L. Boyer Center archives, Messiah College, Mechanicsburg, PA.

Boyer was passionate about educating Upland's student body in terms of their sense of civic duty, devoting many chapel messages to inform them of current events and their responsibility to engage them. He created and coached a college debate team, passing on skills from his own experience at Greenville College.[12] He created the nation's first 4-1-4 academic calendar in 1953, devoting the first interterm to the subject of US-Soviet relations.

Nearing graduation from USC, he met with his faculty advisor, W. Charles Redding, to discuss next steps. Boyer proudly revealed he planned to continue to work for Upland College to help them achieve accreditation. Boyer's advisor looked sternly at him and threatened to withhold the degree should he follow through with this plan. Proudly he boasted, "Our Ph.D.'s go to bigger jobs."[13] Boyer was distraught. He deeply valued the work of Upland College, and had no interest in landing one of his advisor's "real jobs." Boyer reluctantly took an adjunct position at Long Beach State teaching night classes to appease his advisor and keep his day job. He was still awarded his PhD in 1957.[14] Boyer's leadership was successful, as Upland College eventually received accreditation from the Western College Association. Boyer and Martin, eager to replicate their accreditation success, were then instrumental in the founding of the Council for the Advancement of Small Colleges (CASC), a group that helped small colleges navigate through the accreditation process. As a result of the CASC's efforts, ninety small colleges received accreditation, including Boyer's alma mater, Messiah College.

Boyer's work in lobbying accrediting bodies on the merits of small-college higher education planted seeds for his landmark views on scholarship. Boyer's most popular and influential work, *Scholarship Reconsidered*,[15] was largely formed due to his experiences in helping Christian colleges gain accreditation. Time after time, he pleaded the case of Christian college to accreditors. He coached Christian presidents in how to communicate the unique aspects of their institutions. In so doing, he found that there was value in the things Christian colleges did that did not fall into traditional metrics.

Despite Boyer's good work to cultivate a vibrant, quality academic community at Upland, the college was going bankrupt, and it became clear in the early 1960s

---

[12]William and Anna Haldeman, interview by Merle Brubacher, 2004, Box T02, Folder 01, Ernest L. Boyer Center archives, Messiah College, Mechanicsburg, PA.

[13]Martin, interview.

[14]Martin, interview.

[15]Boyer, *Scholarship Reconsidered*.

that the college needed to close.[16] Boyer helped the school through negotiations to send the college library and its seal to Fresno Pacific University. Messiah College would then absorb Upland's remaining debt and officially become recognized as its merging partner in 1964.[17]

Much later in his career, when Boyer was president of the Carnegie Foundation for the Advancement of Teaching, he sought to translate his small-college experience to the broader educational community. He challenged the publish-or-perish focus of the academy, arguing that it was pursued at teaching's expense, neglecting students. This conviction led Boyer and the Carnegie Foundation to publish arguably two of the most important reports during his tenure: *Scholarship Reconsidered: Priorities of the Professoriate*,[18] and the very report you now hold in your hands. He announced the pending release of these reports to a gathering of the American Association of Independent Colleges and Universities in February of 1990. This group was largely inspired from Boyer's own work thirty years prior to his cofounding of the Council for the Advancement of Small Colleges. His experience in championing the benefits of the small-college experience was now coming to fruition, over thirty years later.

In this audience, Boyer knew he was among friends, friends who valued teaching and pursued the development of college students beyond the classroom. Boyer was very excited about the release of both reports, hoping they would help higher education return to where the small, independent colleges had been all along. To this audience, he said, "Your agenda is being legitimized because, I believe, it is absolutely right."[19] It was an affirmation that independent colleges (of which Christian institutions formed a significant part) were the exemplars of the very type of vibrant learning community and broadened, engaged scholarship that Boyer proposed.

In addition to his foundational work in the development of the American Association of Independent Colleges and Universities, his work in cofounding the CASC also influenced the founding of the Council for Christian Colleges and Universities (CCCU).[20]

---

[16]Ernest L. Boyer. Statement about Upland College, 1975, Ernest L. Boyer Center archives, Messiah College, Mechanicsburg, PA; Ray Musser and Fern Musser, interview by Merle Brubacher, 2004, Box T02, Folder 01, Ernest L. Boyer Center archives, Messiah College, Mechanicsburg, PA.

[17]Musser and Musser, interview.

[18] Boyer, *Scholarship Reconsidered*.

[19]Ernest L. Boyer, "Campus Life: In Search of Community" (speech, American Association of Independent Colleges and Universities meeting, February 1990); Ernest L. Boyer Center archives, Messiah College, Mechanicsburg, PA, 8.

[20]"CCCU History," CCCU, www.cccu.org/about/history (accessed July 6, 2013).

CAMPUS LIFE: A REPORT WITH SOUL

In March 1990, the Carnegie Foundation, in cooperation with the American Council on Education (ACE), released *Campus Life: In Search of Community*. The study surveyed five hundred presidents all over the country, along with hundreds of other administrators, faculty, and students. The overall conclusion was generally optimistic: "Campuses are well managed, and we've built in the United States a system of higher learning that's the envy of the world."[21] Yet the campus was not without perils. Student apathy, alcohol abuse, racial tension, and incivility were causes for concern. Boyer felt they were a reflection of the society at large. In the *Campus Life* report, he praised student personnel professionals (now widely referred to as student affairs professionals) for their superb response to the crises besetting the college campus. He also felt concern for these professionals, believing they were asked to carry too much of the responsibility for these issues.

Boyer introduced the results of the *Campus Life* report to the annual gathering of the National Association of Student Personnel Administrators (NASPA) in March 1990.[22] Rather than simply trying to curb bad behavior on college campuses, Boyer cast a larger vision, outlining six principles that captured the essence of higher education. His goal was to provide a framework for the development of a community of learning.

First, Boyer argued that a college campus was a purposeful community, where faculty and students work together. To Boyer, such a community was one where the academic and the cocurricular are integrated: "I'm convinced that the academic and nonacademic cannot be divided and if students do not become intellectually engaged—if they do not take seriously the educational mission of the institution, then all talk about community will be simply a diversion."[23] He encouraged both faculty and student personnel professionals to be viewed as teachers, common educators for a common cause.

Second, Boyer argued that the college campus is a just community, where dignity is affirmed and equality is pursued. Boyer firmly believed that America's colleges could be a shining example to the country of how to bridge what he felt was a widening gap between rich and poor. Third, the college is an open community, where freedom of thought and expression is protected. On this point Boyer reveled in the power of language to exchange ideas. He referred to it as a

---

[21]Boyer, "Campus Life," 1.
[22]Boyer, "Campus Life."
[23]Boyer, "Campus Life," 3.

"sacred trust."[24] Fourth, the college campus was a disciplined community, where governance promotes and protects the common good. Boyer, in spite of his conservative Brethren upbringing, advocated for a more open and inclusive campus. However, he strongly argued that all colleges follow the likes of his alma maters Messiah and Greenville and have some sort of clear code of conduct developed by the campus community. Fifth, the college is a caring community, where members are supported and service is embraced. Boyer felt that a college committed to service would allow students the valuable opportunity for engagement across the generations. Finally, the college campus is a celebrative community. Tradition and heritage are remembered. He quipped that a "community of learning must be held together by something more than a common grievance over parking."[25]

Boyer sent a copy of the report his friend and colleague John W. Gardner, who was then the Mirian and Peter Hass Centennial Professor in Public Service at Stanford University. Gardner then wrote a letter thanking him for the gift and praising the report: "Not only does it cover all aspects of the subject with clarity and wisdom, but it is a wonderfully humane report. It has soul, which is in such short supply these days that I suspect you of having access to some secret source."[26] A reading of the *Campus Life* report does indeed reveal a soul.

THE SEARCH FOR RENEWAL (AGAIN)

Nearly thirty years since the release of *Campus Life*, Christian higher education stands at a critical point in its history. Many institutions face declining enrollments, escalating discount rates, fractured faculties, rises in the mental health needs of student bodies, and ideological clashes over theology, politics, and culture. These colleges and universities, once considered bastions of evangelicalism, are emerging as battlegrounds in a new chapter of the long-standing culture wars, a tension that proved particularly palpable during the 2016 US presidential election.

An unfortunate casualty of such tumult is the peaceful campus life many institutions took for granted. Racial tensions, financial troubles, and theological diversity now continue to threaten the social fabric of these historically small, tight-knit institutions. For such a time, leaders of Christian colleges and universities must reflect on what led their institutions to this precipice and, in turn, cast a new vision for campus life.

---

[24]Boyer, "Campus Life," 8.
[25]Boyer, "Campus Life," 13.
[26]John W. Gardner, letter to Ernest Boyer, August 27, 1990, Ernest L. Boyer Center archives, Messiah College, Mechanicsburg, PA.

In many ways, Boyer devoted his career to translating the formative power of Christian higher education to a wider audience. The concepts championed by Boyer and his associates in *Campus Life*, coupled with the many challenges facing today's campuses, present an opportunity to reconsider and translate those concepts to current and future generations of leaders in Christian higher education.

The communal fabric that long defined Christian colleges and universities is fraying. While many of the virtues once woven into that fabric are timeless and worthy of reinvestment in the present context, some scholars rightfully contend that a number of topics were precluded from taking their place among ones deemed acceptable.

For example, Stanley Hauerwas argued that many Christians allowed the vice of sentimentality to parade as a virtue to the point of precluding conversations to take place that, while needing to be part public discourse, were deemed inadmissible.[27] Underlying that compulsion is the belief that a veneer of niceness is preferable to the discord that may ensue when people engage in conversations in which they may at least initially disagree. As a result, conversations concerning various threads of human identity such as gender, same-sex attraction, and, more recently, transgenderism were not granted the space needed to take their place among other topics deemed more acceptable for discussion.

In contrast, the editors for and contributors to this volume believe a theologically well-woven fabric of community not only withstands but also rightfully frames conversations needing to be addressed as part of the larger process of Christian discipleship. Today's students are not immune to at least an awareness of challenging topics. If anything, social media platforms alone expose them to such ideas in a myriad of ways, ranging from the productive to the unproductive. Christian educators thus have no choice but to wade into any number of substantive topics regardless of how contentious the ensuing conversations might become.

Instead of viewing this challenge as a point of peril, the editors for and contributors to this volume believe this challenge is an opportunity. Undergirding this sense of hope is the belief that well-framed and disciplined discourse is not only how ideas are refined but is also what academe is implicitly called to model for students and society as a whole.

In addition, undergirding this sense of hope is the belief that no topic, regardless of how difficult it may be, is beyond what prayerfully practiced

---

[27]Stanley Hauerwas, "Christianity: It's Not a Religion, It's an Adventure," in *The Hauerwas Reader*, ed. John Berkman and Michael G. Cartwright (Durham, NC: Duke University Press, 2001), 522-35.

theological exploration can handle. The question is thus not whether a topic is controversial but whether it is substantive and thus worthy of consideration. Admittedly, some topics are not worthy of consideration and are simply futile exercises of frivolity. On the other hand, controversy is neither to be avoided nor, by default, embraced. The question needing to be determined is whether the issue at hand is important to the church as it seeks to fulfill its mission to be Christ's body to a world in need and form disciples to carry out that work.

Furthermore, collaborative, generative conversations among curricular and cocurricular leaders are essential to the health of college and university campuses. The editors for and contributors to this volume also believe the fabric that defines campus life more closely approaches an optimal quality when efforts made by educators in the curricular and cocurricular realms are integrated as much as possible. While colleges and universities bureaucratically organized themselves into such categories (and even a seemingly infinite array of other subcategories), few if any of life's most pressing questions can be addressed by resources found within, for example, an academic departments or even the curricular realm as a whole.

Ernest T. Pascarella and Patrick T. Terenzini also repeatedly demonstrated that student learning occurs at higher levels when curricular and cocurricular programs are integrated versus existing in organizational silos.[28] As a result, the introductory chapters to the expanded edition of *Campus Life* were contributed by chief student development and chief academic officers who worked together not only as coauthors but also as partners working on their respective campuses to integrate the cocurricular and curricular programs they lead.

Campus Life also serves as a model for how such conversations and the communities in which they took place were once framed. Some of the qualities that define that model are timeless and thus need to be reintroduced to this generation. Other qualities and in particular the larger context in which those qualities find themselves, are in need of translation. The editors of and contributors to this volume believe such a process is a worthy starting point as they want not only to preserve what is best about the Christian campus but also to help it create disciplined and theologically well-framed spaces for conversations that need to take place.

---

[28]Ernest T. Pascarella and Patrick T. Terenzini, *How College Affects Students: Findings and Insights from Twenty Years of Research* (San Francisco: Jossey-Bass, 1991); and Ernest T. Pascarella and Patrick T. Terenzini, *How College Affects Students: A Third Decade of Research* (San Francisco: Jossey-Bass, 2005).

THIS VOLUME

In particular, this volume includes the original content of *Campus Life* in a new, expanded edition. Preceding the original text are contributions from those curricular and cocurricular leaders who, in pairs, respectively offer an introduction to each one of the original report's chapters. In other words, chief academic officers and the chief student development officers from the same campuses work together to translate these timeless qualities found in *Campus Life* to the realities facing our campuses today.

The essays in this collection thus offer a context in which readers can reflect on the past while also thinking critically about the prospects for the future of campus life at evangelical institutions of higher learning. This expanded edition equips higher education leaders to explore questions such as the following:

> How can the curricular and cocurricular realms of institutions work more effectively together to foster a learning environment that develops whole people?

> How can Christian campuses serve as laboratories for justice?

> Amid the current cultural climate, how can Christian college and university campuses embody convicted civility?

> How can Christian campuses model forms of community that seek individual flourishing and the common good?

> What is an appropriate and biblical ethic of care toward today's students and faculty?

> How does one honor campus traditions while also embracing change?

Part one of what follows includes those six introductory chapters written by pairs of chief student development and chief academic officers. Each chapter unpacks the timeless nature of a theme included in the original edition by Boyer and his associates followed by an effort to translate the relevance of that theme to the present set of realities. Part two includes the full version of the original edition of *Campus Life*. The text from the original edition has been typeset to match the rest of the volume, but it has not been altered in any other way. A discussion guide is then included at the end of this expanded edition of *Campus Life*. The purpose of that guide is to facilitate conversations among audience members who work through the expanded edition together as members of reading groups.

As a whole, what is offered in these pages, however, is not an equation for community. In contrast, what is offered is a series of frameworks through which members of particular campus communities can think through what makes the life they share unique. One of the greatest strengths of the American higher education system is its diversity of institutional offerings. As is hopefully indicated in these pages, one of the most significant components of that diversity involves the way various Christian traditions have invested in the education of the next generation. As a result, community should look different at a historically Quaker institution such as George Fox University in comparison to a historically Anabaptist institution such as Messiah College.

By thinking with our fellow Christian brethren about how they live together, we hope that the fabric of each campus and the church will be strengthened. This side of eternity, no one community can capture all of what it means to live in divine inspired fellowship. By learning from one another, we can catch glimpses that sustain our common calling as members of Christ's body.

PART ONE

. . .

CHAPTER ONE

A PURPOSEFUL COMMUNITY

MARK L. SARGENT AND EDEE SCHULZE

For nearly three weeks the smoke had drifted from the east, rising out of Los Padres National Forest and the grasslands and homes of Ventura County. The Thomas Fire had ignited some forty miles away from our campus in Montecito, and had steadily been consuming the backwoods even as it stretched toward the sea, well on the way to becoming the largest wildfire in California history. By the middle of December 2017, Christmas décor on the streets of Montecito and Santa Barbara was coated with ash. The sun hid behind opaque skies. Pedestrians, far fewer than normal, were wearing masks.

By then, we had already sent students home. Literally hours before the start of finals, we quickly asked faculty to improvise and offer exams remotely. At that time, our primary concern was the impure air and our students' health, not the threat of the flames. Many faculty and staff remembered the Montecito Tea Fire of 2008, a sudden flare-up that rode sundowner winds onto the campus and claimed several buildings and fifteen faculty homes. However, at this moment few of us feared the Thomas Fire would spread as far as Westmont.

But all that changed suddenly one morning nearly a week later, as the winds turned erratic, and the flames jumped the fire line on the Santa Ynez foothills and descended the slopes toward the college. As several of us gathered in a downtown office, we watched the televised images of oaks, eucalyptus, and chaparral engulfed by flames less than a mile above campus. Through our second-story window, we could actually witness the frontline of the wildfire as it raced westward across the hills, flying up ridges and filling the canyons in a matter of seconds. The foliage of the previous spring, such splendor after nearly five years of drought, had become fuel. Fortunately, the winds shifted, the flames reached former burn scars, and the firefighters eventually gained the upper hand. By the end of the day, our prayers for the preservation of the college had turned to prayers of gratitude.

For much of our lives, as we have worked on Christian college campuses, both of us have thought extensively about the purposes of Christian higher education. But in those hours of vulnerability during the fire we actually found new joy in being part of a purposeful community. It came in the urgency of the hour, as we adjusted plans, faced new risks, and spent prayerful moments together. In the future, when we look back at these uncertain days, we may well remember them as occasions when we felt the greatest commitment to the promise of the institution.

Writing after many hard months of ministry in Corinth, the apostle Paul reminded the Romans "that in all things God works for the good of those who love him, who have been called according to his purpose" (Rom 8:28 NIV). That certainly reassures us that good can come from hardship, even threats to our campus. It also affirms that God's purposes are larger than our aspirations, and a purposeful community originates as much in our love for God as in our own calculations. "Many are the plans in a person's heart," the proverb states, "but it is the LORD's purpose that prevails" (Prov 19:21 NIV). A purposeful community needs plans and strategies to set a course, but also the humility to recognize that blueprints, efficiencies, and achievements may be less vital than receptive hearts.

In that respect, we appreciate the notes of collegiality and empathy in Boyer and his collaborators' definition of a purposeful community. Reflecting on their thoughts, we posit such a community has an institutional mission statement that is widely known and shared and is fulfilled collaboratively as a communal activity so all students have access and can achieve their goals.

AN INSTITUTIONAL MISSION STATEMENT
THAT IS WIDELY KNOWN AND SHARED

All told, Christian colleges have done well at crafting mission statements that convey the desire to nurture hearts and minds to contribute to the building of God's kingdom. Quite frequently, when accrediting bodies visit Christian campuses, review teams salute the communities' embrace of their mission statements. At their best, these statements become fundamental drivers of the colleges' planning, and the most eloquent statements offer language that infuses other core documents and practices. Far from simply a bureaucratic obligation or a pragmatic guide, mission statements frequently offer a poetic center.

There are, though, plenty of challenges in using the mission statements as compasses for institutional purposes. Among Christian colleges, most of the statements are sufficiently generic that they do not always differentiate one institution from another. Many colleges could easily swap statements without changing character. Furthermore, budget pressures and the shifting terrain of higher education led many institutions to alter their educational priorities, and at times the new and emerging institution strides less securely within the lanes of the historic mission. The ideals of the liberal arts, still invoked in many mission statements, become hazier as schools move rapidly toward applied programs, even as swelling enrollments, online options, and off-campus sites stretch long-held convictions about community and pedagogy.

Many of these changes, of course, have revitalized colleges, expanded horizons, reached new learners, and renewed faculty. However, most evolving institutions still have work to do to ensure innovations are linked to a shared understanding of mission. It is not merely a matter of justifying new ventures with references to the most elegant or generic themes in the mission statement. That is done often—and easily. It is more difficult to link innovation to the purposeful community. The cultural strands that bind an institution—the traditions of shared governance, familiar roles and responsibilities, curricular and cocurricular partnerships, and commonly prized customs and ceremonies—can fray easily with sudden change. Rapid transformation, fueled by a sense of urgency, can also empower innovators in the midst of greater autonomy, and sometimes less accountability. To sustain a purposeful community, institutional leaders are wise not merely to justify changes by citing mission and necessity, but also to devote the time to finding the language and the practices that preserve and evoke the best of the past.

At Westmont, we have tried to cultivate within faculty members, administrators, and staff members an appreciation for our heritage. The president and other executives host the Westmont Institute for all new staff members, a multi-week seminar on the heritage, mission, purpose, and ethos. A two-year seminar for new faculty, known as Wayfinding, not only covers the familiar topics related to launching an academic career, but also pays considerable attention to defining how current strategic objectives reveal nuances in the five planks of the college's mission.[1] As a strongly traditional, undergraduate, and residential liberal arts college, Westmont fully recognizes the increasing uniqueness of our model as well as the swelling pressures for adaptation in our current landscape. However,

---

[1]The five planks of Westmont are embedded in the mission statement (identified in italics): "Westmont College is an *undergraduate, residential, Christian, liberal arts* community serving God's kingdom by cultivating thoughtful scholars, grateful servants and faithful leaders for *global* engagement with the academy, church and world."

we understand that our conversation about innovation must be rooted in a vision of the liberal arts as an incubator for creativity, not as a threat to a static and revered curricula.

The notion that a mission statement can blend tradition and innovation came up repeatedly during our planning for our newest facility at Westmont—the residence hall and conference center known as the Global Leadership Center. Westmont's mission statement is encapsulated in several key words or planks, two of which are global and residential. Accordingly, during our planning for the building, it was essential to describe what new dimensions the facility would bring to the global and residential planks. How would the center help us cultivate a new four-year residency plan? How would it enable students returning from study abroad (more than half of Westmont students spend a semester off campus) come together in a synthesizing, shared, and transitional senior year that harvested their rich overseas experience for the community and launched new hopes and plans for global citizenship after college?

FULFILLED COLLABORATIVELY AS A COMMUNAL ACTIVITY

Mission statements provide institutions purpose as long as the college can sustain the balance of coherence, community, and liberty. This balance is extraordinarily difficult to maintain, but it is also where many of the healthiest institutions thrive. As citizens of the academic world, we desire to grant scholars the freedom to critique, speculate, and debate without reprisal, even as we expect that scholarly discourse will lead to a multidisciplinary and selfless search for truth rather than simply personal license and autonomy. We want to contribute to the robust search for truth and meaning in the academy and public life, even as we value our faith commitments as a source of coherence. A discourse that clarifies and refines purpose can be ennobling even in the midst of disagreements; a discourse that disregards institutional mission and purpose in the name of personal prerogatives can be dissembling.

How does an institution sustain this balance of coherence, community, and liberty? Above all, it requires breaking down some of the silos in academe that lead to fragmentation. Academic and student life professionals need the discipline to collaborate regularly and candidly. Both of us meet weekly to discuss potentials for new collaboration and the risks of protecting turf. We try to find opportunities—such as in faculty meetings—where student life professionals can be showcased as scholars of undergraduate culture and student behavior and values, even as the student life professionals regularly celebrate faculty members' contributions to the students' emotional and spiritual needs. One of our recent endeavors has been to build much stronger ties between academic advising and the well-established Student Care Team in the student life division so that we can build retention strategies that intervene wisely and appropriately in the lives of students at risk.

The partnership between the curricular and cocurricular divisions of the college is more essential now to institutional purpose because new professional pressures can draw us into separate spheres. Student life divisions have changed dramatically in the last thirty years: more services are provided; more regulations emerged; parental engagement is more frequent; and greater attention is now required for students' needs, not the least of which is centered on the emotions and mental health. In addition, specialization and demands for scholarly production tempt the faculty to embrace isolation.

So often these pressures reshape our communities steadily without sufficient conversation. As the old saying goes, vision leaks, especially under steady, accelerating, and decentralized change. At Westmont, which has the benefits of being a small community, we have endeavored to do all we can to preserve the weekly Faculty Forum—a subsidized lunch and scholarly exchange for professors and student life professionals—as part of the communal glue. During a recent visit to campus, James K. A. Smith noted that the Faculty Forum tradition embodied one of the educational liturgical practices he writes and speaks about when he urges academics to blend inquiry, worship, and moral development.

As greater doubts emerge within the public and in some political quarters about the relevance and value of a college degree, we have greater obligations to make the case that a coherent, interdisciplinary education matters. Nurturing students' sense of vocation and helping them launch well into further study or careers have become increasingly important to us at Westmont, largely to help assure our students and families that a liberal arts education can show a return on investment. We do value the importance of helping students embrace their liberty to think and aspire for themselves.

At the same time, virtually any significant cultural or professional challenge in the coming generation is going to require interdisciplinary solutions. Any serious discourse about the challenges of immigration, for instance, needs the wisdom of the economist, the sociologist, and the ethicist, to name just a few. A purposeful community is one that inculcates in students the conviction that scholars and leaders need one another. They need one another not just for a personal sense of belonging, but also for the pursuit of truth and for the kindling of the moral imagination. How we model that shared pursuit in our forums, our curricular structures, and our academic and cocurricular partnership is critical to our expression of purpose. How we model that shared pursuit will also determine how well our students are prepared to serve the common good.

SO ALL STUDENTS HAVE ACCESS AND
CAN ACHIEVE THEIR GOALS

In more cases than not, discussions about educational goals focus predominantly on our *purposes* for our students rather than on their membership in a *purposeful community*. For all the merits of thinking about learning rather than just teaching, the recent emphasis on learning outcomes can frequently redact the complexities and beauties of the educational process into overly simplistic metrics, more often associated with competency than with discovery. Yet learning flows from context and community. As Alexander Astin and others have shown, peers have as much influence on the cognitive development of students as faculty and staff have, and sometimes more. Strong learning communities are able to organize educational programs around commonly shared learning experiences that promote collaborative inquiry, encourage the transparent exchange of ideas, and promote empathy and moral discernment. The makeup of the student community contributes immensely to a college's educational purpose.

That should resonate in our public discourse about access and diversity. Most of our institutions still struggle to diversify faculty, staff, and students. When discussing our purposeful community, we should acknowledge the commitment we share with other institutions to provide more access. Our diversity goals are part of the larger social endeavor for equity and part of our Christian calling for justice. But it is just as vital that we discuss diversity as the academic and spiritual enrichment of our educational community and purposes. International students, first-generation students, immigrant students, and multicultural students stretch and strengthen the intellectual and moral fabric of the institution.

There are undoubtedly some significant impediments to building this community. Financial needs, fed by growing economic disparities in the United States, are restricting access. Persistence rates remain lower among some ethic and socioeconomic groups than others. To the extent that our budgets are moral statements, a major signpost of our institutional purpose is the investment we make in the support and scholarship programs that bring together a community of learners that will challenge, inspire, confront, and ultimately mature all of us at the institution. We bring our institutions closer to the heartbeat of democracy when we find ways to include students' access to education as among our core purposes, not just our peripheral hopes.

In recent years, discussions of learning, care, and persistence were often structured around the ideal of student success. At Westmont, we have endeavored to use the student success theme as a way of unifying efforts, establishing key metrics, and identifying needs that are currently unmet. Most every educator testifies that students are more likely today to express needs for support, from psychological care to digital addictions. With the usual budget pressures, it is not possible to address these needs simply by expanding staff, but it is also negligent and self-defeating to set these concerns on the margins.

Any discussion of an educational purposeful community will eventually require us to revisit our workloads and pedagogies to ensure that we are meeting students where they can best learn. The focus on student success is a logical expansion of the widespread emphasis on retention, though it is something far more empathetic and visionary. We do not simply keep students enrolled; we want them to thrive. For some students, that will require opportunities to collaborate with faculty on published articles or chances for creative and high-end internships. For others, it will be trying to help them survive their first weeks adapting to the freedoms and rigors of college.

The language of student success is not an assurance but an aspiration, and in many respects a matter of integrity. We admit students and accept their tuition with expectations that they can find joy and value in their experience. One purpose of an American college these days is to equip more graduates for an educated workplace, including a larger portion of underrepresented groups. A vital purpose of the Christian college is to envision for all students who enter our halls a life of meaning.

•   •   •

We began with the story of the fire, and it has a sequel—this one far more tragic. On the first day of the spring semester, we held a chapel of gratitude for those who helped sustain and serve us during the fire. We sang our college hymn: "Great Is Thy Faithfulness." Yet less than twenty-four hours later, a steady drizzle turned suddenly into a fierce downpour. In the middle of the night half an inch of rain fell in five minutes and sliced soil from the burned hillsides, sending a torrent of mud, boulders, and debris into the streets of Montecito. The violent stream sped down a canyon just half a mile east from Westmont.

The irony was stark: on our quiet campus, rejuvenated by rains and the energy of a new semester, it was nearly impossible to imagine the tragedy so close at hand. It would take a few hours before we fully grasped the scope of the storm: hundreds of homes near the college had been destroyed, most of them mercifully evacuated in advance. But more than twenty lives were lost, some of them friends of Westmont families. We learned shortly that water lines had been shattered, including the ones that served the college. The freeway, a main artery between Southern and central California, would be shut down for more than a week. So, only a day after we had opened the second semester on a note of promise, we were forced to evacuate the campus again, unable to provide students potable water. It would take eight days before we could resume the semester; it would take longer for many of our neighbors to return to their homes, or in many cases the few remnants they could find.

In the days that followed, we were keenly aware that our gratitude for Westmont's preservation was matched by the pervasive lament for the devastation of our town. As eager as we were to return to normal, we understood more acutely that this semester would forge a new normal. It was hard to think about our own purposeful community without wondering more fully about our roles as neighbors. There is always the danger that we can lose sight of our interconnections and citizenship in the midst of defining purposes, expressing our uniqueness, and branding our distinctives. For many days, Montecito—one of the wealthiest towns in the nation—faced conditions so familiar to the world's poor: the loss of shelter, clean water, sanitation, and life itself. For us, the resonance between the local and the global may have never been more startling. It was a powerful reminder that conversations about purpose should not simply draw us inward in search of coherence and belonging, but should also force us outward into the discomforting corridors and pathways where Christ was always prone to walk.

CHAPTER TWO

AN OPEN COMMUNITY

RANDALL BASINGER AND KRIS HANSEN-KIEFFER

As clearly and forcefully expressed in *Campus Life: In Search of Community*, "A college or university is an open community, a place where freedom of expression is uncompromisingly protected and where civility is powerfully affirmed." This ideal of "openness" in the context of Christian colleges and universities is no less of an issue in 2018 than it was in 1990. However, while this ideal continues to be a central concern for *all* colleges or universities, this concern plays itself out in a distinctive way at Christian colleges. More foundational to "freedom of expression" and the related notion of civility is what could be described as "freedom of belief." Can there be limits on what educators and students can believe and express? And if so, how can these limits be understood and defended in light of the *Campus Life* call for "an open community . . . where freedom of expression . . . is powerfully affirmed"? The purpose of this essay is to explore this question.

THE PRIMA FACIE TENSION

Christian colleges have theological convictions closely tied to their identities as Christian institutions, and these often directly affect how these institutions function in the educational programming and hiring of employees. On the other hand, Christian colleges are committed to the open pursuit of truth, including the genuine exposure to and exploration of different perspectives and beliefs. In brief, Christian colleges are not *Christian* institutions that happen (accidentally) to also be academic institutions. Conversely, they are not *academic* institutions that happen (accidentally) to be also Christian. They seek to be fully and simultaneously Christian and academic.

How is this accomplished? Aren't firmly held theological commitments in tension with intellectual openness and diversity? Does the up-front, exclusive nature of a Christian college seriously hamper the intellectual openness that a serious commitment to the academic enterprise seemingly demands? Does the openness demanded by the academic enterprise rule out the possibility of core theological commitments central to a Christian college?

This essay explores answers to these questions and how these answers play themselves out in the belief expectations Christian colleges place on educators and students. We will argue that, while the central notion of academic freedom is consistent with the belief expectations Christian colleges place on educators, this works itself out in different and legitimate ways at different Christian colleges in relation both to educators and to students.

A TYPOLOGY OF COLLEGES

But just what do we mean by a Christian college? Following the typology of Robert Benne, we will begin by distinguishing three types of colleges: orthodox, critical mass, and pluralistic.[1] Within pluralistic colleges, there are no belief expectations for educators. Within critical mass colleges, while there are no religious belief expectations for all educators, these colleges have at least some (critical mass) of educators who affirm specific Christian convictions. In contrast, within orthodox colleges, educators must affirm a set of Christian beliefs that are at the core of the theological identity and commitments of these institutions.

These ideal types are on a continuum with pluralistic colleges and orthodox colleges at the opposite ends and critical mass colleges situated in the middle. Pluralistic colleges resolve the tension between theological commitment and academic openness by ruling out any belief expectations for educators and opting for openness. Critical mass colleges resolve the tension by placing belief expectations on only some educators. The tension exists in a straightforward way for orthodox colleges given their belief expectations for all educators.

How can this tension be addressed within orthodox Christian colleges, and what does this mean for these colleges as they live out their mission as Christian colleges? Answering these questions involves first raising the issue of academic freedom.

ORTHODOX CHRISTIAN COLLEGES AND ACADEMIC FREEDOM

Given the fact that orthodox Christian colleges require all educators to affirm a set of Christian beliefs, there is a sense in which orthodox Christian colleges

---

[1]Robert Benne, *Quality with Soul: How Six Premier Colleges and Universities Keep Faith with Their Religious Traditions* (Grand Rapids: Eerdmans, 2001).

place a limit on academic freedom. How can educators be free to explore ideas when they are constrained by the institution's belief system? And how then can an institution that places limits on academic freedom be an authentic academic institution committed to the open pursuit of truth?

In response to this question, some argue that the openness and freedom regularly assigned to educators in pluralistic and critical mass colleges is an illusion. While a pluralistic college does not have a set of explicit beliefs expectations, there are more than likely secular values and worldview commitments that guide and influence, if not control, the pursuit of truth. There are implicit, if not explicit, ideological biases and perspectives in all institutions. Thus it is argued that institutions constrain academic freedom whether the institution is secular or religious. Therefore, if the lack of academic freedom is a problem, it is problem for all colleges, not simply for orthodox Christian colleges. In essence, this argument defends orthodox Christian colleges by deconstructing any difference between the three types of colleges.

While this approach has some legitimacy, it is probably not helpful or realistic to ignore the differences that exist among the three types of colleges. It remains the case that orthodox Christian colleges place very explicit expectations on what educators must believe. It is important to explore how such explicit limitations can be reconciled with the openness required in academic institutions.

Orthodox Christian colleges have distinct Christian missions, and it is certainly reasonable for colleges to hire toward their respective Christian missions. An orthodox Christian college, by definition, is guided by a Christian narrative and implements its academic mission within that narrative. When there is mission fit between the institutional narrative and the personal scholarly narrative of the educators who choose to join the institution, the educators are freely pursuing their academic scholarly projects and intellectual ends within their discipline and, hence, are experiencing academic freedom. When the individual educator's faith/learning narrative is in line with the institution's faith/learning narrative, there is a meaningful and relevant sense of academic freedom.

This understanding of academic freedom aligns with the American Association of University Professor's *1940 Statement of Principles on Academic Freedom and Tenure* when it acknowledges the limits of academic freedom in institutions with a religious mission.[2] However, the 1940 statement rightly adds that the limitations of academic freedom because of religious or other aims of the institution

---

[2]American Association of University Professors, *1940 Statement of Principles on Academic Freedom and Tenure*, www.aaup.org/report/1940-statement-principles-academic-freedom-and-tenure (accessed November 19, 2018).

should be clearly stated in writing at the time of the appointment. In short, for this sense of academic freedom to exist, it is incumbent upon orthodox Christian colleges both to identify and to share any such limitations with educators at the time of hiring and contract renewal.

Assuming that orthodox Christian colleges can be authentic academic institutions with academic freedom, how do orthodox colleges live out this sense of academic freedom? How do orthodox Christian colleges live out their particular faith/learning narratives in their educational programming and in the lives of educators and students? In answering these questions, we will see that there are different ways of being an orthodox Christian college.

QUANTITATIVE DIFFERENCES IN ORTHODOX CHRISTIAN COLLEGES

All orthodox Christian colleges, by definition, place belief expectations on all educators. Those expectations imply a basic distinction between what an orthodox Christian college considers core beliefs (the beliefs that the college affirms and all educators must affirm) and neutral beliefs (beliefs in which the college has no real stake). Orthodox Christian colleges can and actually do differ quantitatively in how they implement this distinction.

This is to say they differ significantly on the actual number of core beliefs and by implication the number of neutral beliefs they recognize. The differences emerging here are purely a function of the faith/learning narrative that guides a particular orthodox college's identity and mission. While all orthodox Christian colleges are Christian, they are Christian in different ways, and the faith/learning narratives will play out accordingly.

We can imagine a core belief/neutral belief continuum of orthodox Christian colleges ranging from those who have a minimal number of core beliefs to those who have a much higher number of core beliefs. There is an inverse relationship between the number of core belief expectations and the corresponding number of neutral beliefs. The more core beliefs an institution affirms, the less diversity will be present. Orthodox Christian colleges are situated at different places on this continuum, and where a college is situated on this continuum is significant.

Is there an optimal location on this continuum? On the assumption that the presence of diversity of beliefs within a college is an academic or educational good, orthodox Christian colleges at the minimal end of the continuum have an advantage. While this way of thinking might be tempting, it is too simplistic. Once we grant that the notion of an orthodox Christian college is coherent, where specific orthodox Christian colleges draw their respective lines between core and neutral beliefs will differ relative to the theological identity and mission that guides the college. There is no objective way of determining where the line between core and neutral beliefs ought to be drawn for all orthodox Christian colleges. There is no universal formula for drawing such lines. Any line that is drawn will be justified from the perspective of that particular mission. Each orthodox Christian college has a right to actualize its mission within the context of its theological identity and mission—within its particular faith/learning narrative.

Therefore, while diversity and openness to different beliefs is an educational good, it is not an absolute good to be pursued at any cost. Taking diversity as an absolute good rules out the very possibility of an orthodox Christian college. Some distinction between core and neutral beliefs must be present in any orthodox Christian college, and the lines that are drawn will be a reflection of its specific Christian identity and mission.

However, for educators to experience academic freedom, orthodox Christian colleges must be clear on and then clearly articulate where they draw their respective lines. Orthodox Christian colleges, wherever they find themselves on the quantitative core belief continuum, must resist any implicit or arbitrary addition of beliefs that, while not officially core, come to function as such in an ad hoc fashion. Such implicit, ad hoc additions undermine the academic freedom of its educators and in so doing undermine the academic mission of the college.

When clear lines are drawn, orthodox Christian colleges can advance their respective academic missions by leveraging their neutral beliefs—the genuine pluralism of beliefs that stand outside of the core beliefs. This provides a context for exploring and grappling with the differences that exist among Christians and others. This can and should be fertile ground for modeling civil disagreement and dialogue that includes respect and tolerance of those with whom we disagree.

THE ADDED COMPLEXITY AND ADVANTAGE
OF PRIVILEGED BELIEFS

Thus far we have been analyzing orthodox Christian colleges in a way that only distinguishes core beliefs (beliefs the college affirms and all educators must affirm) and neutral beliefs (beliefs on which the college has no mission stake). However, there is another way an orthodox Christian colleges can understand its theological commitments and its relation to the belief expectations for educators.

It is possible to add another kind of belief category into the mix: privileged beliefs. Privileged beliefs are neither core beliefs nor neutral beliefs. Unlike neutral beliefs but like core beliefs, the college affirms *privileged* beliefs. They are beliefs in which the college has a theological stake. Unlike core beliefs, the college does not expect all educators to affirm its privileged beliefs. However, since the college has a stake in its privileged beliefs, the college expects all educators at least to support its privileged beliefs. Support entails the notion of respect of the college's views that in turn implies that educators will treat the college's position as a valid and responsible Christian approach and will not demean, seek to undermine, or advocate against the college's privileged beliefs even when educators might not fully affirm them.

Simply stated, within this orthodox Christian belief framework, there are three kinds of beliefs at play:

Core: Beliefs that the college affirms and all educators must also affirm.

Privileged: Beliefs the college affirms, but which educators need not affirm. While all educators are free to disagree among themselves and with the college, all educators must be supportive of the college.

Neutral: Beliefs on which the college is neutral. Educators are free to have their own beliefs. Everyone is free to disagree.

For example, an orthodox Christian college might stipulate the belief that God is the Creator of the world as a core belief while at the same time privileging views that reconcile creation with evolutionary science. This would signal that, while all educators must affirm that God is the Creator, they might differ on how divine creation relates to evolutionary science; therefore, views that reconcile creation and evolution are privileged. This privilege would be manifested in the educators who are hired, the curriculum and cocurriculum that is offered, and the kinds of lectureships that are supported. In contrast, another orthodox Christian college might privilege views that reconcile creation with a very young earth, and its curriculum and cocurriculum and hiring would reflect this privileged perspective.

Similarly, an orthodox Christian college could have a core belief about the authority and trustworthiness of Scripture while at the same time holding privileged views on a given hermeneutical approach that does not affirm inerrancy. Alternatively, another orthodox Christian college could have a core belief about the authority and trustworthiness of Scripture and privilege an inerrantist hermeneutic. In either instance, these privileged views would play themselves out respectively in these colleges' curriculum and hiring.

More generally, various orthodox Christian colleges, given their particular theological commitments and traditions, might affirm particular privileged beliefs on women in ministry, pacifism, human sexuality, eschatology, and so on.

In each of these instances, the college would privilege and hence emphasize specific theological positions on specific—even controversial—issues with the wider Christian community, without making them core beliefs that all educators must affirm.

In these examples, the privileged belief is not a core belief: educators can differ among themselves and with the college. This is acceptable, and perhaps even desirable, as long as all educators are supportive of the college's perspective. Moreover, the privileged belief is not a neutral belief: the college has a stake in this belief, so this belief will shape the educational programming and the hiring of educators.

It is good when there are educators who do affirm the college's privileged beliefs. In fact, it can be argued that the college needs a critical mass of these educators. However, the educators who affirm the college's privileged beliefs must respect the legitimacy of other beliefs and respect educators who hold them because these privileged beliefs are not core. On the other hand, educators who do not affirm the college's privileged perspectives must be supportive of the college, which minimally entails they will not complain about or seek to change the educational programming and delivery and the hiring strategies that flows from the college's privileged perspectives.

There is an important advantage in employing this notion of a privileged belief: the theological particularities of an orthodox Christian college can be advanced without making them a core requirement that everyone who joins this particular community must affirm. Thus room is created for educators outside a college's theological tradition to be in dialogue with the particularities of a college's theological mission without having to be personally committed to the particularities of its theological mission. This entails the possibility of diversity and constructive dialogue and disagreement on campus—even diversity on issues that the college affirms—without compromising the core commitment and privileged perspectives that flow from the college's identity and mission.

Just as it is the case in drawing the line between core and neutral beliefs, we must resist making value judgments about the lines a given orthodox Christian college might draw between core and privileged beliefs. Once again, there is no objective way of drawing lines between core and privileged beliefs. Any line that is drawn will be determined and justified from the perspective of that particular mission. Each orthodox Christian college has a right to actualize its mission within the context of its theological identity and mission—within its particular faith/learning narrative. But as stated earlier, for educators to experience academic freedom, orthodox Christian colleges must be able and willing to clearly articulate where they draw their respective mission lines among core, privileged, and neutral beliefs.

ORTHODOX CHRISTIAN COLLEGES AND STUDENTS

Thus far, we have focused solely on the belief expectations that orthodox Christian colleges place on educators. What is the relevance of the above for understanding the belief expectations orthodox Christian colleges might place on students?

We should first note that orthodox Christian colleges vary in what they expect from students regarding the institutional belief structure. Some colleges require all students to affirm a set of Christian beliefs in the same way that educators are so required. In general, colleges that take this approach have the advantage of common, mission-driven beliefs shared by the college, educators, and students along with the pedagogical advantages that shared beliefs and common learning allow. Students alongside educators who affirm the college's faith/learning narrative will explore the intellectual foundations for and alternative perspectives to the core beliefs of the college. At the same time, the college's privileged and neutral beliefs become a fertile context where both theological and nontheological differences, disagreements, and explorations of alternatives can be intentionally leveraged for student learning.

It is crucial, however, for those orthodox Christian colleges that require a particular faith commitment on the part of students to draw clear lines between core, privileged, and neutral beliefs. It is important for students to understand the belief playing field before they choose a college and as they negotiate their own theological commitments with the curriculum, cocurriculum, and the educators they encounter.

Other orthodox Christian colleges do not place any belief expectations on their students. Rather than expecting affirmation of specific beliefs, the expectation is that all students understand the Christian mission of the college and express a willingness to learn within the context of that mission. The emphasis shifts from the student's ability to affirm the college's basic beliefs to the student's willingness to respect what the college's Christian mission educationally entails.

However, colleges taking this approach face a challenge. It is important to make a distinction between students who assume leadership positions within the college and those who do not. Colleges have an important stake in student leaders since they shape campus culture and educational programming and, in so doing, influence the delivery of the college's mission. However, when a Christian college does not require students to affirm the college's core beliefs, how is it possible for such colleges to have the student leaders necessary to advance the college's mission?

Orthodox Christian colleges who only admit students who affirm the college's core beliefs do not face this problem because any distinction between leaders and nonleaders is simply a function of opportunity and leadership skills, not in the nature of the students' beliefs.

In contrast, orthodox Christian colleges who do not require students to affirm a set of core Christian beliefs have a challenge since they cannot assume a shared set of core Christian beliefs between student leaders and the college. Therefore, the challenge of cultivating student leaders who can advance the college's mission is very real.

The best strategy for these colleges is to hold student leaders to a different and/ or higher standard of commitment to the mission of the college as these leaders actualize their roles as ambassadors and facilitators of the college's mission. Even if a college does not require students to affirm the college's basic beliefs, the college can expect student leaders to be at least *supportive* of the college's core and privileged beliefs. On the one hand, this does not require student leaders to affirm the core or privileged beliefs of the college; but, on the other hand, this expectation to be supportive is more than the minimal respect of the college's mission that admission into the college assumed.

However, there may be some instances where support is not sufficient. Some leadership positions, such as the roles of student chaplain, small group Bible study leader, or residence life leaders, involve programming and relationships that embody the college's theological mission in the life of the college. These positions are so intertwined with the college's Christian mission that having student leaders who align with the college's theological mission is a necessity and thereby requires student affirmation of core beliefs rather than only support.

Supporting a set of beliefs that one does not personally affirm or affirming core beliefs that other students may not share can be a sophisticated and com-plicated role for a student leader. It requires a level of maturity on the student's part and a deep commitment to mentoring and professional development on the part of the advisor/supervisor. The results of this are beneficial to both the college and the student leaders. The college gains effective student leaders who can ad-vance the mission of the college, and the students develop the skill for leadership among peers and colleagues in diverse settings that will extend to their lives beyond graduation.

CONCLUSION

There is no one way of balancing theological commitments with diverse beliefs and genuine openness to alternative points of view. Orthodox Christian colleges, in contrast to pluralistic and critical mass colleges, place explicit Christian belief expectations on their educators. To be an educator in these orthodox colleges means holding specific Christian beliefs. But as we have seen, orthodox Christian colleges differ significantly on how they actualize their respective Christian identities within their academic missions. In particular, we have seen that they can differ on the number of their core beliefs and by implication the neutral beliefs they employ. Orthodox Christian colleges can also differ on whether they recognize privileged beliefs and, if so, what those privileged beliefs might be. Moreover, beyond these belief expectations for educators, orthodox Christian colleges also differ on the belief expectations they place on students, in general, and student leaders, in particular.

There is no one right way of being an orthodox Christian college. The faith/ learning narrative that is rooted in and flows from a college's particular Christian identity and mission will unavoidably and rightly dictate the particular balance the college strikes between its commitment to core beliefs and its openness to diverse perspectives and points of view. The differences that exist among orthodox Christian colleges are a function of their respective faith/learning narratives. And as authentic academic institutions, orthodox Christian colleges must ensure their belief structures are clearly and consistently communicated and administered with students and educators.

CHAPTER THREE

A JUST COMMUNITY

BRAD LAU AND LINDA SAMEK

When I (Brad) was a young professional just beginning my journey as a student life practitioner at a small faith-based institution, I decided that one of the pressing needs for student programming was to plan a series addressing critical concerns for the Christian community. One of the most urgent of these concerns, in my view, was how we actively engage the need for racial justice and reconciliation out of our deep faith in Jesus and his work in the world. I was energized by this task and spent considerable time putting together a compelling program to facilitate this important conversation. I also spent significant energy marketing the upcoming program to students, faculty, and staff.

On the day of the planned program, I arrived at the designated room early to set up for what I thought would be an engaging and important conversation about racial reconciliation. The time arrived and a few students had trickled in so I decided to wait to begin, knowing that college student schedules are not always conducive to an on-time start. After ten minutes passed, I realized that I was sitting in a room with fifteen to twenty students of color and not one white student, faculty member, or staff member other than myself. Needless to say, I was embarrassed for our Christ-centered institution and apologized to the students in the room. Seemingly, there were not white members of our community who cared about this conversation or thought it important enough to show up, even though it was the lived reality for our students of color who were in the room. We went on to have a good discussion, but it was an early lesson for me as a young professional of how far we had to go on this and so many other compelling issues of our day.

Today, one does not have to watch the daily news programs very long to know that we continue to struggle to build a just community that truly looks out for the most vulnerable and marginalized among us. Headlines ripped from the news cycle include the frustrations of the Black Lives Matter movement, concern over the growing gap between rich and poor, countless stories of sexual harassment and assault, and fears of climate change, among so many other compelling issues that call for engagement and "answers." Coupled with these contemporary challenges is the sad reality that we have lost our ability to talk to one another with civility and respect. More often than not, sentiments are shared on social media and met with vitriol and anger rather than a desire to understand another's perspective or story.

The college campus is, of course, a microcosm of this same brokenness. It is our belief that the Christian college has a unique voice to offer in the current cultural milieu, but we must find the courage and will to do so. God still requires the same things of us as he did in the days of the prophet Micah:

> To do justice, to love kindness,
> And to walk humbly with your God. (Mic 6:8 NASB)

So what is a " just" community, and how do we build it?

FOUNDATIONS AND PRIORITIES OF A JUST COMMUNITY

In his book *Campus Life: In Search of Community*, Ernest Boyer indicates that "a college or university is a just community, a place where the sacredness of each person is honored and where diversity is aggressively pursued."[1] It is certainly true that his definition may be too limited and limiting in our current cultural context. For example, it demands the question of "diversity" toward what end and derived from what compelling "idea" or "ideal"? Our pursuit of diversity is about so much more than merely increased numbers or broader representation on our college campuses. It is about a deeply embedded cultural humility, engagement, and responsiveness that goes beyond mere awareness to a deeply felt and compelling responsibility for change. Ultimately, for the Christian college student, this is about living out faith in Jesus in a way that makes a difference in the lives of those around us—our neighbors, our nation, and our world.

In particular, a deeply communal aspect is critical to our Christian faith. Paul calls fellow believers, "costrugglers," "coworkers," and "colaborers." There is no such thing as a faith that is "just my own." It must be lived out in my care and

---

[1]The Carnegie Foundation for the Advancement of Teaching, *Campus Life: In Search of Community*, foreword by Ernest L. Boyer (Princeton, NJ: The Carnegie Foundation for the Advancement of Teaching, 1990), 35.

concern for others, in not showing favoritism, and in caring for the marginalized and oppressed in our society and in our world.

Our increasingly fractured world is seeing a growing focus on the injustices that are all around us. Colleges and universities are caught in the crossfire of cultural and political movements that call for our active engagement and "voice." We have seen an increase in overt acts of bias and discrimination, but much more insidious are the numerous microaggressions that occur on our campuses and in our classrooms every day. The scope and scale of sexual misconduct (defined as sexual assault, stalking, dating and intimate partner violence, domestic violence, and sexual harassment) highlighted by the #MeToo movement is staggering. Controversies and hateful acts due to disagreements around sexuality and gender identity or religious belief or affiliation (or lack thereof) are also very real. Add to this growing list issues such as sex trafficking, creation care and climate change, global poverty, inadequate drinking water, natural disasters across the globe, and numerous other challenges. While the list is daunting, it provides an incredible opportunity for the Christian college to truly live out our individual and corporate faith in Jesus in a powerful way. We can and must do better as we lead the way in standing against injustice and oppression!

To "do better" as Christ-centered college communities requires us to "press into" a few key commitments and priorities. First, we must repeatedly affirm and reaffirm our deeply held belief in the worth and dignity of all people as created in the image of God. Living in a fallen and broken world does not negate this core conviction of Christian faith. It also does not mean that we have to deny other convictions or beliefs that are also true. God calls us as believers to certain things and away from other things. Similar to the "already" and "not yet" tension of the kingdom of God being "here" but not yet fully completed, we always live in a place of tension and paradox this side of eternity. This truth does not negate our responsibility to be the hands and feet of Jesus in bringing shalom and hope to our world as we love those around us. Each and every human being is deeply valued and loved by God. Can we do any less as the people of God?

A second key commitment is to open and civil discourse and understanding on our campuses. While not a Christ-centered university, California State University–San Marcos seeks to "create a community that navigates social justice issues and multiple perspectives through self-reflection, care, respect, and empathy while acknowledging the culture and humanity of others."[2] This seems to

---

[2]"Civility Campaign," California State University San Marcos, www.csusm.edu/civility/index.html (accessed April 2018).

us to be an effective statement of aspiration that easily applies to both faith and non-faith-based institutions. Such an attitude and approach must be modeled for students in the way faculty and staff colleagues interact with one another as well. The problems and challenges we face are not easy, nor are they easily solved, but the way in which we engage one another does matter. It is essential that members of our communities learn to listen well to multiple perspectives and voices around the table. This requires an attitude and posture of humility toward those with whom we might disagree, but the results are amazing. Christena Cleveland writes with great insight about this in her book *Disunity in Christ: Uncovering the Hidden Forces That Keep Us Apart.*[3] The prioritization of relationship over ideology toward shared understanding remains a worthwhile aspiration and commitment.

Third, Christ-centered institutions should see pursuing justice as an institutional commitment and priority tied to our mission, vision, and values. If we are committed to both equipping our students for civic engagement and participation (i.e., making a difference in their communities and world) and providing a truly transformative curricular and cocurricular experience, then doing justice is a part of that unique call of faith. Whether the issue is racial justice, gender equity, creation care, or caring for the orphans and widows, it is impossible to divorce our faith from action. This commitment should be embedded in key statements of the communities of which we are a part. An example from our own institution is a collaborative effort to create a theological statement on diversity that was ultimately approved by the board of trustees. The preamble to this statement reads in part,

> George Fox University is a Christ-centered institution that values diversity as an essential dimension of what it means to be human. As a community we believe that racism and other forms of division are destructive to redemptive community. Scripture is clear that the outpouring of the Holy Spirit following the resurrection of Jesus Christ enacts a form of community that at once embraces and transcends our differences. In Jesus Christ our unique, individual identities are both preserved and liberated to engage in redemptive community and in the reconciling work of Christ in the world. We believe that God values each of us in our uniqueness. Therefore we seek to be a community that celebrates the uniqueness of each of its members, including one's race and ethnicity.[4]

---

[3]Christena Cleveland, *Disunity in Christ: Uncovering the Hidden Forces That Keep Us Apart* (Downers Grove, IL: InterVarsity Press, 2013).

[4]"Theological Imperatives for Racial and Ethnic Diversity," George Fox University, www.georgefox .edu/diversity/Theology%20of%20Racial%20and%20Ethnic%20Diversity.pdf (accessed November 14, 2018).

We believe that commitments of our Christ-centered communities must not just be assumed or "understood" but explicitly stated and embedded in key documents when appropriate.

Finally, it is important for our campuses to truly value differences as contributing to the richness and vitality of the educational experience within clearly defined values of a covenant community. We believe there is great value in learning from diverse perspectives and voices whether in the classroom, around the dining hall table, or late at night in the residence hall. It is also important that such conversations be formed around agreed-on values of civility, respect, listening, humility, and love. The words from the April 1989 report from the University of Michigan still ring true today.[5] This report stated that colleges and universities must "build academic communities in which people learn to respect and value one another for their differences, while at the same time defining the values shared by all those who join the university as scholars and as citizens."[6]

THE PROMISES OF A JUST COMMUNITY

At George Fox University, we make many promises to our students and their families, to our employees, and to our surrounding community about the way we build and live in community. Many of these promises are intended to support equitable opportunities for an excellent education. The most visible promise is to our students, that they will "Be Known" personally, academically, and spiritually. That promise is prominent on our website, on billboards, and in materials we share widely. Included implicitly in the "Be Known" promise is the promise of a community where each person is recognized as an individual created by God for a unique purpose and who can expect to flourish in a just community.

But what is a just community? What should we see in a just community? What should we hear in a just community? How do we enact this promise? In their book *Live Justly*, colleagues from Micah Challenge write, "Biblical justice isn't an action once a year, it is a lifestyle."[7] The promise, then, of a just community is "the state of wholeness due all of God's creation. Justice is required for Shalom."[8] We will explore three promises that must be fulfilled to ensure a just community: That each person will be both host and guest, that each person will have power to move the furniture, and that each person's voice will be honored and included when community decisions are made.

---

[5]James J. Duderstadt, *The Michigan Mandate: A Strategic Linking of Academic Excellence and Social Diversity* (Ann Arbor: University of Michigan Press, 1990).

[6]*Michigan Mandate*, cited in Boyer, *Campus Life*, 35.

[7]Jason Fileta, *Live Justly* (Portland, OR: Micah Challenge USA, 2014), 5.

[8]Fileta, *Live Justly*, 11.

The first promise is that each community member is expected to be both host and guest. Rebecca Hernandez, associate provost for local and global engagement at George Fox University, has several works that address the roles of host and guest. In her chapter "Beyond 'Hospitality': Moving out of the Host-Guest Metaphor into an Intercultural 'World House,'" Hernandez notes that too often we relegate others to the role of guest and never allow them to serve as the host.[9] Guests do not have power in a Western community. They move at the pleasure of the host. Hernandez says, "The guest knows that to enter those spaces requires personal change. In order to make those changes, the guest must know the host well, while the host—who makes no change—never has to truly know the guest."[10] It is incumbent on those of us who have traditionally been identified as host to truly know those who have traditionally been identified as guest. This mutual knowing allows both to be host and guest as they live together in a just community. Each member of the community must be committed to knowing others to enable a just community where everyone participates as host.

The second promise is that each community member will be permitted to move the furniture in the house. In her compelling book, *Designing Transformative Multicultural Initiatives*, Sherry Watt develops the metaphor of moving furniture to explain her experiences in higher education.[11] She describes how she has been welcomed into university communities, given everything she needs to do her job well, and seemingly invited to be a full participant in the community; but then she's only allowed to sit on the furniture, never to move it. Watt explains:

> The partnering message I receive is "do not move the furniture." If you try to move the furniture, we will tell you very quickly and with the most neutral, slightly patronizing, and non-emotional tone, "enough already." This attitude has an air of "who do you think you are to disrupt how things are done here?" In other words, institutional gatekeepers resist deconstructing the traditions and changing its practices to address structural inequities.[12]

A just community promises that all residents will not just be allowed but also invited to move the furniture when they identify unjust practices in the community.

---

[9]Rebecca R. Hernandez, "Beyond 'Hospitality': Moving Out of the Host-Guest Metaphor into an Intercultural 'World House,'" in *Thriving in Leadership: Strategies for Making a Difference in Christian Higher Education*, ed. Karen A. Longman (Abilene, TX: Abilene Christian University Press, 2012), 223-42.

[10]Hernandez, "Beyond 'Hospitality,'" 227.

[11]Sherry K. Watt, *Designing Transformative Multicultural Initiatives: Theoretical Foundations, Practical Applications, and Facilitator Considerations* (Sterling, VA: Stylus Publishing, 2015).

[12]Watt, *Designing Transformative Multicultural Initiatives*, 19.

A third promise of a just community is that each person's voice will be heard, honored, and heeded when decisions that influence the whole community are considered. This means that each community member needs to be included in the conversation that leads up to an important decision, not just informed after the decision has been reached. Each person has experiences, strengths, and wisdom that can inform and improve the decision-making process and the ultimate outcome. Inclusion of diverse voices is critical in maintaining a just community.

In the Quaker tradition, the community process of discernment is where the group invites each person to contribute their insights to the collective conversation. The intention is that decision-making is done by coming to consensus after hearing all voices. In some cases, a community member may choose to stand aside when they are not in full agreement but do not have a strong enough dissent that they wish to delay the decision. Often, the final question asked is, "Are all hearts clear?" to move forward with grace and understanding. This can be a long and difficult process; however, hearing all voices enriches the eventual decision.

There are likely many more promises that are made by communities that strive to be places where justice lives. We cannot afford to only talk about these promises and not make them part of our lifestyle. The word *each* is used in this section rather than *all* to emphasize that every person should be known as a unique creation of God and valued for her or his unique contribution to a just community. Let's make a commitment to keep these promises as we move closer to enacting just communities.

CHALLENGES IN BECOMING A MORE JUST COMMUNITY

Good people talk about the importance of promises of just communities, but we live in a world full of negative -*isms*: racism, sexism, ageism, ableism, ethnocentrism, classism, and more. In our communities we encounter both overt and implicit biases built on our deeply ingrained need for safety with people who are like us. Many readers are likely familiar with Project Implicit, the testing, and attendant research, for implicit biases resident in our hearts and lives.[13] Many of us deny that we are biased toward or against any group of people, because we are good Christians who love everyone. I (Linda) have learned that I have clear preferences for younger, whiter, healthier people. What I choose to do with these biases once they are identified define how I live into creating a just community where I live and work. "Isms" are real, and we are challenged to live beyond those that exist in us.

---

[13]Bethany Teachman and Matt Nock, Project Implicit, www.projectimplicit.net/index.html (accessed 2011).

Becoming a more just community is a process. It is frustrating to know that this side of eternity we may never arrive at a completely just and equitable community. It would be good to be able to declare that "we have arrived." We conduct workshops, we take inventories, we read books, we have lengthy and good conversations, we promise to do better at practicing justice, but we seldom if ever are able to declare victory. Why is that? Should we try harder? Could we read another good book on the subject? Should we have more conversations with more diverse people? Should we just humbly admit that we are imperfect people, ask for forgiveness, and move on? To where? To what end? We have more questions than answers, and living justly is hard work; but we cannot afford to stop that work until we leave this world.

Sometimes, at Christian institutions, we may feel like we are preaching to the choir. But are we really? On the outside, our choir may look like it is in tune with justice. We say the right words and make the right motions in public, but communities only move toward justice when the members are able to be honest about their biases and feelings of inadequacy. It is challenging to confront a community with truth about injustice when they have a different "truth" in mind. Helping each member of the community understand where he or she fails at building a just community is a daunting task and not one to be entered into timidly.

Another challenging barrier to justice occurs when people want to focus on "intent" and ignore the "impact" of their actions. We are all good people, or so we think. God says quite clearly, in many places, that actually we are *not* good people. Romans 3:23 says, "We've compiled this long and sorry record as sinners (both us and them) and proved that we are utterly incapable of living the glorious lives God wills for us" (Rom 3:23 The Message). We are born with sinful natures that lead us too frequently to do the thing that protects us rather than the right thing for others. Excusing our actions by noting that we intended no harm does not mitigate the harm we cause when we behave unjustly. We can start with purity of intent, but we must acknowledge the negative impact that our actions often have on others. That is not their fault or theirs to suffer. It is ours to own and rectify. Understanding the impact of our actions on others is the beginning of building a just community.

An additional barrier to building just communities is our propensity to congregate with others who are very much like us. Cleveland's *Disunity in Christ* also has a lot to say about how we as humans lean toward the safety of those who are like us. She notes how we tend to divide even Christian brothers and sisters into "Right Christians" and "Wrong Christians." Mostly she means Christians who are like us and Christians who are not like us. Think of how much more we do this sorting with those in our circles who are not Christians. Cleveland writes, "Rather than using his power to distance himself from us, Jesus uses it to approach us. He follows his own commandment to love your neighbor as yourself—often to his detriment, I might add—by pursuing us with great tenacity in spite of our differences. He jumps a lot of hurdles to reach us."[14] May we learn to jump hurdles in our pursuit of building just communities for each member of our community.

PRACTICES OF A JUST COMMUNITY

A truly just campus community should go beyond mere theory to praxis. As the writer of the book of James makes abundantly clear, "Don't fool yourself into thinking that you are a listener when you are anything but, letting the Word go in one ear and out the other. *Act* on what you hear!" (Jas 1:22 The Message). Most Christian campuses provide ample opportunities for service and social engagement. We want our students to be focused on the needs of others and not just their own needs.

On our own campus, for twenty years we have devoted the third Wednesday of every fall semester to Serve Day. It is a day when we cancel classes and all students, faculty, and staff are divided into service teams that are assigned to serve at one of over one hundred different nonprofit and service organizations throughout the region. This important tradition is intended to be more than just a day of service, but to create an ethos of service on our campus. This is the call for all Christians to serve those around us in tangible ways, to make a difference in our local and global communities as we carry the light of Jesus with us to those who are hurting, marginalized, or in need of encouragement and hope.

Because George Fox University is connected with the Evangelical Friends, we have benefited from many of the traditional Friends practices and beliefs that inform what it means to be a just community. As the Northwest Yearly Meeting of Friends statement of Faith and Practice indicates,

> Together, we seek to live in obedience to the same Life and Power that called early Friends to courageous evangelism, compassionate service, community, integrity, simplicity, equality and peacemaking in ways that speak to the present culture. . . . We witness to the dignity and worth of all persons before God. We repudiate and seek to remove discrimination based on gender, race, nationality, or class. We deplore the use of selfish ends to gain unfair advantage, and we urge political, economic, and social justice for all peoples. We consider civil order most just when conscience is free and religious faith uncoerced.[15]

---

[14]Cleveland, *Disunity in Christ*, 16.
[15]"Faith and Practice: Vision, Mission, and Values," Northwest Yearly Meeting of Friends, 1997, nwfriends.org/faith-and-practice-revised.

It is hoped that these practices among others are powerfully connected to and frame what it means to be a just campus community that engages our students in things that matter and truly create a transformative student experience.

Another Friends practice that is helpful in matters of justice is the use of "queries." Following are examples of some of the queries used by Friends:

> As followers of Christ do you love and respect each other? Do patience and consideration govern your interactions; and when differences arise, do you resolve them promptly in a spirit of forgiveness and understanding? Are you careful with the reputation of others?

> Is your life marked by simplicity? Are you free from the burden of unnecessary possessions? Do you avoid waste? Do you refuse to let the prevailing culture and media dictate your needs and values?

> Are you careful to live within your income? Do you avoid involving yourself in business beyond your ability to manage or in highly speculative ventures? Are you willing to accept a lower economic standard rather than compromise Christian values?

> Do you speak out for justice and morality, and against oppression, exploitation, and public wrong? Do you recognize the equality of persons regardless of race, gender, or economic status?

> As a Christian steward, do you treat the earth with respect and with a sense of God's splendor in creation, guarding it against abuse by greed, misapplied technology, or your own carelessness?

> Do you observe and teach the Friends testimony against military training and service, making clear that war is incompatible with the spirit and teachings of the Gospel? Do you find appropriate ways to work for peace?[16]

Of course, some of these queries are fairly unique to Friends. It should be noted that our campus community would have a range of perspective on various issues raised by these queries. (In fact, only a small percentage of our forty-one hundred students would identify as Friends.) However, the Friends focus on social justice provides context and language that grounds our campus in understanding the importance of a lived faith that is outward and not just inward. The practices of a just community will demand a level of personal and community engagement with deep and challenging questions. Tony Campolo models his own self-reflection in *Faithful Learning and the Christian Scholarly Vocation* when he writes,

---

[16]"Faith and Practice Queries," Northwest Yearly Meeting of Friends, 2016, nwfriends.org/faith-practice.

As a middle-class American, I would like to dismiss these radical theologians in a cavalier fashion by merely allowing that they have some "interesting" insights into Scripture. Unfortunately, I feel that there is a great deal of truth to their message. I believe that God has identified with the poor and the oppressed. I am coming to see that there is something incongruous about my life of affluence and my claim to be a follower of one who emptied himself of all wealth and became a suffering servant. I am haunted by a Jesus who tells me that unless I deny myself, sell whatever I have, and give to the poor, I cannot be one of his disciples. Increasingly his message to the rich young ruler speaks to me, and I am coming to see that Christian discipleship requires a commitment to the poor and the oppressed, and a readiness to give up my position of wealth and power to follow a humble Galilean.[17]

Campolo goes on to challenge the Christian university to ask new and important questions of students (and faculty and staff) that cause them to think about their role and responsibility in a world filled with need and injustice.

PORTRAIT OF A JUST COMMUNITY

Considering what we have discussed in the preceding pages, let's paint a portrait of a just community. What would you include? Love? Respect? Care? Hope? Peace? Those are just a few of the characteristics that we as Christians might choose to describe a community that is just. These are characteristics that most people strive to share with others. In a just community, they should color everything we think, say, and do. However, as humans, we often fail to display these qualities. How can we do better, knowing how important it is to model love, respect, care, hope, and peace for our colleagues and our students? We would suggest that just communities are only built with full participation of all members of the community. By listening to each other through deep and difficult conversations, we will come to know each other and understand how to practice justice.

Two characteristics that we sometimes neglect in our portrait of a just community are humility and equity. Let's explore humility, particularly cultural humility, which is understood as a lifelong process of self-reflection and self-critique, whereby we learn about another's culture. However, it is critical that we begin by examining our own beliefs and cultural identities. In exploring cultural humility, we will also find the essence of equity. According to Melanie Tervalon

---

[17]Anthony Campolo, "The Challenge of Radical Christianity for the Christian College," in *Faithful Learning and the Christian Scholarly Vocation*, ed. Douglas V. Henry and Bob R. Agee (Grand Rapids: Eerdmans, 2003), 147-48.

and Jann Murray-Garcia,[18] in a portrait of a just community, we should see three practices related to cultural humility:

- Lifelong learning and critical self-reflection
- Recognition and challenging of power imbalances for respectful partnerships
- Institutional accountability

We all have cultural identities, although our white, domestic students sometimes do not realize this truth. It has been interesting over time to have students participate in a poetic form called, "I am from . . ."[19] It guides one through an examination of your cultural roots, and in sharing your poem with others, you learn about the existence of your culture, different from others. In a just community we know each other, learn each other's cultures, and with humility, share community. It is imperative that we constantly examine our beliefs and actions to see if they exemplify humility and justice. If not, why not? What needs to change in our practice?

Cultural humility requires that we recognize and challenge power imbalances. In a host/guest metaphor, we see power imbalances that result in inequitable treatment of those identified as guests.[20] The visual has two panels showing three children outside a fence trying to see a baseball game. The children are varying heights, but in the first panel each child is standing on a single identical box. The tallest child really doesn't need the box to see over the fence. The middle child is just the right height to see over the fence by standing on one box. The shortest child still cannot see over the fence, even when standing on a single box. This is a picture of equality, as each child has an identical box. In the second panel, the tallest child has given his box to the shortest child, and now each of the children has a clear view, over the fence, of the baseball game. The first child has no box, the second has one box, and the third child now has two boxes stacked one on the other. This is equity, with each member of the community able to experience success. As people have struggled with this image, you will find multiple versions that address what comes after equity. Where in your community do you see power imbalances that need to be corrected? What is your responsibility in seeing that this happens?

Twice a year at our university, we engage the faculty in a conference day where we provide professional development around pedagogies that are informed by

---

[18]Melanie Tervalon and Jann Murray-Garcia, "Cultural Humility vs. Cultural Competence: A Critical Distinction in Defining Physician Training Outcomes in Multicultural Education," *Journal of Health-care for the Poor and Underserved* 9, no. 2 (1998): 117-25, dx.doi.org/10.1353/hpu.2010.0233.

[19]"I Am from Poem," Santa Ana Unified School District, www.sausd.us/cms/lib/CA01000471/Centricity/Domain/3043/I%20Am%20From%20Poem.pdf (accessed 2018).

[20]"The Problem with That Equity vs. Equality Graphic You're Using," Cultural Organizing, October 29, 2016, culturalorganizing.org/the-problem-with-that-equity-vs-equality-graphic/.

our Christian faith. Several years ago we were looking for a powerful way to impress on faculty that their classrooms were not always models of justice. To this end, we asked ten senior students of color to participate in a conversation with faculty about their experiences in George Fox University classrooms. Not surprisingly, the students were reluctant to speak directly to two hundred faculty. They agreed to create a video in which they shared their lived experiences with our faculty. Following the showing of the video, we divided the faculty into ten groups of twenty and sent them to breakout rooms, each group with one of the students from the video and a faculty ally. What transpired was enlightening, inspiring, and for some, frightening. The students facilitated a conversation focused on pre-assigned readings, the video presentation, and role plays conducted in the room. Faculty saw themselves in ways they had not before this experience. Although this occurred three years ago, we still hear faculty talk about the impact of hearing directly from students. Many of them understood for the first time the importance of humility and the need for equity in their teaching.

As leaders in Christian institutions of higher education, we have a responsibility to build communities where each of our members experiences justice, equity, and opportunity to flourish. We are accountable for the well-being of our community members. This is a portrait of a just community in action.

CONCLUSION

In conclusion, we encourage you to examine your community to identify where systemic injustices may reside. Who on your campus has power, and who does not? Who experiences anonymity? Who is always relegated to the role of guest and never the host? Who is not allowed to move the furniture? And who is not heard when important decisions are made? What needs to change on your campus for each person to be known as a valued member of the community?

We encourage you not only to talk about building a just community, but to find ways to enact a just community. Who will lead this effort? What practices could you adopt? Who are your best role models? What portrait do you want to paint as you build a more just community?

This is difficult but important work. God admonishes us

> to do justice, to love kindness,
> and to walk humbly with your God. (Mic 6:8 NASB)

We must see justice done in Christian communities if we have any hope of seeing justice in our world. God will hold us accountable for this command, as will our colleagues and our students.

PART ONE

. . .

CHAPTER FOUR

A DISCIPLINED COMMUNITY

STEPHEN T. BEERS AND EDWARD ERICSON III

The Carnegie Foundation's 1989 synopsis of the college campus learning community was an indictment. They reported,

> We conclude that a college or university must be a disciplined community, a place where there are appropriate rules governing campus life, an institution where individuals acknowledge their obligations to the group. Specifically, we suggest an Honor Code for both scholarly *and* the civic dimensions of campus life. Such codes convey a powerful message about how honesty and integrity form a foundation of a community of learning.[1]

In this special report, the authors called to our attention the academy's lack of understanding and resolve in regard to making the critical connection between what happens in and out of the classroom. Specifically, in what may have been an early attempt to throw off the role of in loco parentis, universities missed the impact of what was transpiring outside of the classroom on the students' learning experience. Ernest Boyer and others lamented the lack of leadership in shaping the full community, including what they called the civic dimensions, where students live and learn.

With this backdrop, let us consider what has changed in the past thirty years and explore how a college or university in the first quarter of the twenty-first century can build and foster a disciplined community. We will also start by introducing you to our institution. John Brown University's (JBU) holistic educational foundation includes expectations for both scholarly and civic dimensions of campus life, as

---

[1] The Carnegie Foundation for the Advancement of Teaching, *Campus Life: In Search of Community*, foreword by Ernest L. Boyer (Princeton, NJ: The Carnegie Foundation for the Advancement of Teaching, 1990), 46.

illustrated in one of our two institutional mottos: "Head, Heart, and Hand." This phrase emerged as a simplified summary of the second half of our mission.

Our motto, which can be recited by almost everyone on campus, manifests the agreed-on campus-wide responsibility of developing the whole person. JBU fully embraces a learning community that includes both what is happening in the classroom and what is happening in the residence halls, the choir practice room, the sports fields, and the theatrical stage. This motto calls campus leaders to embrace our responsibility to influence the scholarly and the civic dimensions of a student's learning experience.

Richard Light in *Making the Most of College* highlights the importance of acknowledging all aspects of the student's experience as part of the learning community when he reports that four out of five seniors at Harvard testified that the most important learning experience in their time of study while in the university happened outside of the classroom.[2] Charles Pollard, JBU's current president and past chair of the CCCU board, also notes, "College represents an intense, life-shaping experience for so many people. Young people head to college ready to leave home but often not quite ready to take on adult life. They are searching to understand their place in the world."[3] If the reader is still unsure of the importance of managing the civic component of the college experience on the learning community, one has only to simply look as far as the university's counseling center wait list or the judicial board's records to know that the student's learning environment is influenced by what is happening beyond the classroom.

AN UPDATED VIEW OF THE UNIVERSITY LANDSCAPE

The Carnegie Foundation's special report argues for the adoption of civil expectations. Their report was buoyed by reporting the negative effects of college students' abuse of alcohol and drugs. So what has changed and what remains the same regarding substance abuse and its impact on the college experience? The following paragraph provides a quick update:

> College drinking has been recognized as one of the most important problems facing today's college student. Even though excessive drinking has increased only modestly over the past few decades, concern about its health, behavioral, and safety consequences has risen exponentially. As the concern grew, so did the controversy about how to study college drinking and how to respond to it.[4]

---

[2]Richard J. Light, *Making the Most of College: Students Speak Their Minds* (Cambridge, MA: Harvard University Press, 2004).

[3]Charles W. Pollard, *May It Always Be True: Educating Students in Faith* (Abilene, TX: Abilene Christian University Press, 2010), 221.

[4]George W. Dowdall, *College Drinking: Reframing a Social Problem* (Westport, CT: Praeger, 2009), ix.

Furthermore, raising the issue to national attention are alcohol-related student deaths. *The Economist* reports that "more than 200 university students have died from hazing-related accidents in the United States since 1838—forty in the past decade alone. While some die from drowning or falling, most often the cause of death is alcohol poisoning."[5] These incidents are driving institutional leaders to tighten alcohol-use policies, as exemplified in the current handling of the campus Greek systems. *The Economist* goes on: "Universities have responded to recent hazing accidents by suspending recruiting by fraternities and sororities, cancelling social events and banning hard liquor and kegs of beer at parties. But experts say such restrictions may only drive drinking to even riskier settings."[6]

To be sure, the challenge is not easy nor is the solution simple, but institutions must take this challenge head on. The bad news is that the problem has not abated, but the good news is that society has an increased awareness and concern. Until university administrators fully address the issue, a positive solution is outside of their grasp. Maybe most interesting for the purposes of this chapter is that non-faith-based institutional policies are moving closer to the space Christian universities have inhabited—setting clear civic boundaries. More about this later in the chapter.

What may not have been anticipated in the original report was the impact of the misuse of prescription drugs or the legalization of recreational marijuana. Journalist Avery Stone says, "A new survey released by the Partnership for Drug-Free Kids found that abuse of prescription stimulants is becoming normalized among college students and other young adults."[7] Simultaneously, California legalized recreational marijuana in 2018, making it the sixth US state to do so. Only time will reveal the full impact that this decision will have on the ability of college students to remain fully engaged in the learning process.

Furthermore, the federal government is increasing pressure on universities to accept institutional responsibility for student behavior. The Clary Act requires collecting and publishing crime statistics for the campus, thus providing the public direct access to data about what is happening on campus. This legislation forces accountability, as these published campus crime statistics show the relative safety of the campus. These statistics are profoundly important in an ever-increasing competitive marketplace where students and their parents are making college choices based on a widening array of factors, safety being one of them.

---

[5]"Hazing Deaths on American College Campuses Remain Far Too Common," *The Economist*, October 13, 2017, www.economist.com/blogs/graphicdetail/2017/10/daily-chart-8.

[6]"Hazing Deaths."

[7]Avery Stone, "Survey Finds 1 in 5 College Students Have Abused Prescription Medication," *Huffington Post*, November 14, 2014, www.huffingtonpost.com/2014/11/14/one-fifth-of-college-students -abuse-prescriptionpills_n_6159608.html.

Today we see the increased pressure from the broader culture requiring universities to rein in and address bad behavior. Welcomed or not, new federal legislation places responsibility of the university's handling of sexual assault accusations in a context of civil rights violations. The government's goal is to empower and hold accountable university officials to work against the reported systemic culture of sexual assault. This legislation, in part, is an external application of what the Carnegie Foundation was concerned about: universities abdicating their responsibilities of providing a safe environment for the learning community. External forces have emerged to begin to fill the gap.

Complicating matters for colleges and universities are competing federal and state legislations, seen most recently in navigating new gun laws. Each law is purported to increase student safety, which has been compromised by horrific experiences of shooters on campus. The final impact of these laws is still emerging as the debate continues. In each of these last few illustrations, the local, state, and federal governing bodies believe it is the university's responsibility to manage aspects of the students' overall college experience—basically requiring the university to move toward a disciplined community.

JBU AS A DISCIPLINED LEARNING COMMUNITY

Let's turn our attention back to JBU to illustrate how institutions can develop a learning community where individuals accept their obligations to the group and where well-defined governance procedures guide behavior for the common good.[8] JBU's learning community expectations have always included obligations to the larger community beyond simply encouraging integrity in academic pursuits. This holistic embrace is motivated by our theology, which speaks clearly about human nature and human flourishing. The outline of these directives for guiding student civic behavior is a document we have titled the Community Covenant. The document was originally crafted by a committee of faculty, staff, and students. Covenantal language is related to our Christian heritage, and as a faith-based educational community our students, faculty, and staff are familiar with a posture of being called to sacrifice individual rights in order to facilitate the common good. The Community Covenant has four major civic commitments that guide our community: (1) a commitment to embrace Scripture in word and deed; (2) a commitment to honor the uniqueness of each individual; (3) a commitment to living with integrity; and (4) a commitment to place the

---

[8]Carnegie Foundation, *Campus Life.*

community above oneself.[9] Included in the document are illustrations of how students would live out such an honor code.

The Community Covenant as a civic code is foundational in shaping the experiences of individual students and the educational community. It is not primarily a list of prohibitions; instead it is a document that is aspirational. For example, it calls community members to honor individual differences—more easily said than done. Embracing and honoring the uniqueness of individuals is actually a reference to the New Testament, highlighting the necessary diversity in the body of Christ. In any given year, our institution can be a compilation of students from over forty-four states and forty countries. Needless to say, there are distinct differences in the students that attend. As an open-enrollment university, learning how to honor, celebrate, and manage our unique differences is an obligation of the highest magnitude.

As mentioned earlier in the chapter, the original report spends a significant amount of the chapter on the challenges that emerged in colleges during the 1980s regarding the misuse of alcohol. Our JBU students in the traditional undergraduate program willingly (not always with excitement) commit to abstaining from the use of alcohol during their enrollment period, even those over twenty-one years old. In addition, nonmarried students commit to abstaining from sex, even if it were to be consensual. These obligations that direct the larger community may seem foreign to those outside of our faith-based community, but we maintain that they are rooted in scriptural directives or have emerged from a basic Christian posture of giving up what is a privilege in order to serve others and avoid becoming a stumbling block.

The Carnegie report challenges universities to develop and disseminate the rationale and details of a civic code. To that end, JBU's Community Covenant is actually embedded into the application process; so functionally when students sign the application, they are in fact acknowledging their awareness of the expectations and are agreeing to the covenant policies. During new-student orientation, the student development staff presents the tenants of the covenant and highlights the rationale for their importance. As students return to campus each subsequent year, they are asked to recommit to the covenant by signing a fresh copy.

To be sure, not all students live up to this code, and the campus judicial system manages these violations. When violations occur, the judicial system works diligently in setting a posture of education and restoration in the discipline process—

---

[9]"Community Covenant," John Brown University, www.jbu.edu/assets/student-development/resource
/file/2018/JBU_CommunityCovenant_2018.pdf (accessed November 14, 2018).

virtually extending the learning community into the realm of student discipline. Interestingly, most discipline appeals at JBU do not focus on the student's concern about the code or the civic obligation, but instead usually focus on the type or severity of the discipline rendered.

The Carnegie report continues with a call for practical applications that improve security. To that end, JBU has increased security measures through additional surveillance, improved locks, increased lighting, better emergency communications, and updating our memorandum of understanding with the local police, to name but a few. In addition to the physical improvements, we have increased educational safety programming for disaster preparation, including shooter-on-campus training and drills. In a 2016 national poll, JBU was listed as the safest college in Arkansas. To be sure, there are numerous variables that go into this nonscientific assessment. One of those statistical assessments is our crime statistics. We serve just over twenty-five hundred students on three campuses including graduate, nontraditional, and a growing number of online students. Over the past twenty years, our crime report has been populated mostly by zeros. Tomorrow that may all change, but our campus community is intentional about being a disciplined community, and we believe that this is part of the reason we are a safe community.

Because these various discipline conversations on campus are framed in terms of our theological understandings and because the larger Western culture has continued to move away from its Judeo-Christian heritage, one of the primary means of staying disciplined has been through how we hire, develop, and occasionally discipline faculty and staff. Although not completely synchronized with student expectations, our faculty and staff also have similar civic expectations. Their role, more than any document or mission statement, forms the primary leadership of shaping the university culture. Let's look at our process.

First, we are very focused on hiring for mission, as exemplified in our recruitment process. A committee of senior faculty members, chaired by a member of the Biblical Studies Division, interviews every candidate based on a list of standard personal faith and faith-integration questions. While the interview is not designed to be intimidating, the Inquisition (as it's affectionately known on campus) does have a significant say in whether faculty candidates continue in the process. Similarly, our president interviews every faculty- and director-level-or-higher candidate with mission-related questions primarily in mind. We also ask for faith statements up front on our application, and our search committees spend significant time attempting to discern institutional fit.

Second, we do, however, understand that a lot of people coming to JBU, especially in various professional fields, may not have deep theological backgrounds and, in some cases, are new to the faith. We have, therefore, instituted a series of overlapping mentoring programs, including a new faculty orientation workshop, a semester-long new faculty seminar (for which they get a course release to attend), two different mentors, and various continuing faculty-development efforts. To give a sense of how vital these kinds of programs are to JBU, our faculty-development budget is roughly similar to that of our neighbor, the University of Arkansas, despite being only one-tenth their size.

Furthermore, we have in the last two decades developed a detailed formal evaluation and promotion process for faculty. Ninety-seven percent of the faculty who have gone through the process in the last five years have passed the formal evaluation cutoffs, so it is primarily a formative process. Having said that, a 3-percent failure rate, plus another roughly 3 percent who don't even make it to the formal evaluation stage, means that we are letting go of some faculty for performance, primarily for teaching or mission issues. We have an egalitarian system of three-year contracts instead of tenure, which the faculty have generally supported as a way of avoiding the have and have-not culture of much of higher education, and that has made these kinds of decisions a bit easier at JBU; but make no mistake, letting people go is always hard and painful.

Last, JBU has been more fiscally disciplined than most over the years in not hiring additional people to long-term, full-time positions. We have metrics that we look at both within budget areas and across the institution to try to limit the number of full-time hires, and cost-incentive systems that reinforce that general strategic goal. Budgeting is about mission—that is, putting resources into what matters to an organization—and mission is central to being disciplined, because you have to know what type of community you're trying to develop. So our disciplined budgeting process has been vital to our sense of having a disciplined community.

CONCLUSION

The Carnegie report challenged universities to take seriously the role of providing guidance in and also outside of the classroom. Their rationale was based on the important role the campus community plays in developing the whole student. John Brown University has since its beginning been a place where the full community takes seriously the role of fostering a disciplined community to promote acceptable behavior in order to facilitate the holistic development of our students. Similarly, the modern university must be intentional about finding ways to meet the unique needs of its students by providing great scholarly opportunities but also through shaping and protecting all aspects of the learning community. These sociological constructs that frame our campus communities should be informed and guided by each institution's mission and culture. To be sure, the guidelines and boundaries at each institution will and should look as diverse as the institution, but the ultimate responsibility is for institutional leaders to know their institutional mission, vision, and values in order to establish appropriate disciplines that enable formative and holistic student learning to flourish.

PART ONE

...

CHAPTER FIVE

A CARING COMMUNITY

PAUL O. CHELSEN AND MARGARET DIDDAMS

*A college or university is a caring community, a place where
the well-being of each member is sensitively supported
and where service to others is encouraged.*

ERNEST L. BOYER, *CAMPUS LIFE*

In chapter five of *Campus Life*, Ernest L. Boyer and his colleagues identify a
caring community as the characteristic that helps colleges[1] function as purposeful, just, disciplined, and open communities. He described care as "the
way people relate to each other" so that they "feel they belong." Boyer identified
the outcomes of a caring community as individual affirmation and humane
activity (i.e., faculty who create a supportive climate in the classroom; offices
that treat students with respect; and services that are available to students
when they need them).

Psychologists Ed Deci and Richard Ryan define "well-being" not only as a
disposition, but more importantly as a process where people are free to pursue
meaningful goals in the context of relationships.[2] Not surprisingly, when people
are asked what makes them happy and gives them joy and a sense of meaning,
Beverley Fehr notes that friendships are at or near the top of the list.[3] C. S. Lewis

---

[1]In using the word *colleges* we are being inclusive of both colleges and universities.
[2]Edward L. Deci and Richard M. Ryan, "Hedonia, Eudaimonia, and Well-Being: An Introduction,"
Journal of Happiness Studies 9, no. 1 (2008): 1-11.
[3]Beverley Fehr, "Friendship Formation," in *Handbook of Relationships Initiation*, ed. Susan Sprecher,
Amy Wenzel, and John Harvey (New York: Taylor & Francis, 2008), 29-54.

wrote, "To the Ancients, friendship seemed the happiest and most fully human of all loves; the crown of life and the school of virtue."[4] This is no less true for students. According to Laurie Schreiner, two aspects of social connectedness are important to their thriving: "1) individual relationships; and 2) the sense of being a part of a larger community on college campus."[5] While Boyer and Schreiner do not use the word *friendship*, it is easy to infer that friendship is the major factor in individual relationships needed for social connectedness. In fact, Bree McEwan and Laura Guerrero write that friends are often a primary source of support for incoming freshmen.[6]

Fehr defines friendship as "a voluntary, personal relationship, characterized by equality and mutual involvement, reciprocal liking, self-disclosure, and the provision of various kinds of support."[7] She is careful to point out that it is a combination of these factors that fosters friendship. Consequently, multiple points of engagement make it more likely for friendships to develop in a caring community.

The types of college contexts fostering these points of engagement will be unique to each institution. For a residential Christian college, they are commonly classes, housing, chapel, areas of cocurricular involvement (e.g., student clubs and organizations, athletics, arts and music, service learning), and student care areas (e.g., counseling, health center, academic and disability services) that from a student's perspective can create an interconnected and at times seamless environment. A classmate on someone's floor may be enrolled in the same class as well as being a fellow participant in an off-campus tutoring ministry.

Students' primary point of engagement will be the classroom. The traditional rationale for the liberal arts is to educate the whole person, which liberates that individual to serve the church and society.[8] Scripture describes the freedom that comes as a result of knowing the truth, namely, Jesus Christ.[9] In Christian higher education, faculty support students by helping them integrate faith and learning in the classroom;[10] the intended result will be a closer relationship with Christ as both the center and outcome of academic study. When faculty integrate Christianity in the classroom, they are asking students to engage in higher-order thinking

---

[4]C. S. Lewis, *The Four Loves* (Orlando, FL: Harcourt Brace Jovanovich, 1960), 87.

[5]Laurie A. Schreiner, "Thriving in Community," *About Campus* 15, no. 4 (2010): 4.

[6]Bree McEwan and Laura K. Guerrero, "Freshmen Engagement Through Communication: Predicting Friendship Formation Strategies and Perceived Availability of Network Resources from Communication Skills," *Communication Studies* 61, no. 4 (2010): 445-63.

[7]Fehr, "Friendship Formation," 29.

[8]Jeffry C. Davis, "The Countercultural Quest of the Christian Liberal Arts," in *Liberal Arts for the Christian Life*, ed. Jeffry C. Davis and Philip G. Ryken (Wheaton, IL: Crossway, 2012), 31-44.

[9]"And you will know the truth, and the truth will set you free" (Jn 8:32 ESV).

[10]Arthur Holmes, *The Idea of a Christian College* (Grand Rapids: Eerdmans, 1987).

by creating meaningful connections between the material and their own lives, contributing to transformative learning and identity development. While Boyer did not specifically link student happiness, health, or well-being with identity development, Nevitt Sanford's research suggests that identity development is one of the primary tasks of college students.[11] As any change carries risk, faculty have an opportunity to model their identity in Christ as well as provide supportive relationships as student identities mature. When faculty members support a student's life in and outside the classroom, the college becomes more than a place for knowledge transmission or preparation for a job; intellectual, social, and spiritual support from faculty provides the necessary freedom for students to experience both holistic transformation and social connectedness.

A caring community will nurture student identity development through the bonds of friendship. This aligns with developmental psychologist Erik Erikson's seminal work on identity as an awareness of stability in one's self in relation to others.[12] In his life-stage model, identity development involves a conflict or a crisis between individual needs and the needs of others that must be resolved before moving on to the next stage of development. According to Erikson, the identity development of young adults (ages eighteen to forty) focuses on long-term relationships outside one's family. As college students address the conflict between family relationships and friendships, they are more likely to experience intimacy through happy, committed relationships. Erikson did not write specifically about belonging, but his research suggests that feeling a sense of belonging is a byproduct of intimacy in happy, committed relationships. Failure, according to Erikson, will result in a fear of commitment in relationships and feelings of isolation, which one could argue are a barrier to belonging.

Students are naturally motivated to reflect on their relationships as a way to understand themselves. Consequently Erikson's theory supports the efforts of colleges to foster a caring community through friendships as a way to help students make sense of their relationships and subsequently their identity. According to Glynn Harrison, to be created in God's image and redeemed in the image of Christ are two sides of the same identity coin.[13]

But there are challenges for students, staff, and faculty at Christian institutions to create a caring community where relationships and identity development can thrive. In 1994, just after the time Boyer wrote *Campus Life*, the American College

---

[11]Nevitt Sanford, *Self and Society: Social Change and Individual Development* (New York: Atherton, 1966).

[12]Erik H. Erikson, *Identity, Youth, and Crisis* (New York: W. W. Norton, 1968).

[13]Glynn Harrison, *A Better Story: God, Sex and Human Flourishing* (London: Inter-Varsity Press, 2016).

Personnel Association published *The Student Learning Imperative*, reemphasizing
the prioritization of student learning and development amid major changes in
higher education.[14] Today, higher education is experiencing the full impact of the
changes discussed in *The Student Learning Imperative*: economic constraints,
eroding public confidence, accountability demands, and demographic shifts.
Millennials have not been socialized to develop the attributes of friendship that
Fehr has identified. They are exposed to unprecedented amounts of self-focused,
one-dimensional, personal information on social media to create whatever self-
image desired.[15] Additionally, many more students struggle with anxiety, depression, and suicidal ideation[16] along with a cultural perception that Christianity is a source of discrimination.[17] Students must also contend with
individualism, which for evangelicals may contribute to the preservation of racial
divisions[18] and an abandonment of historic biblical sexual ethics.[19] Colleges must
increasingly divert resources to developing clear policies, training protocols, and
due process investigation procedures to address harassment and discrimination:
barriers in a caring community for friendships to flourish.

If Boyer were conducting his research today, he would likely find just as much
if not more need to support the well-being of staff to balance colleges' environmental challenges. Student development staff are regularly diverted from
mission-focused work with ancillary tasks, external pressures, and limited time.
The last half century of higher education suggests that as student demographics
have changed, so have staffing and structures to support them. Boyer could not
have predicted the robust communication and care networks colleges need to
establish across entire institutions in order to prevent students from taking their
own lives and/or the lives of others. He likely could not have foreseen the well-
meaning but burdensome unfunded mandates from federal and state govern-
ments requiring specific supports for students at a time when national and state
economic climates mean decreasing financial support. Nor did he imagine
several decades of case law and court decisions that may deter college staff

---

[14] *The Student Learning Imperative: Implications for Student Affairs* (Washington, DC: American College Personnel Association, 1994).

[15] Sherry Turkle, *Alone Together: Why We Expect More from Technology and Less from Each Other*
(New York, NY: Basic Books, 2011).

[16] *Annual Survey* (Indianapolis: Association for University and College Counseling Center Directors, 2016).

[17] David Kinnaman and Gabe Lyons, *unChristian: What a New Generation Really Thinks About Christianity, and Why It Matters* (Grand Rapids: Baker Books, 2007).

[18] Michael O. Emerson and Christian Smith, *Divided by Faith: Evangelical Religion and the Problem
of Race in America* (New York: Oxford University Press, 2000).

[19] Harrison, *A Better Story*.

members from having meaningful interactions with students out of fear of costly, time-consuming, reputational-damaging lawsuits, which have long-lasting implications for enrollment, budgets, and institutional image.

Faculty also have their own challenges in supporting student relationships. Historians of higher education tell the story of a time when there was one curriculum, where professors taught a broad range of material, lived with students, and functioned in place of students' parents to oversee their intellectual, spiritual, and moral development.[20] There was a close connection between the challenge and support students experienced in and out of the classroom. Industrialization and the influence of the nineteenth-century German research university introduced specialization of knowledge and academic guilds. Eventually, faculty members began earning advanced degrees and the curriculum was organized into specific disciplines of study and general-education areas of study.[21] As student enrollments grew, more staff members were hired to support students in structures that eventually replaced the holistic support once provided by the faculty and the president.[22] A holistic approach to student support requires a reexamination of organizational structure and culture that is less siloed and hierarchical.

While today's challenges are real, an ethos of care is crucial for holistic student growth and identity development. Christian liberal arts colleges are especially well positioned to look beyond today's prevalent educational models to shape students' souls through a vibrant institutional mission, faculty-staff collaboration, and fostering reciprocal student engagement.

An ethos of care begins with a dynamic and well-understood institutional mission. Caring college campuses, according to Boyer's research, encourage membership in small campus groups that help students connect with others. David Brooks writes that an organization which leaves a mark on its members becomes part of a person's identity and engages the whole person: head, hands, heart, and soul. Thick organizations marry their missions with their members' desires to work toward a higher good. Brooks ends the piece by emphasizing that intimacy and identity in thick organizations are borne out of a common love.[23] Given this common vision, the most important activity to create a strong

---

[20]David Kelsey, *Between Athens and Berlin: The Theological Education Debate* (Eugene, OR: Wipf & Stock, 2011).

[21]Chad Wellmon, "Knowledge, Virtue and the Research University," *The Hedgehog Review* 15, no. 2 (2013): 79-91.

[22]John R. Thelin, *A History of American Higher Education* (Baltimore: Johns Hopkins University Press, 2004).

[23]David Brooks, "How to Leave a Mark on People," *New York Times*, April 18, 2017, www.nytimes.com/2017/04/18/opinion/how-to-leave-a-mark-on-people.html.

commitment to institutional mission is through hiring and new employee orientation.[24] According to Brooks, leaders continue to strengthen mission through physical setting, regular gatherings, collective rituals, and commonly known stories about the origins of the organization. Senior administrative leadership must endorse and model the cooperative nature that is part of a Christian college's mission, vision, and/or community value statement. Each member's contribution to the work of a particular department should be seen as supporting the institution overall, which, according to Schreiner, is the second factor contributing to social connectedness.[25]

But in a fallen world, such common cause can seem idyllic. Self-interested members who function outside the institutional mission contradict the goal of being a supportive community by fostering conflict, which diverts time and energy from cultivating a healthy institution. Boyer wrote that campus groups can also be counterproductive if they do not support the institutional mission, or the reason for its existence. Scripture warns that a house divided against itself will fall (Mk 3:25). Thus there must also be supervision processes for missional accountability as well as the creation of a corrective process when self-interest is pursued to the exclusion of institutional mission.

Faculty and staff build an ethos of care in collaborating to live out the institutional mission. Students can easily expect this partnership, as they often do not come to college aware of how faculty differ from staff. The 1937 "Student Personnel Point of View" states that students flourish with holistic support, an idea Boyer echoed when he wrote, "A modern college or university should be a place where every individual feels affirmed."[26] Sanford theorized that student development occurs when there is a balance of support in the environment to offset the challenges.[27] If faculty and staff affirm each other in their roles as student club advisors, music ensemble directors, athletic coaches, residence life staff, and chaplain's staff, then students are more likely to experience the same holistic affirmation and support in their relationships with individual faculty and staff.

Students must also see themselves as not just the beneficiaries of this ethos but as being responsible, in part, for its health. College students will struggle to develop their self-identity while at the same time establishing their first long-term relationships outside of their family,[28] which is why Sanford's theory stresses

---

[24]Richard D. Breslin, "Hiring to Maintain Mission," *Journal of Catholic Education* 4, no. 2 (2000): 227-38, digitalcommons.lmu.edu/cgi/viewcontent.cgi?article=1215&context=ce.

[25]Schreiner, "Thriving in Community."

[26]*The Student Personnel Point of View* (Washington, DC: American Council on Education Studies, 1937).

[27]Sanford, *Self and Society.*

[28]Murray Bowen, *Family Therapy in Clinical Practice* (New York: Jason Aronson, 1978).

the need for a balance of support.[29] Students are most likely to build strong friendships when they share information about themselves while asking questions of others. Reciprocal vulnerability, trust, and other-oriented listening are all important aspects for students to contribute to an ethos of care.[30] When the writer of Hebrews exhorts Christ followers to "stir up one another to love and good works" (Heb 10:24 ESV), his words are aligned with Boyer's concern that students must be taught about mutual dependence in part through community service, which helps them to see and act in response to human needs.

Colleges cannot assume that students have the foundational skills to create friendships. Try observing a group of college students at a local coffee shop and pay particular attention to how much speaking and listening appears to be occurring. It is likely that most students' gazes are fixed on a computer or phone screen. Students need to be guided in how to ask discerning questions of themselves and others while creating authentic dialogue with each other. In our technological age, embodied listening does not come naturally. Yet Greg Tanaka's research demonstrates the importance of reflecting on one's cultural narrative in order, for example, to encourage storytelling among culturally diverse students on a multicultural campus.[31] Such storytelling can foster interdependent relationships while prompting reflection on personal positions of power. Storytelling for Christian college students can become even more meaningful for identity development when they understand God's invitation to participate in his metanarrative of love, mercy, and justice.

Encouraging personal storytelling must be coupled with listening to others. Dietrich Bonhoeffer wrote that listening to someone is the first step in expressing patience and kindness to that person, just as listening to God's Word is the first step in loving God.[32] Similarly, Max DePree wrote that we do not learn by knowing the answers but by learning how to ask questions.[33] Students learn about themselves not only in telling their own story but also in learning to listen and ask questions of others to facilitate reflective learning about relationships.

Asking questions, storytelling, and listening are especially important for students who are in developmental distress. It's not unusual for distressed students to experience anxiety, depression, and/or suicidal thoughts, which negatively

---

[29]Sanford, *Self and Society.*

[30]Irwin Altman and Dalmas A. Taylor, *Social Penetration: The Development of Interpersonal Relationships* (New York: Holt, 1973).

[31]Gregory Tanaka, *The Intercultural Campus: Transcending Culture and Power in American Higher Education* (New York: Peter Lang, 2007).

[32]Dietrich Bonhoeffer, *Life Together*, trans. John W. Doberstein (New York: Harper & Row, 1954).

[33]Max DePree, *Leadership Jazz* (New York: Currency Doubleday, 1992).

influence their basic life functions (e.g., eating, sleeping, hygiene, and class attendance). If faculty and staff engage students with God's patience and kindness, students can experience the hope in Jesus Christ as the one who has committed to never leave or withdraw support (Heb 13:5). Sometimes students disclose sinful thoughts and/or actions in response to their developmental distress, which James teaches can lead to healing, especially when such confession is followed by prayer (Jas 5:16). Faculty and staff need to be alert to uncharacteristic changes in students' basic life functions and how sharing such a concern with student development staff can help mobilize support from highly trained professionals to care for students. Such training assumes and perhaps stretches institutions of higher education to organize student-support offices under the leadership structure of one dean who can help foster an overall institutional ethos of support.

What Boyer did not address in his chapter on building a caring college community was what happens when uncaring actions occur. If crisis is part of identity development for students, as Erikson's research concludes, then it is likely that the development of a campus identity around an ethic of support will be negatively shaped over time by uncaring moments on a college campus.

Unfortunately, most colleges have recently experienced a greater number of unexpected painful, uncaring moments on their campuses and in the media, both traditional and social. Yet if colleges are prepared to live into community to reflect on and learn from them, uncaring moments do not necessarily lead to diminishing an ethos of care. Christine Pohl has written about developing practices of (1) embracing gratitude as a way of life, (2) making and keeping promises, (3) living truthfully, and (4) practicing hospitality, which may be particularly helpful for the organizational sense-making that often follows conflict and tragedy.[34] When painful conflicts or tragedies are lived out in public, an ethos of care has the potential of becoming systemic. There is no hiding. All eyes are waiting and watching for how members of the college community will respond to the situation and to each other. Just as students need to learn to engage with each other, so also college administrators, faculty, and staff must have the training to foster institutional identity around an ethos of care by engaging in authentic dialogue following conflicts and tragedies; these practices can in turn promote reflection, listening, and prayer. A campus-wide conflict or tragedy creates an unexpected opportunity to learn mutual dependence.

---

[34]Christine D. Pohl, *Living into Community: Cultivating Practices That Sustain Us* (Grand Rapids: Eerdmans, 2012).

Christians know that serving each other under duress is only possible through the help of the Holy Spirit, through whom we find a way to bear, believe, hope, and endure all things, necessary actions the apostle Paul teaches about love (1 Cor 13:7). Love is the most essential element for sensitively supporting the well-being of each member, and it is the foundation of service to others. An ethos of care requires the deep soak of time and commitment on the part of all. For a Christian, such care is rooted in Scripture. The apostle Paul, in 1 Corinthians 13, defines love as patient and kind. Along with patience and kindness, James instructs, "be quick to hear, slow to speak, slow to anger" (Jas 1:19 ESV).

Scripture promotes a robust vision for unity (Ps 133:1; Eph 4:1-3) and peace (Ps 34:14; Rom 14:17-19; 12:18; Heb 12:14). If Christ followers are to realize this unity and peace, they must treat one another in loving-kindness, especially in conflict and tragedy, which are opportunities to be a living testimony of God's patience and kindness through the person of Jesus Christ and in the helping power of the Holy Spirit (Jn 17:20-23). Gathering together for corporate questions and listening through civil dialogue, worship, and prayer with each other and with Jesus Christ are important attributes of Christian community, particularly in the aftermath of campus tragedy or conflict. Such gatherings are embodied reminders of gratitude for God's presence in all things, the blessings of his Word, and the fellowship that is possible through the Holy Spirit. God's promise to make all things new (Rev 21:5) can begin to plant a seed of hope in the midst of lament.

Boyer's words about the importance of a caring college community sound almost prophetic when read today. Racial tensions are rife on campuses across the country. Polarization saturates state and national politics, while the space between the wealthy and the poor expands. Natural disasters fill the pages of the news, as do acts of violence committed against innocent and unsuspecting individuals and groups. International conflicts have created unprecedented displacement among millions of people when at the same time US politicians are restricting its borders to immigrants. Genocidal patterns repeat themselves in countries around the world.

With the advent of the internet after Boyer penned *Campus Life*, college students arrive with a constant awareness of how uncaring the world can be. And yet, these are the same students who, along with faculty and staff, are created in the image of a Triune God who lives in relational unity with distinctions, and who is the source of patience, kindness, and support for daily life—a true and faithful friend who is committed to the well-being of his followers forever. A caring community strives to reflect this love.

PART ONE

...

CHAPTER SIX

A CELEBRATIVE COMMUNITY

DORETHA O'QUINN AND TIM YOUNG

In 2012, Vanguard University launched a new summer bridge program to promote the recruitment, retention, and success of incoming Hispanic students at risk of failing due to poor high school academic performance. As a burgeoning Hispanic-Serving Institution, this demographic was becoming a more prominent component of institutional enrollment. Twenty students were admitted to the program and given extra support through the summer bridge program. At the end of the academic year, only one of these first bridge students remained at the institution; most were not able to thrive academically. Upon reflection and evaluation, it became clear that the institution was not equipped to support the needs of this new demographic of students and needed to improve the systems dedicated to supporting the success and retention of all students.

Six years later, seventy students entered the university bridge program as part of a revamped science summer bridge program. Over the last six years, as the university has engaged in an intentional process of focusing on updated programs and services designed to meet the needs of current students, the retention of these students increased to match the overall institutional retention rate. The lessons learned from the initial failure and subsequent institutional reflection helped Vanguard transition into an institution more effective at supporting and celebrating all students.

In *Campus Life: In Search of Community*, Ernest Boyer and his colleagues describe a "Celebrative Community"[1] as one in which the heritage, traditions, achievements, and beliefs of the institution are remembered, and where shared

---

[1] The Carnegie Foundation for the Advancement of Teaching, *Campus Life: In Search of Community*, foreword by Ernest L. Boyer (Princeton, NJ: The Carnegie Foundation for the Advancement of Teaching, 1990).

rituals affirm both tradition and change. This focus, they write, creates a vibrant and life-giving environment for students. They then posit that a college must never forget its foundations and history and should engage students in intentionally creating the campus culture. While this value is still true today, much has changed since their initial writing, including an increased national aversion to the high costs of college tuition, students wrestling with whether college is worth the cost, and shifting demographics that radically change student-body composition. Today, institutions must wrestle with how to best be a celebrative community in view of these changes.

Being a celebrative community is even more important today and perhaps more difficult as universities navigate the difficult tensions shared by upholding transition and managing change. Institutions may not be prepared to bridge the gap between alumni and today's students. Legacy traditions and celebrations that once created culture may no longer connect to current students. To remain relevant, colleges must explore innovative ways to allow students to thrive by reexamining culture, rituals, and traditions to ensure the current student population is actively engaged while also honoring lessons of the past. The goal is to truly be an institution where "rituals affirming both tradition and change are widely shared."[2]

The purpose of this chapter is to create a discussion about navigating the tension between tradition and change and to explore how institutions can thrive while also honoring lessons of the past. This discussion will include lessons learned in Vanguard's transition to a majority-minority-serving institution and a Hispanic-Serving Institution.

Vanguard was a predominantly white institution for most of the past ninety years. Gradually, as demographics began to change and reflected the demographic development in Southern California, Vanguard changed as well. In 2012, more than 25 percent of students were Hispanic. By 2017, 45 percent of freshmen were Hispanic, and 63 percent were students of color. These demographic shifts paralleled what was happening across the United States, yet Vanguard was not prepared or ready for the transition. Many institutions are in the same situation and must now wrestle with a similar tension of navigating demographic changes with students who are different from student populations of previous years. As a predominantly white institution, connecting students through common rituals was a simple process, as both students and staff and faculty came from a largely monocultural background.

---

[2]Carnegie Foundation, *Campus Life*, 8.

As cultural and ethnic differences began to emerge, finding new ways to connect students from diverse backgrounds created new opportunities and challenges. Once-meaningful rituals that met the needs of students from a predominantly white cultural heritage began to lose meaning. One specific example was found in a residence hall, where new freshmen female students gathered together in the gym, yelled and screamed, and cheered for their floors. Some students felt isolated from the residence hall community as a result of this event, as this experience did not fit their personal or cultural preference. Rather than bringing students together, this traditional event created more of a division between students from different cultural backgrounds. This demographic and cultural transition created opportunities for faculty and staff to identify new ways to implement historical rituals while still striving to maintain a cohesive institutional identify.

These new students brought experiences to the community that informed their worldview, but frequently they could not see themselves in the history of the college as captured in pictures, on walls and yearbooks, campus images, or viewbooks. One simple resolution was to complete a marketing audit and ensure all publications, websites, and printed materials reflected current students. To resolve this larger tension, the institution began to examine all aspects of the student experience, including classroom instruction, chapel, residence life, and annual university events, to name a few, and examined the ways students experienced the institutional heritage. Findings indicated that many students felt isolated by their classroom experience or what happened in chapel.

In the classroom, students reported experiencing faculty who used classroom examples that didn't relate to their cultural background. They described how this made them feel isolated and disconnected from other students. They often felt like second-class students due to this isolation. In chapel, the teaching or worship styles differed from their home churches and made the students feel unwelcome. They reported frequently not seeing people who looked like them teaching or leading worship. These responses began a thorough process of modifying chapel to include more diverse worship styles and speakers. In addition, a chief diversity officer was hired to ensure that inclusive excellence occurred at all levels of the institution.

Over time, resolving these tensions strengthened the institutional ability to support a more diverse student population. As alumni return to Vanguard, they see and notice the differences, yet still recognize the values that initially connected them to the Vanguard community. Although the university and its programs and services look different, there is an ongoing commitment to ensure the heritage message is inclusive for all.

To begin this process of reflection, institutions must identify and then navigate the tensions shared by tradition and change. As Vanguard engaged a process of reflection, a few principles emerged that helped bridge the gap between the past and the present and maintain what Boyer has called the celebrative community. Vanguard learned the following lessons through this process of reflection: (1) learn from institutional history; (2) revise tradition for current students; (3) align academic and student affairs; (4) enhance campus storytelling; and (5) train faculty and staff. We'll look at each of these in turn.

LEARN FROM INSTITUTIONAL HISTORY

There is much wisdom to be gained in honoring lessons from the past. Contextualizing university history for current students is an essential contribution to truly becoming a celebrative community today. A core question to consider is, how do history and legacy connect to what the institution is today? By reviewing the mission, rituals, and traditions through the lens of current students, much can be learned.

To this end, revisiting institutional history is an essential aspect of being a celebrative community today. Vanguard's founder was a woman, Huldah Needham, who desired to address social justice issues locally and internationally. She was discouraged by the difficult requirements and immense resources necessary to begin a Bible school for Christian workers.[3] Still, she pushed forward, sharing her vision to develop an institution, Vanguard, that integrated academic learning with an emphasis on social justice. During the 1920s, most enterprises were founded by men; women encountered more barriers. Through grit and fortitude, Needham persisted in this vision and the institution that exists today is a result of her vision and perseverance.

Needham's story is told to new students at Vanguard in a manner that encourages students to see themselves in what she accomplished—breaking down social barriers, pursuing a vision and calling, and accomplishing difficult goals. This social justice emphasis has been integral to the DNA of Vanguard since 1920. Many alumni have started organizations dedicated to helping others as a part of their educational experience. These students and their experiences are immersed in a culture that focuses on social justice issues, which can be traced back to the founding of the institution. By teaching all students this history, institutional values are kept alive and nurtured in the lives of students in vibrant and living ways.

---

[3]Lewis Wilson, *A Vine of His Own Planting* (Costa Mesa, CA: Vanguard University, n.d.).

REVISE TRADITIONS FOR CURRENT STUDENTS

How are values, rituals, and practices transmitted and communicated to new students? How is this different from thirty years ago? These questions are important to consider and reflect on in order to ensure that traditions and rituals meet the needs of current students. Boyer and his colleagues describe rituals as "what unites the campus and gives students a sense of belonging." If rituals are to be maintained, they need to affirm the institutional history while also embracing the changing university environment. Institutional legacy, history, and traditions are initially about current students. However, when they are lived out in a transformational way, their impact will continue in the lives of alumni who will choose to value and embrace them for a lifetime.

As students change, traditions must change from a monocultural focus to one that represents diverse cultural perspectives. New-student orientation is an important tradition for building legacy and heritage. As a result, orientation at Vanguard now includes an intentional focus placed on ethnically diverse and inclusive orientation practices to ensure family members and students are welcomed. The increase in first-generation students has also resulted in an orientation more focused on sharing how to navigate college, access resources, and ask for help.

For most Christian institutions, chapel provides an important foundation for enhancing community and maintaining a common conversation. An important question to consider is, how can chapel provide a space to cultivate a community that includes and celebrates all community members and identify how difficult conversations can serve as a bridge to enhancing community? At Vanguard, a chapel council was developed composed of diverse representation from across campus to speak into the planning and implementation of worship and chapel speakers. By cultivating diverse voices, the university created a more effective and representative chapel program that cultivated and deepened community.

Another strategy to bring new students into the history, traditions, and rituals of the institution was the launch of a new club called First to VU. This group brings first-generation faculty and staff together with students to ensure these students understand that they are an important part of the campus. By allowing faculty and staff to share their success stories and failures, students see aspirational individuals who become mentors. More importantly, students can see people like them who have successfully navigated the college experience.

ALIGN ACADEMIC AND STUDENT AFFAIRS

Many institutions operate as silos in their efforts to serve students. The academic enterprise now functions in semi-autonomous regions that, on their own, are quite busy and self-sufficient. Consider any institutional registrar, academic support, student development, or grounds/maintenance office. Yet students are holistic individuals who often have trouble navigating a dichotomized organization. Mastery of learning requires instructional integration. Students learn most effectively about community on campus, specifically a celebrative community, through alignment of the curricular and cocurricular. To be effective, student success must be central.

As campus services have expanded, the institutional mission can easily become diluted and students may receive an incoherent educational experience. Aligning student-learning outcomes inside and outside the classroom ensures a more integrated, holistic approach. W. Norton Grubb and Rebecca Cox developed a framework to assist institutions with *pedagogical alignment*, focusing on the relationship between teachers and learners and the ability to integrate curricular and cocurricular practices.[4] This is an essential but difficult practice.

Vanguard sought to answer the question, what do we desire our students to look like after attending Vanguard? This question guided an update and revision of core student-learning outcomes and the corresponding student affairs learning outcomes. These aligned learning outcomes became the foundation for a four-year discipleship plan, an intentional programmatic and academic strategy to ensure the Vanguard experience was imparted to all students. More importantly, this plan ensured that the values, legacy, and tradition of the institution were transmitted to all students in a meaningful way.

Having a clear framework of pedagogical alignment with academic and student affairs has ultimately strengthened the institution. Alignment creates consistency in both the curricular and cocurricular learning environments and moves students in one common direction to reach success. A second component of this alignment involves ensuring that faculty, staff, and students understand academic and student affairs goals and expected outcomes. Such outcomes must be clear, measurable, and student focused in ways that advance the mission of the institution.

ENHANCE CAMPUS STORYTELLING

Storytelling—institutional and personal—is an important component of developing and curating a strong community. At Vanguard, the institutional byline is "your story matters," which places a high value on the individual

---

[4]W. Norton Grubb and Rebecca Cox, "Pedagogical Alignment and Curricular Consistency: The Challenges for Developmental Education," in *Responding to the Challenges of Developmental Education*, ed. Carol Kozerecki, special issue of *New Directions for Community Colleges* 129 (Spring): 93-103.

narrative. For some individuals from diverse ethnic backgrounds, the focus is less on the individual narrative and more value is placed on the communal narrative. To navigate this tension, an important question to consider is, what institutional stories should be told? Crosscultural perspectives of narrative and storytelling must be understood to fully tap into legacy and history. George C. Rosenwald and Richard L. Ochberg describe personal stories as not merely ways of telling about one's life; they are how identity is constructed.[5] Understanding identity as a narrative construction is another way of conceptualizing personal change. People understand themselves and how they change over the course of their lives by describing a narrative. Telling a story that matters is a uniquely human way of meaning-making and helps to create an understanding that makes sense.

At Vanguard, an emphasis has been placed on allowing all students to share their story in a way they find most beneficial. Students utilize life maps, which are an intentional process of identifying important people, places, events, and experiences, to cultivate a common conversation and allow them to share their personal and cultural narratives. In addition to this storytelling tool, cultural graduation celebrations were also developed to allow different cultural groups to share their corporate stories.

The purpose of these celebrations is to honor the challenges, traditions, and values of students from different cultures. These celebrations allow the narratives of students from different cultural backgrounds to be heard and understood by others. While initially confusing to majority students, these events have created helpful conversations about commonality and difference. The first event was a Hispanic graduation celebration to honor the hard work and determination of students, many who were first-generation. This celebration honored the culture of *la Familia*—the family—where the entire family was a part of college selection, paying for it, and ultimately supporting students to graduation.

After this first celebration, a Black Graduation Celebration and Asian Pacific Islander Celebration were implemented as well. These celebrations created space to honor students and allowed them to tell their own stories of their journey through the institution. These celebrations and other events like them help Vanguard be mindful of what the institution was and what it is becoming. A truly celebrative community is inclusive of all student stories and allows them to join the institutional legacy, heritage, and rituals.

---

[5]George C. Rosenwald and Richard L. Ochberg, *Storied Lives: The Cultural Politics of Self-Understanding* (New Haven, CT: Yale University Press, 1992).

TRAIN FACULTY AND STAFF

A significant barrier that emerges as a student population transitions from one majority to another is the long-standing faculty and staff who might not change as rapidly as the student population. It is imperative that faculty and staff of the dominant campus community learn to identify their biases and blind spots in their ability to navigate diverse experiences successfully. To respond to this challenge, Vanguard engaged an intentional plan to educate faculty and staff regarding how to bring heritage rituals and traditions to present students.

The first training component was focused on developing capacity among faculty and staff to meet the needs of diverse community members. The Intercultural Development Inventory[6] is an assessment tool developed to enhance the cultural competency of faculty and staff members, measuring cultural competence on a continuum (denial, polarization, minimalization, acceptance, adaptation)[7] along with an individual development plan (IDP) for support to ensure ongoing process and growth toward cultural competence. This assessment ensures continual progress of cultural growth if it is taken seriously and there is commitment to the process.

The second component included launching an Institute for Faculty Development with the goal of equipping faculty members with the skills necessary to modify their instructional practices and pedagogy, align curriculum, and bridge the gap from past practices to the needs of current students. The institution has committed to these practices to create inclusive teaching and learning experiences that create space for a diversity of views and ideas that can be shared and honored and where sustainable relationships are formed.

Vanguard also launched a Compassion Retreat with the goal of bringing together faculty, staff, and students from a variety of cultural groups to cultivate a common conversation about navigating differences and to ultimately cultivate a culture of compassion and caring in the community. A secondary purpose has been to cultivate diversity allies, majority-culture members who choose to confront difficult issues alongside those not in the majority. These retreats have deepened the community conversation regarding the institutional commitment to supporting students and have created an environment focused on student success.

---

[6]Mitchell R. Hammer, "A Measure of Intercultural Sensitivity: The Intercultural Development Inventory," in *The Intercultural Sourcebook*, ed. Sandra M. Fowler and Monica G. Mumford (Yarmouth, ME: Intercultural Press, 1999), 2:61-72.

[7]Raymond D. Terrell and Randall B. Lindsey, *Culturally Proficient Leadership: The Personal Journey Begins Within* (Thousand Oaks, CA: Corwin Press, 2009).

An important focus of campus training also extends to understanding the campus climate. An important question to reflect on is, how does the institution build capacity among faculty, staff, and students to cultivate cultural competency? which is the ability and capacity to successfully navigate differences. To believe that all community members will naturally know how to relate to each other is naive and at times countercultural. The institution must develop within its leadership, faculty, and staff a capacity for crosscultural sensitivity and culturally proficient leadership. It is important that students learn about historical rituals and how new rituals become culturally relevant to the community. Recognition, education, and celebration of cultural holidays (Martin Luther King, Hispanic Heritage Month, Women's History Month, etc.) create a rich awareness of diverse campus needs and cultures.

By engaging the entire community in this journey toward enhanced competence and inclusive practices, all students will engage in learning experiences meaningful to them, heritage remains strong, and the celebrative community now embodies and is practiced by each student, faculty member, and staff member. As individuals learn to navigate culture more effectively and identify areas of personal development, diverse faculty, staff, and students are engaged in redefining and creating a healthy institutional celebrative community.

CONCLUSION AND CHALLENGE

The dissonance between who students are today and the culture of the institution make the concept of being a celebrative community an essential yet difficult conversation. Thirty years later, the work Boyer and his colleagues offered is still relevant. As institutions wrestle with how to navigate the tension of cultivating a celebrative community, the key seems to be making practices inclusive for all faculty, staff, and students by acknowledging that society and culture have changed. The most effective institutions at cultivating a celebrative community will be ones where there is an intentional cultivation of curricular and cocurricular practices that identify ways to bring the campus together. Finding ways to connect diverse students and alumni who bring a unique heritage with meaningful rituals seems to be one of the central challenges for institutions today. If thoughtfully implemented, rituals, heritage, and tradition will adequately transcend any organizational or demographic change.

WALKING THE "NARROW RIDGE" OF CHRISTIAN CALLING AND ACADEMIC EXCELLENCE

BECK A. TAYLOR

Imagine an institution of higher learning located atop a beautiful but craggy mountain ridge. Its location gives the institution matchless views, scenic perspectives, and a winsome and palpable sense of something bigger than itself that inspires those who work and study there to bring their full selves—professional, personal, spiritual—to the important work at hand.

The educational institution located there is strikingly lonely. There are few other similarly located colleges and universities that share its vantages. Down one side of the "narrow ridge" that locates our conspicuously lonesome institution are located many other colleges and universities that, despite their variety, resources, and relative modern successes, represent a bygone age in American higher education. These institutions are among scores of private colleges and universities founded by the church and for the church, yet these colleges and universities slowly, beginning in the early part of the twentieth century, began to jettison their faithful missions and slide down the steep slope toward secularism.

The reasons why these institutions made the choices that eventually distinguished them from the relatively few remaining church-affiliated colleges and universities, ones like our isolated institution, are many and complex. Perhaps they sought greater academic prestige and found the historic linkages to their founding denominations too restraining for that goal. Or, perhaps, without presumably burdensome theological and doctrinal constraints, the leaders of these institutions hoped that they could navigate more deftly the increasingly pluralistic forces at play on their campuses and among their constituencies. Regardless, these once faithful institutions hardly resemble the places they were created to be.

Our solitary institution located atop our imaginary ridge isn't alone just because some of its former neighbors walked too closely to the slippery slope of secularism. There is another slope just as dangerous—the slope of rigid and anti-intellectual sectarianism. You see, located at various points on the other side of the narrow ridge are institutions that have at times neglected their academic missions in pursuit of dogmatically constructed sets of beliefs, beliefs that are to be protected at all costs, even at the risk of losing the essence of what it means to be a place of liberal (or liberating, if you like) learning.

Even if these faithful institutions also aspire to locate on the ridge, too common at these places are proverbial hedges cultivated to grow thick and high enough to keep out those who are drawn to faithful conversations and learning and who have much to contribute to that discourse, but whose perspectives and views of the world don't match with those espoused and protected by the institutions that find themselves on this slope. These institutions often lack rigorous debate, academic freedom, liberty of conscious, civil discourse, and sadly, any real student learning.

At Whitworth, we use the "narrow ridge" metaphor to describe our institution's aspirational goals within the vast and diverse landscape of higher education. Before I offend many of my Christian college colleagues, especially those friends who have contributed so brilliantly to the present volume, I want to be sure to say that I think the vast majority of Christ-professing institutions today, whether they lie closer to the "critical mass" or to the "orthodox" points on the spectrum offered by Robert Benne,[1] have avoided the temptations to slide very far down either of the two slopes our metaphor has offered. Indeed, Whitworth and many other Christian colleges and universities have rejected to a large degree either of the alternatives chased by the institutions that now find themselves closer to the mountain's valleys.

My predecessor at Whitworth, Bill Robinson, began using the narrow ridge metaphor in the 1990s, when Whitworth needed to center its own historical pendulum swing between the forces of relativism and fundamentalism. Robinson correctly and wisely discerned that Whitworth needed a new vocabulary by which to define itself, and to do so he borrowed a metaphor from twentieth-century Jewish philosopher Martin Buber.[2] Buber constructed his narrow ridge

[1]Robert Benne, *Quality with Soul: How Six Premier Colleges and Universities Keep Faith with Their Religious Traditions* (Grand Rapids: Eerdmans, 2001).
[2]Martin Buber, *Between Man and Man*, trans. Ronald Gregor Smith (London: Kegan Paul, 1947).

metaphor to illustrate how two opposing parties in a debate could come to-gether to find common ground. Mind you, the ridge was no "happy middle" where competing ideas and perspectives simply sought safety and neutral ground. Rather, Buber described the ridge as sometimes precarious, always potentially dangerous, and a place where the topology could potentially cause missteps and stumbles.

But, as Buber argued, the ground there was also fertile for discourse, under-standing, and discernment—the basic ingredients for learning. Paradox and contradiction could be explored on the ridge, and competing "truths" could be fully vetted. As Whitworth has adapted the metaphor's aspirational meaning, the narrow ridge has come to be symbolic of the place where faith and reason meet—the perfect geography, I would argue, for the modern Christian university inter-ested in both mind and heart, however difficult for Whitworth or any other in-stitution to perfectly navigate and summit.

BOYER'S VISION FOR (CHRISTIAN) ACADEMIC COMMUNITY

We cannot know whether Boyer knew of Buber's narrow ridge imagery, but I will argue that the essential elements of academic community Boyer articulates in *Campus Life*—being purposeful, open, just, disciplined, caring, and celebrative—fit well within my use and understanding of the aspirational language Buber of-fered. I am grateful for the additional insights and examples contributors to this volume have so generously provided, insights that serve to broaden our under-standing and realization of Boyer's ideals, and also to help us map Boyer's gener-alized constructs of community into our more specific Christian campus contexts.

Given my colleagues' contributions and extensions found within these pages, and given my own reading and understanding of Boyer's works and professional life, I'm persuaded that Boyer would have argued for exactly the kind of Christian institution that would set its sights on the narrow ridge. Boyer was first and foremost a true scholar and academic. He loved the academy, and he loved the search for truth. And as a product of and contributor to Christian higher edu-cation himself, he undoubtedly valued the faithful institutions that shaped and molded him.

For those Christian institutions that continue to value our cherished missional and church-related commitments, I suspect Boyer would encourage us to hold tightly to our pledges to be institutions of higher learning and to our commit-ments to remaining beacons of light and knowledge within the Christian intel-lectual tradition. As such, Boyer would have lamented the slow decay of Christian commitment among many colleges and universities. Boyer would not see faith and reason as so incompatible as to necessitate sacrificing faith in order to salvage academic credibility.

Equally vexing to Boyer, I contend, would be the choices some institutions might be tempted to make to protect their privileged values and beliefs so vigorously as to shut down the academic project altogether. Indeed, Boyer's community descriptors can and should be the vehicles by which faithful academic institutions remain faithful *and* academic. My colleagues who contributed to this volume have made many of those arguments well. In what follows, I briefly apply each of Boyer's community descriptors to the narrow ridge metaphor I've introduced.

BEING PURPOSEFUL ON THE NARROW RIDGE

The narrow ridge that connects faith and reason isn't the easiest to traverse, but it remains our aspirational goal. To mix metaphors, the intersection at the crossroads that connect Athens and Jerusalem is just out of the way enough that one might miss it altogether. Perhaps that's why so many institutions that once embraced faith and learning have fallen away, and why remaining faithful to mission and purpose is so critical to Christian colleges and universities today.

Our institutional missions must be the lenses through which all decisions are made. Whitworth's mission statement reads, in part, that the university will "provide its diverse students with an education of mind and heart, equipping graduates to honor God, follow Christ, and serve humanity." Not only does that mission consistently call us back to our faithful traditions and commitments, but it also reminds us of our desire to provide the very best education possible because doing so honors God and serves the world. Faithful institutions like ours see inherent complementarity between mind and heart education, although the world would often have us believe the two are mutually exclusive. In the university's history, one can find periods of time when Whitworth was better at elevating the *mind* component of its mission. During other periods, Whitworth excelled at *heart*. But as I like to remind our community, the conjunction *and* is an important one.

Institutions aspiring to the narrow ridge value *and*s far more than *or*s as they navigate important choices. Although often difficult to live out, the commitments to embrace faith *and* reason, grace *and* truth, curiosity *and* conviction, and freedom *and* responsibility are what set our kinds of institutions apart from those places where only one set of values prevails. Purposefully living out a mission that embraces complexity and nuance in the learning process, and in which paradox and difficulty are often uncovered and even celebrated when searching for truth, takes real resolve, particularly when many of our institutions' constituencies are arguing for easy answers and simplistic ways of thinking about the complex issues that dominate our culture.

I find it difficult to know how Christian colleges and universities can fully live into their missions to embrace faith and reason without a concerted effort to integrate Christian faith into the curricular and cocurricular experiences of all students. Perhaps there are successful Christian institutions that see the primary expression of their faithfulness confined only to cocurricular spaces, but I'm persuaded that the institutions that also expressly require Christian faculty to contend with how biblical and moral standards of the Christian tradition shape and inform their own disciplines are those that are best equipped to serve students well.

For an economist, for example, to ask her students to grapple with how embedded assumptions of self-interest used in neoclassical economic models of market behavior are in tension with more altruistic mandates from Scripture is a useful and illuminating exercise as students begin to wrap their heads around the difference between positive and normative scientific approaches. The Christian biologist who spends important time helping students see the tensions and complementarities between complex evolutionary processes and the divine creative narrative is helping his students navigate some of the most complex questions any human being can ask about meaning and order in the universe. Institutions move closer to the narrow ridge as they chase the most difficult questions by integrating faith and learning with the confidence that God will meet them on that exciting journey.

COMBINING OPENNESS AND FAITH ON THE NARROW RIDGE

The institutions that have eschewed their faithful foundations have done so presumably because they valued openness much more, and they didn't have the resolve to live into the challenges inherent in pursuing faith just as rigorously. Alternatively, the colleges and universities that chose to diminish their commitments to liberality decided, I presume, that to be more open as an academic community introduces potentially unwelcome views and perspectives into the mix. Those perspectives could pit their institutional positions on various doctrinal and ethical issues against those who argue for different perspectives, albeit often faithful ones, and it is feared that the institution's mission and witness could be diluted as a result.

Institutions that seek to locate themselves on the narrow ridge are both open *and* faithful. They are not open at the expense of their beloved values and commitments, but rather in service to them and to the academic tradition of testing ideas and positions for weakness and error. Practicing the virtues of intellectual and spiritual humility must be a part of our regular diet. The premise that for an institution to invite contrary ideas and viewpoints to campus necessarily conveys legitimacy or privilege to those who espouse such is simply wrongheaded. Our students will have to contend with opposing worldviews for the rest of their lives, and in much less nurturing environments. Why not expose them to the best ideas the world has to offer when they are with us? In addition, why not expose those ideas to rigorous thinking and critical questions with the added benefit of having thoughtful Christians alongside?

For instance, if a college or university takes an orthodox perspective on human sexuality and marriage, I would encourage it to host faithful and thoughtful Christians who see things differently. I would then encourage it to engage the community and its guests on the fundamental questions and resources found within the Christian tradition on the topic while discussing the strengths and weaknesses of various hermeneutical approaches. To be sure, students walk away with no less understanding of the institution's position on the issue, but they now have a more informed agency to formulate their own opinions and are better able to back them up with reasonable arguments.

I would even argue that if an institution's position on any controversial issue is well-formulated and articulated, it wouldn't be a threat to employ faculty members who explicitly hold competing perspectives, but who are also content to support and abide by the institution's place on the matter. Doing so internalizes the kind of commitments to openness and faithfulness about which we are talking. Whether on the part of the institution or an individual faculty member, *being wrong* on a subject is an important tradition and right within the academy. Although being incorrect on anything is nothing to celebrate, where would the world be without those who were willing to be wrong on any number of subjects, and where are we as a society because some of them actually ended up being right?

PURSUING JUSTICE ON THE NARROW RIDGE

One of the most common *ors* among many Christians today is the tension between the personal gospel of righteousness and salvation and the social gospel of truth and justice. Too many of our students at Whitworth and many other faithful institutions are divided along lines that separate those who feel their primary purpose on campus and in the world is to evangelize and bring souls to Christ and those who are most called to bringing peace and justice to a fractured society. Of course, Jesus embodied both commitments fully. The gospel of Christ is one that calls each of us, as individuals, to account for our sin and to seek the salvation offered only through Christ's death and resurrection. Jesus does indeed offer his commission to make disciples in his name and by the Spirit. Jesus also spent the majority of his time among the outcasts of society, preaching to and healing those whom culture saw as worthless. In many ways, Jesus was a champion of social justice. Jesus also offers his commandment to love others and to help the marginalized realize the kingdom of God.

Whitworth has been recognized by both religious and secular organizations for our work in relation to diversity, equity, and inclusion. Whitworth was one of the first institutions within the Council of Christian Colleges and Universities to hire a chief diversity officer. The mere mention of "diversity," however, raises suspicions in the minds of many Christians still today. "Inclusion" can be seen as a slippery slope that undermines many moral standards that have long been associated with Christian living. And "equity" can evoke memories of political interventions that have divided Americans and Christians for decades.

This language is loaded to be sure, but that shouldn't prevent institutions who seek to reflect Christ's truth and grace from seeing their roles, in part, as instruments for Christ's redeeming work as we seek to identify and remove structural and systemic causes for racism, sexism, classism, ableism, and many other forms of social and economic segregation. And our work to address these social ills in our society needn't compete with our desire for our students and others to come closer to Christ as a result of interacting with our institutions.

Is there a tension in reconciling standards for righteousness embedded within the Bible and the world's advocacy for diversity and inclusion in their fullest sense? Of course there is. But the institution aspiring to the narrow ridge embraces complexity, seeks both biblical and worldly resources as it approaches difficult issues, and equips its community members to ask and answer complex questions. In doing so, the faithful institution also unambiguously names discrimination, abuse, and subjugation as among the most evil things the world can produce, and it stands in sharp opposition to any and all who would demean the humanity of others rather than seeing in them the sacred image of God.

FINDING DISCIPLINE ON THE NARROW RIDGE

Harry Lewis, former dean of Harvard College, once famously said that educators mustn't forget that college is about turning eighteen- and nineteen-year-olds into twenty-one- and twenty-two-year-olds. For most of our students, college is a coming-of-age experience. As such, discipline is a developmentally appropriate ingredient for thriving students and healthy communities. Additionally, students and other community members must recognize a cogent and logical connection between community standards and the institution's mission and values. It would be consistent, for instance, for a college or university that elevates healthy living and campus safety to prohibit alcohol or tobacco consumption within its boundaries. Similarly, it would be inconsistent for an institution that values freedom of expression and liberty of conscience to deny students the right to protest peacefully on campus.

At Whitworth, we've decided that less is more when it comes to articulating campus rules. Although such rules and standards are critically important to creating and sustaining community, Whitworth's members have reasoned that the world needs better decision-makers rather than more rule followers, and that value for individual responsibility and personal agency has shaped our approach. "The Big Three," as Whitworth's students have named them, articulate the three broad and encompassing standards that largely shape the expectations of students while they are on campus. We've distilled what could be a very large number of rules and expectations to these: (1) students will refrain from alcohol, marijuana, or illegal drug use when on campus; (2) students will not engage in extramarital sexual behavior when on campus; and (3) students will sustain community by refraining from any behavior that injures another, whether socially, academically, spiritually, physically, or psychologically. When you get right down to it, we at Whitworth have reasoned that almost all other rules can be subsumed into these three. Of course, Whitworth has all kinds of policies that govern things like parking, registration priority, and academic honesty, to name a few, but even most of those policies can be reduced into our system. Whitworth's student handbook is, in turn, surprisingly short when it comes to articulating rules.

Again, at the heart of Whitworth's approach are the values we uphold. Different institutions will place varying accent marks on the dimensions they desire to elevate, and those decisions will shape the ways these institutions create and sustain discipline of all kinds on campus. But if we take Lewis's observation about creating adults seriously, we will begin to treat our students like adults in appropriate and timely ways. As I mentioned, agency and responsibility are core values at Whitworth, so we give our students a lot of both.

For example, students sit on all hiring committees of the university, whether for a groundskeeper or for a senior faculty position. Our student newspaper conducts its business with independence and autonomy—never once have I made an editorial decision in my time as president. Twice-weekly chapel services are not required of students, but our worship space is often standing-room only. And students in our residence halls set their own rules concerning quiet times and visiting hours. Institutions seeking to occupy the narrow ridge will value freedom *and* responsibility and give students plenty of opportunities to exercise both.

CARING FOR OTHERS ON THE NARROW RIDGE

Perhaps there is no other more unique or consistent dimension of our students' shared campus experiences than the caring and nurturing relationships they develop while at our institutions. Students often report that their relationships outside of the classroom with faculty, staff, administrators, and peers are what shape their largely positive impressions of their time with us. Many of our students point to strong community and personal attention when they boast about us, and our own marketing and admissions materials certainly seem to take them at their word.

Despite these positive outcomes, I'm reminded daily that there are some students who simply do not have this experience at Whitworth. These students don't feel like they've been cared for, at least not completely. The reasons for the less than enthusiastic response to their time with us are many and varied. Perhaps they are first-generation college students and the university didn't do a great job helping them to navigate the complex nature of our largely bureaucratic and cumbersome institution. Or they are students of color who represent racial and ethnic populations that have historically had little or no access to our historically white and relatively affluent campus. These students saw far too few faculty members with their own diverse experiences, and their racial or ethnic histories and traditions were largely absent from our curricula. Or they are students with physical disabilities, or students with learning differences, for whom carrying a normal schedule without appropriate accommodations made their time with us more difficult and less encouraging than it should have been. Simply put, Whitworth wasn't made with these students in mind. We shouldn't be surprised, then, when we don't serve them as well as we'd like or should.

The narrow ridge metaphor is a powerful one, but like all useful metaphors, it can break down on some important dimensions. Primarily, "narrow" is not a term I'd like to associate with my university. If anything, I've argued for a broader and more expansive Christian university, not one defined by its limiting boundaries. If by narrow we mean to imply less welcoming, or not designed to serve the needs of all students whom we invite onto our campuses, then our work should be centered on turning the narrow ridge into the wide ridge, or something like it. On a very practical level, if institutions like ours are to survive, then we will have to attend to the work of including more diverse student populations. But, on a moral level, we have the imperative to break down barriers, real and perceived, that lessen the experience of some students while eliminating old models of education that cannot serve the needs of all students.

CELEBRATING ON THE NARROW RIDGE

For the first 125 years of Whitworth's history, it had no ceremonial icon to use at academic processionals and commencement ceremonies. Many universities our age have historic items that serve such purposes, such as a ceremonial mace or other object. These items represent both the historical significance of the institution and the connections with generations past as students participate in ceremonies and events that connect them to their institution's identity and culture.

For Whitworth's quasquicentennial anniversary, my wife and I wanted to commission such an icon to use for future celebrations. I had in mind to design a mace, along with input from our campus historians and from Whitworth's students in history and art. Every other institution I had served prior to coming to Whitworth used a mace. As the project began, an art student wrote a paper on the history and symbolic meanings of ceremonial maces. In that research, the student taught me that such items cannot be removed from their practical and symbolic references to war and violence and to patriarchal cultures. The mace's phallic shape and its connection to violent symbols of power caused this young student to boldly and courageously recommend to me that we look elsewhere for a symbol to use at a Christian university devoted to peace and the full inclusion of women. I was easily persuaded. We eventually decided to use a pinecone instead, beautifully made with glass and bronze. There's a lot of symbolism to that iconic shape, and if you've ever been on our beautiful treed campus in eastern Washington, you'll have a better understanding of its resonance within our community.

I tell this final story because it highlights so much of what I've tried to emphasize for those of us leading institutions gutting it out on the narrow ridge. As I've argued, the scenic views and inspirational location atop our metaphorical mountain are awesome, but practical life on the ridge—where faith and reason meet—is much harder to navigate, even if the rewards are great. You see, in that relatively small but hugely symbolic decision to choose a pinecone over a mace were the elements of community that Boyer called us to: a deference to mission and purpose, a reliance on liberal learning, a desire to seek and model justice and inclusion, a willingness to give freedom and responsibility to students, a deep care for our community members and their personhood, and, yes, a desire to celebrate all that our institutions have to offer. The type of community that Boyer championed so many years ago is the kind of community that comes naturally to those of us who aspire to live deeply into our commitments to honor God, follow Christ, and serve humanity through higher education. By the grace of God, may we ever populate the narrow ridge that educates and inspires, for the glory of God!

PART TWO

. . .

*CAMPUS
LIFE*

. . .

BY THE CARNEGIE
FOUNDATION
FOR THE ADVANCEMENT
OF TEACHING (1990)

TABLES

ACKNOWLEDGMENTS

This special report is the result of a year-long effort by many people. Irving Spitzberg and Virginia Thorndike, assisted by Mariam Kurtz, were the key research team, helping to organize the project from the very start. They participated in campus visits, conducted research, and drafted text. We are very grateful for their long and thorough effort.

Also conducting the site visits were Steve Diner, Martin Finkelstein, J. Eugene Haas, Gene I. Maeroff, Barbara Moran, and Jack Schuster. Their site work added vitality and immediacy to the study as well as invaluable information.

This project was in every respect a collaborative endeavor. We thank Robert H. Atwell, President of the American Council on Education, and the ACE Board of Directors, chaired by James Whalen, for suggesting this study in the first place, and for providing great encouragement and support throughout.

The American Council on Education joined with The Carnegie Foundation to conduct the survey of college and university presidents. Special recognition must be given Donna Shavlik, Blandina Cardenas Ramirez, and Russel C. Jones, and most especially to Elaine El-Khawas, who rendered invaluable editorial service. These colleagues provided rich additional information and extensive editorial comment as the manuscript was being shaped.

The National Association of Student Personnel Administrators and the Student Affairs Research, Evaluation and Testing Office of the University of Arizona joined with the American Council on Education to conduct the National Survey of Chief Student Affairs Officers. They contributed enormous energy and resources to our project, and we especially recognize the Executive Directors Elizabeth Nuss and Richard Kroc for their crucial role.

This project would not have been possible without the generous grant we received from The Henry Luce Foundation. I'm especially grateful to Robert Armstrong, Executive Director, for his great encouragement and wise counsel, which reinforced our conviction that this is a timely study.

As always I am most grateful to the staff of The Carnegie Foundation, whose work was particularly crucial to the final shape of the report. Charles Glassick, Mary Huber, and Gene Maeroff contributed immeasurably to drafting and editing the manuscript, as well as Dale Coye in the final stages. Mary Jean Whitelaw, assisted by Lois Harwood, kept track of the data and organized all of the tabular material. Hinda Greenberg and Patricia Klensch-Balmer provided invaluable support from the library. Dawn Ott and Laura Bell produced miracles of speed and quality under tight deadlines in word processing the numerous revisions, and Laura assisted with producing and proofreading the book as well. Dee Sanders not only supervised word processing, but also assisted with the design and accomplished the painstaking work of formatting and producing camera-ready pages on the desktop publisher. Jan Hempel, with great skill and under an impossibly tight deadline, edited, copyedited, and designed the book, oversaw its production, and proofread it, as well.

Ernest L. Boyer
President
The Carnegie Foundation for the Advancement of Teaching

FOREWORD

BY ERNEST L. BOYER

While preparing this report on campus life, I've reflected frequently on the nearly four decades of higher education history I've observed firsthand. The longer I thought about it, the more I was struck by the fact that typical college-age students certainly learn outside the classroom as well as within it, and that each decade, from the fifties to the eighties, seemed to have its own distinctive flavor in relation to student life. We human beings like to slice up our lives into little segments, often defining epochs where they don't exist. But in this case the categories seem to hold.

Consider the 1950s. I was in California during this exhilarating era, and the mood was optimism unrestrained. The emphasis was on buildings, on faculty recruitment, and on the much-applauded master plan for higher education. As for students, they came in ever larger numbers, but the preoccupation at the time was focused on expansion, not the quality of campus life. Those who enrolled— even the G.I.'s—were expected to behave themselves and live by the rules. And campus regulations, though somewhat outdated, were rarely challenged.

Then came the 1960s and, almost overnight, the mood shifted from optimism to survival. The academy hunkered down as angry students folded, spindled, and mutilated computer cards, challenging the huge, impersonal enterprise higher education had become. "I'm not a number," students shouted, "I'm a person." "By what authority," they asked, "can the university arbitrarily regulate our lives?"

I recall those days with mixed emotions. There were times of anger, fear, and sadness. But I also remember those fleeting moments when the intense, yet honest, discourse with caring students revealed what a true community of learning is all about. For example, the "teach-ins," at their best, brought faculty and students out of little boxes into forums where larger, more consequential issues were considered.

Still, the 1960s will always be remembered more for the Kent State killings than for the dialogue about student life or the efforts at educational reform. Indeed, while old rules were abolished, changes were made more out of compromise than conviction, and few colleges had the imagination or the courage to replace abandoned rules with more creative views of campus life.

Perhaps the 1970s are best left unremembered. What, in fact, did happen during this uninspired decade? The good news was that higher education had survived and that serious effort was being made to open college doors to traditionally bypassed students. But in the public mind, the academy had lost its innocence, and while recovering from the onslaughts of the sixties, higher education experienced new pressures imposed by an economic downturn. Further, the baby boom was over, and college leaders heard alarming predictions that enrollments would decline and that hundreds of colleges would close.

In the 1970s, the role of students was ambiguous, at best. Faculty moved quickly to regain control over academic life, tightening general education requirements that had been reluctantly relaxed. In social matters, however, there was no comparable effort to either reestablish rules or to think about a new model of community that could replace the old. Further, the sense of urgency and altruism faded, and confronted by the harsh realities of the economic downturn, students became more concerned about credentials than confrontation.

The 1980s brought another mood to campus. The euphoria of the 1950s did not return, but neither did the anger of the 1960s, nor the depression of the 1970s. The new climate experienced by higher education was a mix of confidence and caution. Finances moderately improved, enrollments did not precipitously decline as had been predicted, faculty saw an upturn in their fortunes, and the second half of the 1980s emerged as a period of renewal.

I'm impressed that colleges and universities are focusing once again on undergraduates and on the quality of collegiate education, and today I hear more talk about the curriculum, about teaching, and about the quality of campus life than I've heard for years.

This focus on renewal is motivated, at least in part, by concerns about the darker side of student life. Confusion about governance and incidents of excessive drunkenness, incivility, and sexual and racial harassment could no longer be ignored, but more inspired motives also are involved. Everywhere, campus leaders have been asking how to make their institution a more intellectually and socially vital place. They understand that, in today's climate, new ways of imagining and creating community must be found.

The start of the new decade now presents, at least from my perspective, perhaps the most challenging moment in higher education in forty years. It affords us an unusual opportunity for American colleges and universities to return to their roots and to consider not more regulations, but the enduring values of a true learning community.

And I'm convinced that the challenge of building community reaches far beyond the campus, as well. Higher education has an important obligation not only to celebrate diversity but also to define larger, more inspired goals, and in so doing serve as a model for the nation and the world.

SEARCH FOR RENEWAL

American higher education is, by almost any measure, a remarkable success. In recent decades, new campuses have been built, enrollments have exploded, and today, many of our research centers are ranked world class. Still, with all of our achievements, there are tensions just below the surface and nowhere are the strains of change more apparent than in campus life.

College officials know they are no longer "parents," but they also know that their responsibilities, both legal and moral, extend far beyond the classroom, and many are now asking how to balance the claims of freedom and responsibility on the campus. At a recent meeting of college and university presidents, one participant explained his frustration this way: "We have growing racial tensions at our place. There's more crime, and I'm really frustrated about how the university should respond." Another president noted that white, black, and Asian students at his university have organized themselves into "separate worlds." "The 1990s," he said, "will be a time of confrontation."

The president of a large public university confessed: "I've been around a long time and frankly I'm more worried today than in the 1960s. Back then, you could meet with critics and confront problems head on. Today, there seems to be a lot of unspoken frustration which could explode anytime." And at the heart of these concerns was what yet another president called "the loss of community," a feeling that colleges are administratively and socially so divided that common purposes are blurred, or lost altogether.

These worries did not appear to be sentimental yearnings for a return to the days when colleges were isolated islands, tightly managed, serving the sons, and occasionally the daughters, of the privileged. Today's college and university leaders understand and celebrate the dramatic transformations that have re-shaped American higher education. Rather, these presidents with whom we spoke were reflecting the deep ambivalence many college leaders feel about how the campus should be governed. Every institution has clearly defined academic rules, but what about the social and civic dimensions of collegiate life? In these areas, where does the college responsibility begin and end?

It was in this context, then, that The Carnegie Foundation for the Advancement of Teaching, in cooperation with the American Council on Education, launched a study to consider social conditions on the campus. We found, first, a deep concern at most institutions about student conduct. College officials consider alcohol and drug abuse a very serious matter, one that poses both administrative and legal problems.

There is also a growing worry about crime. And while robberies and assaults have not reached the epidemic proportions recent headlines would suggest, many institutions are increasingly troubled about the safety of their students.

Especially disturbing is the breakdown of civility on campus. We were told that incidents of abusive language are occurring more frequently these days, and while efforts are being made to regulate offensive speech, such moves frequently compromise the university's commitment to free expression.

We also found that deeply rooted prejudices not only persist, but appear to be increasing. Students are separating themselves in unhealthy ways. Racial tensions have become a crisis on some campuses, and, sadly, we gained the unmistakable impression that the push for social justice that so shaped the priorities of higher education during the 1960s has dramatically diminished.

Further, even though bias against women is no longer institutionalized, sex discrimination in higher education persists in subtle and not-so-subtle forms. It shows up informally, we were told, in the classroom and occasionally in tenure and promotion decisions, too.

Finally, very early in our study, we observed an unhealthy separation between in-class and out-of-class activities. Many students, we discovered, are spending little time pursuing intellectual interests beyond the classroom. The goal of many is getting a credential, and while undergraduates worry about good grades, their commitment to the academic life is often shallow. Thus, it became increasingly apparent during our study that the quality of campus life has been declining, at least in part, because the commitment to teaching and learning is diminished.

Putting it all together, we conclude that the idyllic vision so routinely portrayed in college promotional materials often masks disturbing realities of student life. On most campuses expectations regarding the personal conduct of students are ambiguous, at best. The deep social divisions that all too often divide campuses racially and ethnically undermine the integrity of higher education. Sexism continues to restrict women. The lack of commitment to serious learning among students often saps the vitality of the undergraduate experience, and we ask: If students and faculty cannot join together in common cause, if the university cannot come together in a shared vision of its central mission, how can we hope to sustain community in society at large?

These concerns about campus life are not new, but surely they reveal themselves in strikingly new ways. Consider the students. Today's undergraduates are, by every measure, more mature than the teenagers who enrolled a century or two ago. They bring sophistication and a determined independence to the campus. But we also were told that, increasingly, many students come to college with personal problems that can work against their full participation in college life. And administrators are now asking: Is it possible for colleges to intervene constructively in the lives of students whose special needs and personal lifestyles are already well-established?

Further, lots of older people now populate the campus. These nontraditional students return to college to update job-related skills or to find a new direction for their lives. Often they enroll part-time, only attend a class or two each week, and because of complicated schedules, they are unable to participate fully in campus life. Given these profound changes in the composition of today's student body, administrators are now asking: Is it realistic even to talk about community in higher education when students have changed so much and when their commitments are so divided?

Diversity has also dramatically changed the culture of American higher education. America's first colleges were guided by a vision of coherence, and for the first two hundred years, college students appeared socially and economically to be very much alike. Campuses were populated mostly by men, drawn primarily from the privileged class. Virtually no black or ethnic minority students were enrolled and, at most of these colleges, a female student was "as welcome as an uninvited guest."[1]

Today, men and women students come from almost every racial and ethnic group in the country and from every other nation in the world. While colleges and universities celebrate this pluralism, the harsh truth is that, thus far, many campuses have not been particularly successful in building larger loyalties within a diverse student body, and there is disturbing evidence that deeply ingrained prejudices persist. Faculty, administrators, and students are now asking whether community can be achieved.

Consider also how the organization of higher education has been transformed. At first, the nation's colleges were small, face-to-face communities, places where the president, a few instructors, and the students all knew each other well—too well perhaps. As late as 1870, the typical American campus had, on average, only

---

[1]Helen Lefkowitz Horowitz, *Campus Life* (New York: Alfred A. Knopf, 1987), p. 68.

ten faculty and ninety students.[2] The president and instructors were responsible for everything involving the students.

With nineteenth century expansion, librarians were hired, then registrars. Deans became common in the 1890s and, at about the same time, vice presidents were appointed. Still, an intimate, informal atmosphere prevailed.

Colleges and universities today have become administratively complex. They are often organized into bureaucratic fiefdoms. Especially disturbing, the academic and nonacademic functions are now divided into almost wholly separate worlds, and student life concerns have become the province of a separate staff, with a dizzying array of "services" provided. The question is: How can the overall interests of students be well served in the face of such administrative fragmentation?

Most significant, perhaps, is the way campus governance has changed. Colonial colleges were, in the beginning, tightly regulated places, and the first college leaders did not doubt their responsibility to educate the whole person—body, mind, and spirit. One historian describes the climate this way: "Most members of these communities had been expected to gather permanently within their walls and to remain isolated from adult society for long periods; they were to dine together and share common lodgings in buildings sufficiently compact and secluded to permit officials to exercise a constant surveillance *in loco parentis*."[3]

By the late nineteenth century priorities had changed. Inspired by the European university model, faculty increasingly were rewarded for research, not teaching, and professional loyalty gradually shifted from the campus to the guild. Still, college leaders did not fully free themselves from concern for the "whole person," and presidents and faculty could not escape the feeling that their responsibility went beyond the classroom. Well into the twentieth century, many colleges, both public and private, continued to require daily chapel of all students. Residence halls were still closely monitored, and women, in particular, were strictly regulated. Even when the G.I.s came to campus, colleges kept student life affairs tightly reined.

The 1960s brought historic changes. During that decade, *in loco parentis* all but disappeared. Undergraduates enjoyed almost unlimited freedom in personal and social matters, and responsibility for residence hall living was delegated far down the administrative ladder, with resident assistants on the front lines of

---

[2]Calculated from U.S. Bureau of Census, *Historical Statistics of the United States, Colonial Times to 1970, Bicentennial Edition, Part 1* (Washington, D.C.: 1975), pp. 382-85. Also Victor J. Baldridge, et al., *Policy Making and Effective Leadership* (San Francisco: Jossey-Bass, 1978), p. 253.

[3]David F. Allmandinger, Jr., "New England Students and the Revolution in Higher Education, 1800-1900," in *The Social History of American Higher Education*, ed. B. Edward McClellan and William J. Reese (Urbana and Chicago: University of Illinois Press, 1988), p. 67.

supervision. Top administrators were often out of touch with day-to-day conditions on the campus.

The problem was, however, that while colleges were no longer parents, no new theory of campus governance emerged to replace the old assumptions. Regulations could not be arbitrarily imposed—on that everyone agreed—but what was left in doubt was whether codes of conduct should be established and, if so, who should take the lead. Unclear about what standards to maintain, many administrators sought to sidestep rather than confront the issue.

To complicate matters further, while college and university officials understood that their authority had forever changed, this shift toward a freer climate was not understood or accepted by either parents or the public. The assumption persists today that when an undergraduate "goes off to college," he or she will, in some general manner, be "cared for" by the institution. And it's understandable that parents feel the institution has betrayed them if a son or daughter is physically or emotionally harmed while attending college.

Even state legislators and the courts are not willing to take colleges off the hook. When a crime hits the campus, as in the widely publicized drug overdose Len Bias case several years ago, the university is held responsible, at least in the court of public opinion. And many administrators now confront these urgent questions: Where does the responsibility of the college begin and end? What standards should be used to judge conduct, especially if behavior is personally and socially destructive? How can an appropriate balance be struck between the personal rights and responsibilities of students and institutional concerns?

We do not wish to suggest that colleges and universities have been unresponsive to the new realities of campus life. Indeed, our study of campus life convinced us that quite the opposite is true. We found that almost all institutions have, in recent years, expanded dramatically their student services and recruited more professional staff—counselors, financial aid officers, residence hall supervisors, and the like. Further, colleges and universities have slowly shaped new codes of conduct, often in consultation with students. Many institutions also have created imaginative new orientation programs, and have introduced workshops on social issues and all-college forums throughout the year. Student personnel administrators especially deserve high praise for their sensitive and creative work, often making decisions under difficult conditions.

Still, hardly anyone is fully satisfied with the current situation. Good work is being done to improve the quality of campus life, but student personnel professionals, who carry most of the responsibility for student conduct, are expected to "keep the lid on" with no overall strategy to guide them. No one expects the campus to be problem free, and surely it's unrealistic to view the modern college as an island divorced from the outside world. But neither can colleges and universities live comfortably with a climate of endless ambiguity about how campus life decisions should be made.

How then should we proceed?

What is needed, we believe, is a larger, more integrative vision of community in higher education, one that focuses not on the length of time students spend on campus, but on the quality of the encounter, and relates not only to social activities, but to the classroom, too. The goal as we see it is to clarify both academic and civic standards, and above all, to define with some precision the enduring values that undergird a community of learning.

In response to this challenge, we propose six principles that provide an effective formula for day-to-day decision making on the campus and, taken together, define the kind of community every college and university should strive to be.

First, a college or university is an educationally *purposeful* community, a place where faculty and students share academic goals and work together to strengthen teaching and learning on the campus.

Second, a college or university is an *open* community, a place where freedom of expression is uncompromisingly protected and where civility is powerfully affirmed.

Third, a college or university is a *just* community, a place where the sacredness of the person is honored and where diversity is aggressively pursued.

Fourth, a college or university is a *disciplined* community, a place where individuals accept their obligations to the group and where well-defined governance procedures guide behavior for the common good.

Fifth, a college or university is a *caring* community, a place where the well-being of each member is sensitively supported and where service to others is encouraged.

Sixth, a college or university is a *celebrative* community, one in which the heritage of the institution is remembered and where rituals affirming both tradition and change are widely shared.

We recognize that these principles have to some degree informed decision making in higher education throughout the years. Our purpose in this report is to urge that they be adopted more formally as a *campus compact,* and be used more consistently as the basis for day-to-day decision making on the campus. With this in mind, we discuss in the following chapters just how the principles of community might be defined and how they might provide a new *post-in loco parentis* framework for governance in higher education, a framework that not only could strengthen the spirit of community on campus, but also provide, perhaps, a model for the nation.

PART TWO

• • •

CHAPTER ONE

A PURPOSEFUL COMMUNITY

First, a college or university is an educationally *purposeful* community, a place where faculty and students share academic goals and work together to strengthen teaching and learning on the campus.

We list the principle of educational purposefulness first because it is fundamental to all others. When we began this study, our primary aim was to focus on what one president called "the social pathologies on campus," issues that had little to do, it seemed, with the academic mission. However, as we visited campuses, it soon became clear that the academic and nonacademic could not be divided. At a college or university, teaching and learning are the central functions, and if faculty and students do not join in a common intellectual quest, if they do not take the educational mission of the institution seriously, then all talk about strengthening community is simply a diversion.

It may seem unnecessary to make this point. After all, an institution of higher education is, by definition, a place for learning. But it is precisely this priority that was, we found, too often undermined. Consider the matter of how students spend their time. A recent study revealed that about half of today's full-time students are employed and that they work, on average, twenty hours every week; for part-timers, it's thirty-six hours.[1] Even more revealing, only 23 percent of today's students spend sixteen or more hours each week in out-of-class study.[2] And during campus visits, when we asked under-graduates what engaged them after class, many spoke about social life and jobs, not the academic.

---

[1] American Council on Education, "More College Students Combine Work and Study," news release, Washington, D.C., 4 Sept. 1989.
[2] Alexander W. Astin, Follow-up Trends for 1985-1988, Four Years After Entry. Unpublished information provided to the Carnegie Foundation for the Advancement of Teaching.

Table 1. Percentage of Students Who Study Outside of Class

Per Week	1985	1988
6 or more hours	81%	70%
16 or more hours	33%	23%

Source: Alexander W. Astin, Follow-up Trends for 1985-1988, Four Years After Entry. Unpublished data provided to The Carnegie Foundation for the Advancement of Teaching.

In an earlier Carnegie Foundation study of undergraduates, we found that about one out of every four students at four-year institutions say they spend *no* time in the library during a normal week; 65 percent use the library four hours or less.[3] Further, in a more recent survey of faculty, about two-thirds said they are teaching undergraduates basic skills they should have learned in school. Fifty-five percent believe undergraduates are "doing just enough to get by" and over half the faculty feel today's students are less willing to work hard in their studies.[4]

Several faculty members we talked with described a deficiency in the preparedness of students, especially in language skills and mathematics. One business professor told us, "I have noticed a serious decline in the ability of students to perform simple math or even arithmetic. They also seem less able to do creative thinking. In turn, the university has adjusted standards downward to accommodate these students."

A professor at a liberal arts institution said, "I do feel sorry for these young students in the 1980s, as I feel that the majority of them are grossly underprepared for coping with college-level academic study. In general, their powers of concentration are poor, their cultural literacy is poor, their scientific and technological literacy is poor, and their capacity for logical thinking, analysis, and synthesis has not been properly developed."

In addition to complaints about student preparation, faculty say that students are not always willing to work hard in college. One professor at a doctorate-granting institution said, "A large percentage of students today seem to want to succeed (in school, in life) without making a substantial effort to really comprehend. As unlikely as it may seem, students frequently *say* that some subordinate will do their detail/analysis work for them, therefore, they do not have to understand."

---

[3]The Carnegie Foundation for the Advancement of Teaching, National Survey of Undergraduates, 1984.
[4]The Carnegie Foundation for the Advancement of Teaching, *The Condition of the Professoriate: Attitudes and Trends, 1989* (Princeton, NJ: Carnegie Foundation for the Advancement of Teaching, 1989), pp. 19, 21-22.

These generalizations don't apply, of course, to all institutions. Many are successful academically and others are brilliantly succeeding. Further, no one expects undergraduates to be round-the-clock academic grinds. Students need open spaces, moments alone, occasions to relax with friends. Still, as the first priority, a college should be committed to excellence in education, and college, at its best, is a place where students, through creative teaching, are intellectually engaged.

Table 2. Faculty Attitudes Toward Undergraduate Preparedness and Diligence *(Percentage Agreeing)*

All Institutions	Research	Doctorate-Granting	Comprehensive	Liberal Arts	Two-Year
This institution spends too much time and money teaching students what they should have learned in high school					
68%	60%	64%	73%	56%	73%
Most undergraduates at my institution only do enough to get by					
55%	47%	49%	57%	46%	63%
On the whole, undergraduates are now more willing to work hard in their studies					
24%	30%	23%	26%	23%	21%

Source: The Carnegie Foundation for the Advancement of Teaching, *The Condition of the Professoriate, Attitudes and Trends, 1989* (Princeton, NJ: Carnegie Foundation for the Advancement of Teaching, 1989), pp. 20-22.

But there is another side to the equation. Faculty, because of the reward system, are often not able to spend time with students, especially undergraduates. We found that, on too many campuses, teaching frequently is not well rewarded, and especially for young professors seeking tenure, it's much safer to present a paper at a national convention than it is to spend time with undergraduates back home.

And yet at a college or university of quality, the classroom should be the place where community begins. Educator Parker Palmer strikes precisely the right note when he says, "Knowing and learning are communal acts."[5] If we view student life from *this* perspective, then strengthening community rests not just with counselors, chaplains, residence hall supervisors, or the deans, but also with faculty who care about students and engage them in active learning.

With this vision, the great teachers not only transmit information, but also create the common ground of intellectual commitment. They stimulate active, not passive, learning in the classroom, encourage students to be creative, not conforming, and inspire them to go on learning long after college days are over. We urge, therefore, that colleges and universities reward not only research and publication, but great teaching, too.

---

[5]Parker Palmer, *To Know As We Are Known* (New York: Harper & Row, 1983).

Faculty may sometimes find the lecture format appropriate, but small seminars are also needed so that undergraduates can have more direct access to
professors in a setting where dialogues thrive and relationships grow, not just
between teachers and students, but among the students themselves. In the
classroom, students should learn to cooperate, not just compete, and we recommend, therefore, that all lower-division students have at least one course each
semester with an enrollment of no more than thirty students each. Further, we
urge that all students work together occasionally on group assignments, within
large lecture sections, to underscore the point that cooperation in the classroom
is as essential as competition.

Beyond the classroom, community can be strengthened by academic departments that bring students and faculty together. The department is, perhaps, the
most familiar, most widely accepted organizational unit on campus. As students
select a major, they join with faculty to pursue common academic interests and
often forge social loyalties, too. In addition to their advising role, departments
can become a creative intellectual and social unit on the campus through special
seminars, lectures, and social events for students and faculty. Many academic
departments already do these things, and we urge that the commitment to make
the department a powerful unit of community be broadened.

All college events—those that cut across departmental interests—can be especially valuable in stirring a common intellectual purpose on the campus. Ohio
Wesleyan University, for example, selects a theme each year to be studied by everyone on campus for an entire term. In the fall of 1989, the theme was "The
Impact of Technology on Culture." Every Wednesday at noon, visiting speakers
addressed such topics as "Technology's Impact on the Amish" and "Weaponry
Over the Years." Also there were days when everyone came together in all-college
seminars and forums. The entire campus became a classroom.

The Red Barn, located on the edge of the University of Louisville, has, for
twenty years, sponsored arts and educational programs that bring together students, faculty, staff, and Louisville residents of all ages. On the campus of the
University of California, Berkeley, students hold forth almost daily from the steps
of Sproul Hall. At Earlham College in Indiana, tables in the dining hall often are
covered with hand-outs on social issues, and the Opinion Board in the Earlham
Student Union is another forum for vigorous exchange. Weber State College in
Utah, a campus where most students commute, has set aside one morning every
week for a wide range of student activities, and for a campuswide convocation.

Residence halls can be classrooms, too. At the University of Vermont, a
Living-Learning Center—a kind of college-within-a-college—houses more than

five hundred students who work together. The Center has faculty apartments, classrooms, and its own dining room; students go on field trips and attend special seminars in addition to their regular academic work. Indiana University has sections set aside in some residence halls where faculty meet with students. Several years ago the University of Miami renovated residence halls so senior faculty and administration could "live in." Examples such as these can be found on campuses from coast to coast.

Ideally, a commitment to learning—a shared sense of intellectual excitement—pervades the entire campus. Lectures, informal debates, singing groups, orchestras and bands, theater productions, dance concerts, the student radio and newspaper, literary journals, film societies, debate clubs—all richly promote a community of learning through an "out-of-class curriculum" where the intellectual, aesthetic, and social dimensions of campus life thrive. In such a climate the purposefulness of the college or university is apparent everywhere.

Finally, a discussion of the intellectual life of a community of learning must focus on the curriculum itself. The course of study a college offers provides students an academic road map, and a shared intellectual discourse can be achieved most successfully, perhaps, through a well-planned general education sequence, a core curriculum with coherence.

The sad truth is, however, that at far too many institutions the "distribution requirements" of general education are unfocused. They encourage randomness, not coherence, and create the strong impression that the college has no larger sense of purpose. At one institution in our study, students and faculty compared the curriculum to a fast food restaurant. "We're kind of like a McUniversity," one student told us. "A smorgasbord of fast food."

We conclude that if the spirit of community is to be renewed—if the intellectual life is to be central—the curriculum must illuminate larger, more integrative ends. A coherent general education sequence should introduce all students, not only to the essential fields of knowledge, but also to connections across the disciplines, and help them apply knowledge to their own lives.

We are encouraged that, in recent years, colleges and universities all across the country are, in fact, redesigning general education to achieve these essential aims. At Brooklyn College, the core curriculum consists of ten areas that every student, regardless of major, must study. These include: mathematical reasoning; sciences; art and music; philosophy; western culture; the study of power and social organization in America; European and American history; landmarks of literature; third world cultures; and a foreign language. This cluster provides a solid grounding in academic inquiry and also becomes a base of common learning for all students.

Bethany College in West Virginia has a perspectives program that organizes general education into eight categories: aesthetic judgment, experimental science, global awareness, historical foundations, human personality and behavior, Judeo-Christian tradition, quantitative reasoning, and social institutions. This core curriculum also introduces students to the disciplines, while relating liberal arts education to the working world and to consequential issues in students' lives.

Saint Anselm College in New Hampshire has a cluster of courses built on the theme "Portraits of Human Greatness." Two freshmen core courses cover the many ways "human greatness" has been described from ancient to modern times. One recent unit included a study of the warrior, the prophet, the philosopher, the lawgiver, the disciple, the knight, the townsman, and the medieval scholar. Another unit used Dante's *Divine Comedy* to inquire about God and humanity. Two other courses focused on the lives of noteworthy individuals—Michelangelo, Martin Luther, Queen Elizabeth I, Cervantes, Pascal, Thomas Jefferson, Beethoven, Darwin, Lenin, Gandhi, Sartre, and Pope John XXIII.

Recently, the State University of New York at Buffalo proposed a new general education curriculum for arts and science students. The plan begins with a foundation course in language and writing skills. There are "common experience" courses in world civilization, American pluralism and the search for equality, scientific inquiry, great discoveries in science, mathematical science, physical or biological science, literature and the arts, and social and behavioral sciences. All students in their fourth year also would complete an "integrative course," thus running general education vertically from the freshman to the senior year. These are only a few examples of curricular changes in a national push to revitalize the core of common learning.

We conclude that the quality of a college or university must be measured first by the commitment of its members to the *educational* mission of the institution. It is in the classroom where community begins, but learning also reaches out to departments, to residential halls, to the campus commons. The curriculum, too, if properly designed, should intellectually integrate the campus. In a *purposeful* community, learning is pervasive.

PART TWO

...

CHAPTER TWO

AN OPEN COMMUNITY

Second, a college or university is an open community, a place where freedom of expression is uncompromisingly protected and where civility is powerfully affirmed.

The educational mission of higher learning is carried on through reasoned discourse. The free expression of ideas in a community of learning is essential, and integrity in the use of symbols, both written and oral, must be continuously affirmed if both scholarship and civility are to flourish. The quality of a college, therefore, must be measured by the quality of communication on campus.

Proficiency in language means, first, the ability to read with comprehension, write with clarity, and effectively speak and listen. This is the minimum. But if a higher learning institution is to fulfill a larger function—if it is to sustain a climate of reasoned discourse—the quality of communication on campus must be measured not just by *clarity* of expression, but by *civility* as well.

That's the goal, to be assured that students speak and listen carefully to each other. But during our study, we were troubled to discover that, on too many campuses, incivility is a problem and, all too frequently, words are used, not as the key to understanding, but as weapons of assault. Especially disturbing is the fact that abusive language is revealed most strikingly in racial, ethnic, and sexual slurs.

Offensive language can crop up almost anywhere, but the problem appears to be most acute at large research and doctorate institutions, where more than 60 percent of the presidents we surveyed said "sexual harassment" is a problem, and where half also listed "racial intimidation and harassment." Further, when presidents were asked how they would improve campus life, 86 percent of those at large universities said there should be "new and revised statements on civility and respect for others."[1]

---

[1] The Carnegie Foundation for the Advancement of Teaching and the American Council on Education, National Survey of College and University Presidents, 1989.

Table 3. Percentage of Presidents Who Say Harassment Is a "Moderate" to "Major" Problem on Their Campus

All Institutions	Research & Doctorate-Granting	Comprehensive	Liberal Arts	Two-Year
Sexual harassment				
28%	62%	32%	30%	20%
Racial intimidation/harassment				
16%	48%	18%	15%	13%

Source: The Carnegie Foundation for the Advancement of Teaching and the American Council on Education, National Survey of College and University Presidents, 1989.

Outside speakers often pose a special problem. At a large state university, the black student union invited Louis Farrakhan to speak. Some students and state legislators opposed the use of student fees to pay a speaker they considered a "black racist," and objected to using state money to provide security. The university defended the students' right to invite any speaker, regardless of his views, and also declared that the threat of disruption should not abridge free speech. The event occurred without serious incident.

At another place the drama department invited a black actress to perform a one-woman show called "Nigger Cafe." The dean who approved the performance felt it would help students better understand racial issues. The invitation was opposed, however, by a senior black faculty member and members of the black student union, who found the title offensive. Pressure against the performance became so great that the dean withdrew the invitation.

Elsewhere, students erected a shantytown to express their displeasure with the trustees' stand on South African investment. The shanties, standing at the very heart of the campus, made a powerful visual statement, dividing the college down the middle. Opposing students tore the buildings down. The president said this abridged free expression and the next morning helped rebuild the shanties.

No one wants to be cast in the role of censor. Still, civility and courtesy lie at the very heart of academic life, and many college and university presidents are urgently looking for ways to define the boundaries of acceptable speech. Academic leaders have both an educational and moral obligation to be concerned about abusive language, and 60 percent of the chief student affairs officers we surveyed report that their campus now has a written policy on bigotry, racial harassment or intimidation. Another 11 percent say they are working on one.[2]

---

[2]The American Council on Education and the National Association of Student Personnel Administrators, National Survey of Chief Student Affairs Officers, 1989.

But colleges are finding it difficult to balance free speech with constraint. Several years ago, Tufts University sought to prohibit verbal and written expression that could be viewed as harassment. This move was sparked by the appearance on campus of a T-shirt imprinted with a message judged by many to be demeaning to women. Under the new rule, a student could not wear the offensive shirt in a public space. Students, in demonstrating against the rule, divided the campus with chalk lines—into restricted and free speech zones. The policy was withdrawn.

Several years ago, the University of Michigan adopted guidelines that defined appropriate speech standards in various campus settings—public, educational, and residential. The policy seemed carefully crafted, but subsequent cases reveal, once again, just how hard it is to establish boundaries.

- In a classroom, a student stated his belief that homosexuality is a disease, and said he intended to develop a counseling plan for helping gays become straight. A classmate filed a charge of sexual harassment. A hearing panel unanimously found that the student had, indeed, violated the university's policy—but he was not convicted. A court later found that the student should not have had to endure the process in the first place, since his remark was a part of a legitimate classroom discussion.

- A white student in a pre-dentistry course stated that he had heard that minorities had a difficult time in the course and were not treated fairly. The minority professor who taught the class filed a complaint, believing the comment was unfair and hurt her chances for tenure. The student was then counseled about the policy and wrote a letter apologizing for his comments.

The Court, in reviewing these incidents, ruled that the university policy violated the First Amendment rights of free speech. Specifically, the judge wrote: "It is clear that the policy was overbroad both on its face and as applied. . . ." He concluded that "it is an unfortunate fact of our constitutional system that the ideals of freedom and equality are often in conflict. The difficult and sometimes painful task of our political and legal institutions is to mediate the appropriate balance between these two competing values."[3]

Given conflicting signals, how should colleges proceed? Is it possible to protect freedom of speech and also keep abusive language from poisoning the campus? Since the 1960s, it has been widely accepted law and practice that campuses can regulate the time, place, and manner of speech. They cannot, however,

---

[3]John Doe v. University of Michigan, *No. 89-71683, U.S. District Court, Eastern Division of Michigan, Southern Division, 1989.*

regulate content without violating the spirit of inquiry upon which both scholarship and a free society depend. Indeed, the necessity of assuring free expression on campus derives not only from values rooted in the United States Constitution, but also from the very nature of the university itself.

We conclude that restrictive codes, for practical as well as legal reasons, do not provide a satisfactory response to offensive language. Such codes may be expedient, even grounded in conviction, but the university cannot submit the two cherished ideals of freedom and equality to the legal system and expect both to be returned intact. What the university *can* and *should* do, we believe, is define high standards of civility and condemn, in the strongest possible terms, any violation of such standards.

Perhaps the most enduring policy statement on freedom of expression has been the 1975 report of a Yale University committee, chaired by Professor C. Vann Woodward, and incorporated into the Yale Undergraduate Regulations. The committee wrote:

> No member of the community with a decent respect for others should use, or encourage others to use, slurs and epithets intended to discredit another's race, ethnic group, religion, or sex. It may sometimes be necessary in a university for civility and mutual respect to be superseded by the need to guarantee free expression. The values superseded are nevertheless important and every member of the university community should consider them in exercising the fundamental right to free expression. . . . The conclusions we draw, then, are these: even when some members of the university community fail to meet their social and ethical responsibilities, the paramount obligation of the university is to protect their right to free expression. . . . If the university's overriding commitment to free expression is to be sustained, secondary social and ethical responsibilities must be left to the informal processes of suasion, example, and argument.[4]

Above all, campus leaders must not only protect freedom of expression, but also affirm civility by the force of their own example. Stephen B. Sample, president of the State University of New York at Buffalo, made the point powerfully in a call he made to the entire university community to speak out against intolerance. President Sample put it this way:

> As long as we let those small moments pass without calling attention to the injustice they represent, the threat to justice everywhere will continue. Thus, I call upon all of us to remember our responsibilities to ourselves and each other by speaking out

---

[4]The 1975 Report of the Committee on Freedom of Expression at Yale, chaired by Professor C. Vann Woodward, pp. 10-12.

against bigotry and intolerance whenever and wherever they occur. Only by this vigilance in our daily lives can we help make justice everywhere possible.[5]

Derek Bok, president of Harvard University, in response to a grossly demeaning letter about women circulated by a student club, argued that such communication, while offensive, should not be suppressed:

> Although such statements are deplorable, they are presumed to be protected under the Constitution and should be equally so on the campus as well. Why? The critical question is: Whom will we trust to censor communications and decide which ones are "too offensive" or "too inflammatory" or too devoid of intellectual content? . . . As a former president of the University of California once said: "The University is not engaged in making ideas safe for students. It is engaged in making students safe for ideas."[6]

President Bok then issued a strong and public denunciation of the letter and its authors:

> The wording of the letter was so extreme and derogatory to women that I wanted to communicate my disapproval publicly, if only to make sure that no one could gain the false impression that the Harvard administration harbored any sympathy or complacency toward the tone and substance of the letter. Such action does not infringe on free speech. Indeed, statements of disagreement are part and parcel of the open debate that freedom of speech is meant to encourage; the right to condemn a point of view is as protected as the right to express it.[7]

We cannot leave our inquiry into the uses of language without pointing to a higher standard. During campus visits we were troubled that debates about the limits of expression were often argued in administrative, even legalistic terms. Rarely was attention given to the fact that careless words can be deeply wounding. Words were being analyzed with insufficient care being given to the painful feelings they evoked.

We believe that standards of communication, especially on a college campus, must go far beyond correct grammar or syntax; they even must extend beyond the "civility" of the message being sent. A higher standard is to view communication as a sacred trust. The goal of human discourse must be to both speak and listen with great care and seek understanding at the

---

[5]Steven B. Sample, "Viewpoint of the President," *The Spectrum* (State University of New York at Buffalo), 4 Dec. 1989, p. 11.
[6]Derek C. Bok, "Reflections on Free Speech: An Open Letter to the Harvard Community," *Educational Record*, Winter 1985, pp. 4-8.
[7]Ibid.

deepest level, and this expectation takes on special significance as the nation's campuses become increasingly diverse.

Many students, because of their own cultural isolation, bring prejudices to campus that serve to filter out the feelings of people from racial, ethnic, and religious backgrounds different than their own. But if communication does not go beyond the formality of the words and yield a deeper understanding of who people really *are*, prejudice persists. Wayne Booth of the University of Chicago captured this high standard when he wrote: "All too often our efforts to speak and listen seem to be a vicious spiral moving downward. But we have all experienced moments when the spiral moved upward, when one party's efforts to listen and speak just a little bit better, produced a similar response, making it possible to move on up the spiral to moments of genuine understanding."[8]

In an *open* community, freedom of expression must be uncompromisingly defended. Offensive language must be vigorously denounced. But in the end, good communication means listening carefully, as well, and achieving moments of genuine understanding. "No law can mandate that everyone adore everyone else," as President Sample notes, "but especially in the university community we *can* expect everyone to respect the rights and dignity of everyone else. Indeed, we must demand it."[9]

---

[8]Wayne Booth, "Mere Rhetoric, and the Search for Common Learning," *Common Learning* (Washington, D.C.: Carnegie Foundation for the Advancement of Teaching, 1981), p. 54.
[9]Steven B. Sample, ibid.

CHAPTER THREE

A JUST COMMUNITY

Third, a college or university is a *just* community, a place where the sacredness of each person is honored and where diversity is aggressively pursued.

Higher learning builds community out of the rich resources of its members. It rejects prejudicial judgments, celebrates diversity, and seeks to serve the full range of citizens in our society effectively. In strengthening campus life, colleges and universities must commit themselves to building a just community, one that is both equitable and fair.

For almost two centuries colleges were, with few exceptions, a haven for the privileged. They catered to the most advantaged, enrolling young men who, upon graduation, were often placed in still higher positions of privilege and power. Slowly the admission doors swung wider and more women and minority students came to campus, and during the 1960s, the nation's colleges and universities, in response to the eloquent call for simple justice, pushed aggressively to broaden opportunities for historically by-passed students.

Sadly, this sense of urgency has, in recent years, diminished and the nation's colleges and universities have largely failed to provide sustained leadership in the drive for equality of opportunity in the nation. Rather than push vigorously their own affirmative action programs, aggressively recruiting minority students into higher education, they turned to other matters, and a historically important opportunity to advance the course of human justice was forever lost.

America and the nation's campuses are, once again, afflicted by a deepening polarization along racial and ethnic lines as young blacks and Hispanics remain socially isolated and economically deprived. Recently the American Council on Education reported that the number of low-income, black high school graduates going on to college actually dropped from 40 percent in 1976, to 30 percent in 1988; for low-income Hispanics, the college participation rate fell from 50 percent in 1976, to 35 percent in 1988.[1] This represents an educational failure of intolerable proportions.

We strongly recommend that, during the decade of the nineties, every college and university reaffirm its commitment to equality of opportunity, establish goals for minority enrollment, and select precise timetables, too. This means working closely with the schools, and we propose that colleges begin recruiting black and Hispanic students when they're still in junior high.

But the issue is more than access; it has to do with the lack of support minority students feel once they have enrolled, and there are alarming signals that racial and ethnic divisions are deepening on the nation's campuses. College and university presidents told us that suspicions are intense, and the black student body president at the University of Massachusetts, Amherst, expressed herself this way: "I think within the next decade we will see an increase in racial altercations, not just white on black, but black on white."[2]

In our administrative survey, one in four of all college and university presidents reported that racial tensions are a problem on campus. And the issue is especially troublesome at large universities, where more than two-thirds of the presidents at research and doctorate institutions said "racial tensions and hostilities" are a problem. When asked their views for improving campus life, presidents at these institutions said "greater racial understanding" was a priority.[3]

Many administrators and faculty can recall the 1950s when Rosa Parks boarded a bus and made history with her decision to take a seat up front. They remember the sixties when black students sat at a lunch counter and defied centuries of prejudice with a simple request for service. They recall the decade when United States Marshals had to escort James Meredith onto the campus of "Ole Miss." This was the decade when Martin Luther King, Jr., led a great crusade to affirm the dignity of all.

Table 4. Percentage of Presidents Who Say Racial Tensions and Hostilities Are a "Moderate" to "Major" Problem on Their Campus

All Institutions	Research & Doctorate-Granting	Comprehensive	Liberal Arts	Two-Year
24%	68%	20%	28%	15%

Source: The Carnegie Foundation for the Advancement of Teaching and the American Council on Education, National Survey of College and University Presidents, 1989.

[1] American Council on Education, "Minorities in Higher Education," Sixth Annual Status Report, Washington, D.C., 1987, p. 3.

[2] David Maraniss, "Hard Choices in Black and White," *The Washington Post*, 7 March 1990, p. A16.

[3] The Carnegie Foundation for the Advancement of Teaching and the American Council on Education, National Survey of College and University Presidents, 1989.

College leaders may recall these historic times, but many students do not, and today some reject, even resent, the idea of inclusion. "We carry a stigma," said one Chicano student. ". . . When I first came here as a freshman, a white undergraduate said to me, 'You're here but my friend, who is better qualified, is not.'"[4] At a research university in the Southwest, an assistant dean of students commented: "Most white students don't understand why white applicants are being left out. Black students are asked, 'Did you get in here because you are black?'"

Prejudice was reported elsewhere. During one of our campus visits, the black homecoming queen said there was graffiti in the women's restroom attacking her. At another place, a black candidate for a student government position said a white student he had asked to vote for him responded: "Is the other candidate on your ticket a nigger too?" A Mexican-American student at a southern university was quoted in *Change* magazine as saying: "People will joke around—at least I hope they are joking—and say, 'Oh, he's Mexican, hide your wallet.' Or, 'Do you have a switchblade?'"[5]

At Stanford University several years ago, two white freshmen and a black sophomore had a debate about the influence of blacks on music. As part of the conversation, the black student said that Beethoven was a mulatto. The white students were skeptical and later, after a drinking bout, put a poster outside the black student's room depicting Beethoven as a stereotyped black. Although the white students described their intent as parody, the black student and his friends interpreted the act as racist, leading to a major confrontation.[6]

Virulent forms of anti-Semitism are flaring up as well. A recent front-page article in *The Chronicle of Higher Education* said that Jewish students and faculty members are reporting more anti-Semitic acts on their campuses than at any other time in the past ten years. Among the offensive acts described were the appearance of catalogs promoting neo-Nazi literature, the painting of swastikas on a Hillel building, and the mocking of Jews as the *theme* of a fraternity party.[7]

Incidents such as these speak volumes about the hostile climate many minorities feel on campus. Professor Patricia Williams, the first black woman to teach at Stanford's school of law, described in moving language the deep, personal hurt, as well as insult, such encounters can elicit:

---

[4]Edward B. Fiske, "The Undergraduate Hispanic Experience: A Case of Juggling Two Cultures," *Change*, May/June 1988, p. 31.

[5]Ibid., p. 32.

[6]"Final Report on Recent Incidents at Ujama House," *Stanford Daily*, 18 Jan. 1989, pp. 7-10.

[7]Courtney Leatherman, "More Anti-Semitism Is Being Reported on Campuses, but Educators Disagree on How to Respond to It," *Chronicle of Higher Education*, 7 Feb. 1990, p. 1.

The most deeply offending part of the injury of the Beethoven defacement is its message that if I ever manage to create something as significant, as monumental, and as important as Beethoven's music, or the literature of the mulatto Alexandre Dumas or the mulatto Aleksandr Pushkin's literature—if I am that great in genius, and perfect in ability—then the best reward to which I can aspire, and the most cherishing gesture with which my recognition will be preserved, is that I will be remembered as white. . . . The issue is about the ability of black and brown and red and yellow people to name their rightful contributions to the universe of music or any other field. It is the right to claim that we are, after all, part of Western Civilization. It is the right to claim our existence.[8]

Throughout higher education we found that Hispanic, Jewish, Polish, Italian, Muslim, Arab, Vietnamese, and Haitian student associations have organized themselves in their own separate groups—and on at least one campus a white student union has been formed. Organizations that celebrate diversity have an important role to play, but exclusive groups can generate conflict.

Black student organizations seem to stir the most misunderstandings, even heated controversy, on campuses. And yet those criticizing blacks for being "separatist" were themselves often grouped together, in less obvious ways, so that black students were effectively being held to a double standard. At a small liberal arts college in the East, a white student suggested that the mere existence of a black student union "polarized the students." A black student at an elite private university agreed with this position. He told one of our researchers: "I get a lot of flack because I don't belong to the black student union. I think it's stupid to have a Drama Association and a Black Drama Association" on this campus.

On the other hand, an officer of the student union responded aggressively to the charge that blacks were "separatists." "If black students were inclined toward separation," he insisted, "they never would have come to this predominantly white institution in the first place. The problem is that blacks, once they come to this campus, discover that they need support from fellow blacks to emotionally survive."

This student then told us his experience. "Soon after I got here I found out that I was one of only twelve black people in the freshman class. I did not expect that to be a problem. I was wrong. As the semester progressed, I realized that many whites on campus were not making the same effort to continue relationships that I was. I then realized that the 'black separatists' were the only people who took me at face value and at the same time were themselves with me. I still have white

---

[8]Quoted in Martha Minow, "On Neutrality, Equality, and Tolerance: New Norms for a Decade of Distinction," *Change*, Jan./Feb. 1990, pp. 19-20.

friends, but they are the exceptions who take me for what I am. Basically, we 'black separatists' have set ourselves apart, on one level, because we were forced to do so."

Here's how another student expressed his concern: "Minority students tend to all come together, because they are so small in number and black students just don't feel welcome. Everything is separate for us. We have a totally different idea of what a party is. We don't get together with whites. It's kind of hard when you don't see anyone who can really understand you."

Striking a balance between special groups and the larger community is, we found, one of the most difficult challenges administrators now confront. The president of one elite university described his concern to us this way:

> The question which intrigues me is the role of any homogeneous subset of students who wish through some exclusive arrangement to spend some of their time together. This could be groups of women or men or blacks or athletes. The key point is that membership in these groups is selective and exclusive. My own observation is that as diversity on our campuses increases, many students feel an increasing desire to participate in some homogeneous group.
>
> Last week I asked a student what her main disappointment and her best experience on campus had been. Her chief complaint was the lack of sufficient diversity, but her best experience was her participation in an all-female social club!
>
> Almost every month I'm asked by an exclusively black organization to give them official recognition. Their claim is usually that these organizations give them strength to participate in the larger community. I'm trying to understand how a university that's committed to diversity can have official interactions with organizations that are avowedly *exclusive*, even if they have desirable ends.

It's understandable that students, especially those who feel vulnerable, want to meet together. Indeed, self-generated activity by student groups bring vitality to the campus. Frequently they are the most effective means of creating a fundamental sense of belonging, and through them students gain a feeling of belonging to the larger campus community. But we're also impressed by the tensions created as subgroups organize themselves along racial, ethnic, or gender lines. And we worry about the racial tensions on the campus, the lack of trust, the singular lack of success many colleges and universities have had in creating a climate in which minority students feel fully accepted on the campus.

There is no easy answer. On the one hand, we believe students should join together, as they have always done, to pursue special interests. Minority students especially have a need to organize themselves for support in an environment that is often perceived to be insensitive, even hostile. But we also urge that student groups reach out, authentically, to one another. They should try to explain their own purposes and understand the purposes of others and meet, if possible, as individuals, one on one.

For example, would the student leaders of campus organizations be willing to spend time together, in a summer retreat, in search of common ground? Could we expect that all subgroups also would affirm the larger purposes of the institution? And could the six principles set forth in this report provide a framework by which the legitimacy of every campus group might be judged?

We also suggest that every college and university conduct a detailed study of the racial climate on its campus, to learn more about itself. The goal of such an inventory would be to gather more precise information about the depth of ethnic and racial tensions, to better understand how students from various groups really feel about their situation, how administrative officers and academic groups are viewed, and to hear how various minority students feel the climate might be improved. This information should be shared in an organized way with the campus community at every level—students, faculty, and administrators.

The president at Wellesley College, several years ago, named a Task Force on Racism to study the experiences of racial minorities at that institution and make recommendations for change. The Task Force not only probed academic and nonacademic activities, but also inquired into the sensitivity of administrative officers. The results revealed how various student groups can view the same campus in strikingly different ways.

Upon receiving the report, the president made the following declaration. "It is important that we confront racism, recognizing its complexities and its deep-rootedness in our culture. We must face up to its particular manifestations at Wellesley, not treat it gingerly and pretend it's irrelevant to us."[9] As poet Adrienne Rich has said so well in *Lies, Secrets, and Silence:*

> I believe the word *racism* must be seized; grasped in our bare hands, ripped up out of the sterile or defensive consciousness in which it so often grows, and transplanted so that it can yield new insights for our lives. . . . I am convinced that we must go on using that sharp, sibilant word, not to paralyze ourselves and each other with repetitious, stagnant doses of guilt, but to break it down into its elements. . . . Our stake . . . in making these connections, is not abstract justice; it is integrity and survival.[10]

---

[9]Nannerl Keohane, "Response from the President to the Report of the Task Force on Racism: Progress Report and Working Plan," Wellesley College, 24 Oct. 1989.

[10]Adrienne Rich, *On Lies, Secrets and Silence: Selected Prose 1966-1978* (New York: W. W. Norton & Co., Inc. 1980).

Above all, colleges and universities should seek to build racial and cultural understanding, not just socially, but *educationally* as well. Students should take time in their formal program of instruction to learn about the heritage and traditions of other racial and ethnic groups, so that social relationships can be put in context. The University of Minnesota requires that all students take at least two courses on different American cultures. Mt. Holyoke and Tufts University have a similar requirement. The University of California, Berkeley, Faculty Senate recently ruled that all undergraduates take at least one course in American Cultures. This broader view of the curriculum is necessary, we believe, for every higher learning institution.

Affirming diversity touches the community in other ways as well. It was not until the late 1960s that women in significant numbers entered higher learning institutions and pursued fields of study traditionally reserved for males. Prospects for the professional advancement of women also improved and funds for women's studies programs became available. Today, according to recent studies, freshmen women have higher intellectual and social self-confidence. Their degree aspirations and career choices in such fields as business, law, medicine, dentistry, and computer programming are quite similar to those of men.[11]

Still, it was regularly apparent during our study that sexist attitudes persist. An adult student at a community college in the Southwest recalled: "My professor told me I should not be an engineer because I am Hispanic and a woman. I went home and cried. Then, I decided not to complain. I'd get my degree and show him." A younger undergraduate in an elite university in the Northeast said: "My professor told me not to bother to apply to business school because they never take women." At this same institution, another woman reported that when she registered for an upper-level calculus course the male instructor said: "This is an advanced course. Why are you taking it?"

Men still seem to talk most often in class, and women students, who are often overshadowed, may submit excellent written work, yet wait until after class to approach a teacher privately about issues raised in the discussion. Not only do men talk more, but what they say often appears to carry more weight with some professors, and this pattern of classroom leaders and followers is set very early in the term.[12]

More blatant acts of prejudice are frequently reported. In a 1983 study, 40 percent of undergraduate women reported experiencing sexual harassment[13] and

---

[11]Carol S. Pearson, Donna L. Shavlik, and Judith G. Touchton, eds., *Educating the Majority: Women Challenge Tradition in Higher Education* (New York: American Council on Education/Macmillan, 1989), pp. 32-45.

[12]Edward B. Fiske, citing the work of Catherine G. Krupnics, "Lessons," *The New York Times,* 11 April 1990, p. B8.

[13]Mary M. Leonard and Brenda Alpert Sigall, "Empowering Women Student Leaders: A Leadership

a Harvard University survey found that 34 percent of women undergraduates at that institution reported harassment from a person in authority.[14] At a small eastern university in our study, a sophomore reported that members of the women's caucus "get insults shouted at them." And at a southern research university, the managing editor of the newspaper complained about T-shirts reading "Ten reasons why beer is better than women." At yet another campus, a female student who worked part-time with the maintenance crew complained of lewd remarks.

Defining sexual harassment is a critical step toward its elimination, and we recommend that every college and university codify its own policy and consider sexual harassment as it affects the full range of campus life. Princeton University has a policy that is implemented through education, confidential counseling, procedures for lodging formal complaints, and remedies ranging from mediation to disciplinary action. The Princeton code, which is similar to that of other campuses, defines sexual harassment as:

> unwelcome sexual advances, requests for sexual favors, and other verbal or physical conduct of a sexual nature when submission to or rejection of such conduct is made implicitly or explicitly a term or condition of instruction, employment, or participation in University activity; when submission to or rejection of such conduct by an individual is used as a basis for evaluation in making academic or personnel decisions affecting an individual; or when such verbal or physical conduct has the effect of unreasonably interfering with an individual's work, academic performance, or living conditions by creating an intimidating, hostile, or offensive environment.[15]

Sexual insults and prejudicial acts are intolerable, but most shocking are the physical assaults against women, which were reported on nearly a third of the campuses we visited. There was, for example, a widely publicized fraternity gang rape on one, and at another university 20 percent of the women surveyed reported having had unwanted sexual intercourse.[16]

In response, most colleges have focused on security *and* education. Colorado College, for example, offers free self-defense classes for women and provides

---

Development Model," in Carol S. Pearson, et al., eds., *Educating the Majority: Women Challenge Tradition in Higher Education* (New York: American Council on Education/Macmillan, 1989), p. 231.

[14]Roberta M. Hall and Bernice R. Sandler, *Out of the Classroom: A Chilly Campus Climate for Women?* A publication of the Project on the States and Education of Women, Association of American Colleges, Washington, D.C., October 1984.

[15]SHARE office (Sexual Harassment/Assault Advising, Resources, and Education), Princeton University, "What You Should Know About Sexual Harassment," brochure. Credit to Harvard University, "Tell Someone," brochure, and the University of Massachusetts at Amherst, "Sexual Harassment: the Problem, the Policy, the Procedure."

[16]The Carnegie Foundation for the Advancement of Teaching, National Survey of Undergraduates, 1984.

them with whistles, while the State University of New York, Brockport, like many institutions, has installed "blue light" telephones around campus and initiated a student escort patrol.

At many colleges, "Take Back the Night" rallies have been organized, and health centers sensitize students to date rape. At the University of Richmond, a mandatory session at freshman orientation includes skits that address what's called the "Triple Whammy" of drugs, sex, and alcohol. And women's centers are helpful, too. The University of Minnesota has one of the nation's oldest and best-established centers. Programs include counseling for those who have been sexually harassed and abused both on and off campus. There are meetings for older students, support groups for minority women, and a speaker series featuring artists, authors, and activists. Such actions deserve strong support on every campus.

Finally, women's studies programs, which seek to improve campus climate through education, have made impressive gains, increasing from a handful in the early 1970s to more than five hundred today. Such courses, which cut across the disciplines, share a common intellectual interest in the role of gender in society, in science, in literature, and the arts. We conclude that if women are to participate, without prejudice, in campus life, colleges must not only welcome them into the classroom, but into the curriculum.

A just community is a place where diversity is aggressively pursued. In the coming decade colleges and universities must commit themselves to increase the enrollment of minority students so that their participation in higher education at least matches their representation in the population.

But tolerance, in the sense of inclusion, is simply not enough. Martha Minow, professor of law at Harvard University, has observed that: "To many people who have been made marginal in the past, inclusion sounds like, 'come on in, but don't change anything.'"[17] The larger goal for higher education must be to "build academic communities in which people learn to respect and value one another for their differences, while at the same time defining the values shared by all those who join the university as scholars and as citizens."[18]

This vision of the college or university as a just community must be aggressively pursued, since it is becoming increasingly apparent that time is running out.

---

[17]Martha Minow, p. 24.
[18]*The Michigan Mandate: A Strategie Linking of Academic Excellence and Social Diversity*, a report from the University of Michigan, April 1989.

CHAPTER FOUR

A DISCIPLINED COMMUNITY

Fourth, a college or university is a *disciplined* community, a place where individuals accept their obligations to the group and where well-defined governance procedures guide behavior for the common good.

A community of learning, at its best, is guided by standards of student conduct that define acceptable behavior and integrate the academic and nonacademic dimensions of campus life. We found, however, that when it comes to regulations, students live in two separate worlds. In academic matters, requirements are spelled out in great detail. Undergraduates are told how many graduation "units" to complete. They're given a schedule dictating when to show up for class, and they receive firm deadlines for term papers. But when it comes to life outside the classroom, the strategy is reversed. In nonacademic matters, standards are ambiguous, at best, and what we found particularly disturbing is the ambivalence college administrators feel about their overall responsibility for student behavior.

In just thirty years colleges have gone from being parents to clinicians, and today many are not sure where the oversight responsibility of the institution begins and ends. Many of us remember the days when there were enforced study hours and early lights out, except on weekends. We also can remember the sea change that occurred in the 1960s when too-rigid rules, belatedly, were abolished. No one would argue that colleges can or should return to the days of tight control. But does this mean that there are no standards by which conduct can be measured? Does it mean that colleges have no obligation to define with clarity their expectations for the students in matters beyond the academic?

Consider alcohol abuse. Pushed to the wall by legal and social factors, colleges are being forced to reappraise the legendary college figure of the boozing, boisterous undergraduate. Two-thirds of today's presidents called alcohol abuse a problem on their campuses. "Substance abuse, primarily alcohol" was mentioned most frequently when presidents were asked, "What three campus-life issues have given you the greatest concern?"[1] Further, in a recent Carnegie survey of faculty, 33 percent of those responding said that alcohol abuse by students has increased.[2]

Table 5. Percentage of Presidents Who Rate Alcohol Abuse a "Moderate" to "Major" Problem on Their Campus

All Institutions	Research & Doctorate-Granting	Comprehensive	Liberal Arts	Two-Year
67%	82%	84%	75%	53%

Source: The Carnegie Foundation for the Advancement of Teaching and the American Council on Education, National Survey of College and University Presidents, 1989.

A recent University of Michigan study found that the reported use of illegal drugs by college students has gone down, from 56 percent in 1980 to 37 percent in 1989, but clearly substance abuse remains a serious concern.[3] At a prestigious southern university, we were told that drinking is the most popular "unofficial student activity" on campus.[4] The dean of students, who estimated that between 6 and 10 percent of undergraduates on his campus were alcoholics, speculated that another 30 to 40 percent were serious weekend drinkers.[5]

No one underestimates the difficulty of fighting alcohol abuse. Men and women proudly drinking to excess is as old as Bacchus and Beowulf. On campus, alcohol also has a long history of public acceptance and public consumption—from faculty sherry hours to fraternity beer parties. It's also true that many undergraduates have experience with alcohol and drugs long before they come to college.

Table 6. Campus Life Issues of Greatest Concern Listed Most Frequently by Presidents *(Open-ended Question)*

Substance Abuse (primarily alcohol)
Student Apathy
Campus Security and Crime
Inadequate Facilities
Interracial/Intercultural Relations

Source: The Carnegie Foundation for the Advancement of Teaching and the American Council on Education, National Survey of College and University Presidents, 1989.

---

[1] The Carnegie Foundation for the Advancement of Teaching and the American Council on Education, National Survey of College and University Presidents, 1989.

[2] The Carnegie Foundation for the Advancement of Teaching, *The Condition of the Professoriate: Attitudes and Trends, 1989* (Princeton, NJ: Carnegie Foundation for the Advancement of Teaching, 1989), p. 36.

[3] "Drug Use by Students Has Declined, Study Finds," *The Chronicle of Higher Education,* 21 Feb. 1990, p. A2.

[4] The Carnegie Foundation for the Advancement of Teaching, National Survey of Undergraduates, 1984.

[5] The American Council on Education and the National Association of Student Personnel Administrators, National Survey of Chief Student Affairs Officers, 1989.

Many others, leaving home for the first time, are eager to exercise their new-found freedom, and social drinking and drug use fit in perfectly with this desire.

Still, we conclude that clearly stated alcohol and drug policies are required. If state laws say alcohol use is illegal for those under twenty-one, colleges should make this fact clearly known to students and declare that it will support the law, rather than ignore it. Such a stand is not only a legal mandate, it is in the interest of the students, too. They need models of integrity, not equivocation.

Colleges and universities are, in fact, responding to the crisis of drug and alcohol abuse in a variety of ways. Some institutions, especially those in states where the legal age for drinking has been raised, have banned alcohol altogether. Others insist that it be served only in designated places, while still other colleges now require students to wear wrist bands or badges to identify their age. A few places issue "drink tickets" to limit consumption and many require that when alcohol is served, nonalcoholic drinks also be made available at all college functions.

When rules are tightened, undergraduates often go off campus to drink. A private Southwest university in our study passed a rule forbidding all alcohol consumption on campus. In response, students presented an ultimatum: "If we can't drink on campus, we'll drive drunk"—a position the administrator called "blackmail." The moratorium was lifted but the university ruled that a uniformed police officer and four nondrinking chaperones must be present at all parties where alcohol is served.

Above all, education about the dangers of excessive drinking is important. Today, well over 90 percent of all colleges and universities have alcohol education programs, and more than 70 percent are making special efforts to reduce substance abuse.[6] Counselors, health officers, and chaplains are widely available on campus. We consider it quite remarkable that higher education institutions—in addition to academic, social, and residential programs—offer such a wide range of psychological support. And we were greatly impressed by the creative steps campuses are taking to hold off potential crises.

Each April, Indiana University holds a famous bike race—the Little 500—the biggest social weekend of the year. In 1988 the event was followed by a rock-throwing melee involving drunken students at an off-campus apartment complex. Students were arrested. For the 1989 festivities, the university scheduled extra entertainment events to discourage excessive drinking. Free bus service was also provided so students would not have to drive. Local bar owners offered free nonalcoholic beverages to designated drivers. A possible crisis was averted.

---

[6]"Students Still Drink, Fewer Drive Drunk," *Notes*, the newsletter of the Association of Governing Boards of Universities and Colleges, Washington, D.C., Feb./March 1989, p. 1.

While campuses are safer than city streets, the frequency of criminal acts, for many colleges, is another cause for worry. Indeed, one in four of the student affairs officers responding to our survey say that the number of reported crimes on their campus has increased over the last five years. Forty-three percent of those responding at research and doctorate-granting institutions believe the number of reported crimes on campus has increased over the last five years.[7] One liberal arts college in our study reported a 27 percent rise in vandalism in just one year.[8] Thefts are considered a problem by about two-thirds of the presidents at doctorate-granting institutions; 38 percent of liberal arts college presidents; and 44 percent at two-year institutions.[9]

Table 7. Five-Year Change in Campus Crime As Perceived by Student Affairs Officers *(Percentage Responding "Increase")*

All Institutions	Research & Doctorate-Granting	Comprehensive	Liberal Arts	Two-Year
Number of reported crimes on campus				
26%	43%	35%	32%	16%
Severity of crimes on campus				
14%	20%	16%	14%	11%
Number of reported crimes in surrounding community				
50%	59%	54%	42%	49%
Severity of crimes in surrounding community				
41%	56%	46%	30%	41%

Source: The American Council on Education and the National Association of Student Personnel Administrators, National Survey of Chief Student Affairs Officers, 1989.

We also found a close connection between alcohol abuse and campus crime. One administrator reported that 80 percent of all cases heard by the student judiciary at his institution were alcohol related. Still another told us that the recent increase in vandalism on his campus was caused by excessive drinking. The head of security at a midwestern land-grant university told one of our researchers: "The majority of crime on this campus comes from too much drinking."

Further, contrary to conventional wisdom, most criminal activity on campus is committed not by "outsiders" but by students. Students are, according to a

---

[7]The American Council on Education and the National Association of Student Personnel Administrators, National Survey of Chief Student Affairs Officers, 1989.

[8]The Carnegie Foundation for the Advancement of Teaching, Campus Visits, 1989.

[9]The Carnegie Foundation for the Advancement of Teaching and the American Council on Education, National Survey of College and University Presidents, 1989.

recent report, responsible for 78 percent of sexual assaults, 52 percent of physical assaults, two-thirds of strong-arm robberies, more than 90 percent of arsons, and 85 percent of incidents of vandalism.[10]

Table 8. Percentage of Presidents Who Say Crime Is a "Moderate" to "Major" Problem on Their Campus

All Institutions	Research & Doctorate-Granting	Comprehensive	Liberal Arts	Two-Year
Thefts				
47%	63%	57%	38%	44%
Inadequate security				
38%	34%	34%	41%	39%
Vandalism and destruction of property				
36%	56%	44%	36%	29%

Source: The Carnegie Foundation for the Advancement of Teaching and the American Council on Education, National Survey of College and University Presidents, 1989.

What everyone fears most, of course, are crimes of violence. Despite the shocking headlines that report rape and murder, the campus is still a relatively safe place to be. But the problem is growing, especially for urban institutions. At one residential college, students told us it's just not safe to move about at night, and the dean of students advised those living in high-rise dormitories not to ride the elevators alone. At an urban university where several murders have occurred, students joke, with gallows humor, about living long enough to get their diplomas.

In 1986, a university student in Pennsylvania was raped and strangled in her dorm. The parents sued. An out-of-court settlement was reached when the university agreed to invest in improved lighting and other security precautions. The state legislature, responding to this and other incidents, passed a bill requiring every college and university in the state to publish its campus crime rates. Other states have enacted, or are considering, similar legislation. These anecdotes, while exceptions, reflect the levels of concern about campus safety.

Once again, we found that colleges and universities are moving aggressively to improve security—with better lighting, escort services, emergency phone systems, and a strengthened police force. One eastern university actually established a state-certified police academy on campus to train its own recruits. Student security patrols supervised by campus police also are widely used. And a northeastern university we visited has an "Operation ID" program to mark and register personal property. This, too, is becoming commonplace.

---

[10]National Campus Violence Survey, General Report 1988. A report of the Center for the Study and Prevention of Campus Violence, Towson State University, Towson, Maryland, 1988.

A few years ago, the University of Rochester hired a full-time staff member to direct its crime-prevention programs. The university now employs two full-time and two part-time people who conducted 120 crime-prevention seminars in one year. Rochester also has an "Operation ID" property identification, and about four years ago launched a Blue Light Escort Service in which students accompany colleagues at night. Working with the Women's Caucus, the community began a series of "Walks for Light," a project in which students and staff go around campus at night with security officials to identify places needing improved lighting. Twenty-two blue light phones and fifteen service phones have been added.

Every campus should have a comprehensive security plan, and we urge that during orientation all incoming students participate in a crime-awareness program. Residence hall leaders and other campus officials should offer seminars on safety, date rape, and the art of self-defense throughout the year. Academic departments should discuss safety issues with faculty and students, focusing especially on the use of facilities at night.

Finally, to give overall direction to campus life, all campuses should have a clearly stated code of conduct, one that is widely disseminated and consistently enforced. In our national survey of undergraduates, about half said they support a code of conduct; at liberal arts colleges it was 60 percent. The same percentage of undergraduates at liberal arts colleges said that known drug offenders should be suspended or dismissed. This was a dramatic increase from 1976. Sixty-six percent of the students also agreed that the drinking age in all states should be raised to twenty-one.[11]

In drawing up a campus code, simple courtesy and the rights of others must be affirmed. For example, privacy should be respected, and excessively loud noise should be restricted. And we also urge that every campus should involve faculty and students in the periodic review and update of campus codes. Such involvement provides an important opportunity to reaffirm the institution's commitment to high standards in all aspects of campus life.

Chancellor Kenneth R. R. Gros Louis at Indiana University, Bloomington, described the responsibility of the university this way:

> We must not back down in our attempts to create a climate in which the fundamental business of learning can go on unimpeded. We must make sure that we can guarantee basic needs and services, that we see the loss of personal safety—whether we mean sexual harassment or assault, racial harassment or assault, or even as mundane a

---

[11]The Carnegie Foundation for the Advancement of Teaching, National Survey of Undergraduates, 1984.

violation as bicycle theft—as, at the least, a basic assault—a personal, individual violation of the rights that we all have as citizens, as students, as faculty and staff.[12]

Table 9. Undergraduate Attitudes Toward Moral Issues on Campus *(Percentage Agreeing)*

All Institutions	Research	Doctorate-Granting	Comprehensive	Liberal Arts	Two-Year
Colleges should provide a code of conduct for students					
56%	44%	47%	49%	60%	67%
Undergraduates known to use illegal drugs should be suspended or dismissed					
56%	51%	52%	55%	62%	59%
Drinking age should be 21 in all states					
66%	51%	58%	64%	64%	74%

Source: The Carnegie Foundation for the Advancement of Teaching, National Survey of Undergraduates, 1984.

On many of the campuses we visited administrators are, in fact, working closely with students to shape new rules regarding quiet hours, security procedures, the use of appliances, and parking restrictions, for example. More than half of the chief student affairs officers say that during the past five years student conduct regulations have become more explicit and enforcement more systematic. This pattern held true for all types of institutions, but it was highest at liberal arts colleges and research universities, where almost two-thirds of the student affairs officers report that such actions have been taken.[13]

In the end, a campus code of conduct should define standards of behavior in both social and academic matters. And yet there is disturbing evidence that here, too, behavior is deficient. Fraternities have long been known to keep old term papers on file for their members to copy, and it is possible for students to purchase papers on almost any topic from unscrupulous commercial organizations. Further, various surveys revealed anywhere from 40 percent to nearly 90 percent of students cheat on tests or papers,[14] and 43 percent of today's faculty feel students are ready to cheat in order to get better grades.[15]

---

[12]Kenneth R. R. Gros Louis, Chancellor, Speech to the Faculty Council of the Indiana University at Bloomington, 18 Oct. 1988.

[13]The Carnegie Foundation for the Advancement of Teaching and the American Council on Education, National Survey of Chief Student Affairs Officers, 1989.

[14]Margaret Platt Jendrek, "Faculty Reactions to Academic Dishonesty," *Journal of College Student Development*, Sept. 1989, vol. 30, p. 401.

[15]The Carnegie Foundation for the Advancement of Teaching, *The Condition of the Professoriate: Attitudes and Trends, 1989* (Princeton, NJ: Carnegie Foundation for the Advancement of Teaching, 1989) p. 26.

Table 10. Student Affairs Officers' Views on the Five-Year Change in Regulation of Student Conduct

All Institutions	Research & Doctorate-Granting	Comprehensive	Liberal Arts	Two-Year
More explicit				
54%	63%	55%	66%	48%
About the same				
45%	37%	45%	31%	52%
Less explicit				
1%	0%	0%	3%	0%
More systematic enforcement				
54%	61%	65%	68%	40%
About the same				
44%	38%	34%	27%	59%
Less systematic enforcement				
2%	1%	1%	5%	1%

Source: The American Council on Education and the National Association of Student Personnel Administrators, National Survey of Chief Student Affairs Officers, 1989.

Faculty members are the first line of defense in holding students to high academic standards. And yet a recent study showed that 53 percent of faculty said they rarely or never discussed university procedures on dishonesty with students.[16] And a report from one university revealed that while nearly 60 percent of the faculty observed students cheating, only 20 percent actually met with the student and the departmental chairman, as called for in the university's code of conduct.[17]

We conclude that a college or university must be a *disciplined* community, a place where there are appropriate rules governing campus life, an institution where individuals acknowledge their obligations to the group. Specifically, we suggest an Honor Code for both the scholarly *and* the civic dimensions of campus life. Such codes convey a powerful message about how honesty and integrity form the foundation of a community of learning. Further, procedures for investigating and disciplining offenders must be in place.

Just as in social matters, all universities or colleges should have clear standards governing academic conduct, and all students on entrance must be absolutely clear about those policies and standards. The goal is not to have a list of unenforceable commandments. Rather, it is to assure that all parts of college life are governed by high standards.

---

[16]Margaret Platt Jendrek, p. 402.
[17]Ibid., p. 404.

PART TWO

...

CHAPTER FIVE

A CARING COMMUNITY

Fifth, a college or university is a *caring* community, a place where the well-being of each member is sensitively supported and where service to others is encouraged.

While colleges should be purposeful, and just, and disciplined—as well as open—the unique characteristic that makes these objectives work, the glue that holds it all together, is the way people relate to one another. As impossible as the goal may seem to be, a modern college or university should be a place where every individual feels affirmed and where every activity of the community is humane. Caring is the key.

At first blush, the term "caring" seems soft, almost sentimental. Yet, as human beings we have an absolute need for social bonding, from the first to the last moments of our lives. Professor Mary Clark, San Diego State University, puts the matter this way: "Social bonds," she writes, "are not temporary contracts entered into simply for the convenience of an individual, but are absolute requirements for human existence. Social embeddedness," Clark concludes, "is the essence of our nature."[1]

Students cherish their independence and accept as commonplace a campus environment that is more open, more relaxed. But undergraduates, like the rest of us, still need to feel that they belong. One student captured this paradox when she said, "We don't want the university to be involved in our lives, but we would like someone to be concerned occasionally about our lives."

We found, however, that at all too many institutions the connections students feel are tenuous, at best. No one expects the modern campus to have the intimacy of a family. Students are older, living self-directed lives. Yet, when we surveyed undergraduates several years ago, we were troubled to discover that about 50

---

[1]Mary E. Clark, "Meaningful Social Bonding as a Universal Human Need," in *Conflict: Human Needs Theory*, ed. John W. Burton (New York: St. Martin's Press, in press, 1990).

percent said they "feel like a number in a book." About 40 percent said they do not feel a sense of community on campus, and about two-thirds said they have no professor "interested in their personal lives."[2]

And last year over three-quarters of college presidents we surveyed rated the lack or student involvement as one of the most serious campus life problems they confront. At two-year institutions it was 82 percent.[3]

Table 11. Percentage of Presidents Who Rate Nonparticipation by Students in Events a "Moderate" to "Major" Problem on Their Campus

All Institutions	Research & Doctorate-Granting	Comprehensive	Liberal Arts	Two-Year
Few students participate in campus events				
76%	52%	78%	70%	82%

Source: The Carnegie Foundation for the Advancement of Teaching and the American Council on Education, National Survey of College and University Presidents, 1989.

Many students, perhaps most, experience the academic community in only marginal and momentary ways. The common ground they share with others is the wish to get ahead, the goal of getting a credential, acquiring a degree. As a sophomore at a huge university in the Southwest said: "Yes, I think of this school as a community. People have common goals. Everyone's here to get a degree."

Students did, however, cite with satisfaction their membership in sororities and fraternities, the women's center, the student union, the newspaper, sports teams, the radio club, and the jazz club—groups that helped them feel connected. Students also spoke of connecting through living-learning centers, and through academic majors and clubs. And we were struck by the frequency with which students at two-year institutions spoke of experiencing community at their institution, places that often were described as "truly caring."

Many faculty and administrators, especially those at large universities, feel that campus subgroups—such as those we've just cited—are the prerequisite for a healthy community. They argue that it's too much to expect students to feel bonded to a sprawling campus. A political scientist at a large western institution remarked: "Loyalty to the big institution develops only after these little loyalties." Even at colleges with smaller enrollments, most loyalties are formed to subgroups first. A student at a liberal arts college of eighteen hundred students echoed this view: "You can't have a community of the whole without the smaller groups."

---

[2]The Carnegie Foundation for the Advancement of Teaching, National Survey of Undergraduates, 1984.

[3]The Carnegie Foundation for the Advancement of Teaching and the American Council on Education, National Survey of College and University Presidents, 1989.

Still, as we went from place to place, we also encountered concern about the negative influence of "little loyalties." There's a feeling, as we mentioned earlier, that the very organizations that give security to students can also create isolation and even generate friction on the campus. Fraternities and sororities, we found, are especially inclined to separate themselves too much from others for the wrong reasons.

When we asked college and university presidents about Greek life on their campus, more than half at research and doctorate institutions cited it as a problem.[4] The head of the Panhellenic Council at a small university in the Northeast put it this way: "The freshmen who rush want a place to belong. I joined a sorority because I had no girlfriends. I wanted some friends but Greeks form a sense of community for themselves."[5]

The problem of Greek houses, especially fraternities, is not just isolation, it's also bad behavior. At one liberal arts college that is 30 percent Greek, the faculty recommended disaffiliation to the Board of Trustees on three separate occasions, and cited the use and sale of drugs and alcohol abuse as cause. Even the President of the National Interfraternity Conference, a confederation of fifty-nine fraternities, spoke of the crisis: "Chapters that have gone undisciplined for years now resent our discussion of basic standards and expectations. They cannot begin to relate to our dialogues about 'values and ethics' of fraternity membership."[6]

Table 12. Percentage of Presidents Who Say Fraternities and Sororities Are a "Moderate" to "Major" Problem on Their Campus

All Institutions	Research & Doctorate-Granting	Comprehensive	Liberal Arts	Two-Year
19%	54%	34%	25%	3%

Source: The Carnegie Foundation for the Advancement of Teaching and the American Council on Education, National Survey of College and University Presidents, 1989.

A college or university is diminished when students divide themselves, prejudicially, from one another or engage in destructive behavior, and unless Greeks function as purposeful, just, open, disciplined, and caring organizations, unless they commit themselves to supporting the larger purposes of the institution, they have no place in higher education. Recently, the Board of Directors of the American Council on Education adopted guidelines which stated: "As colleges

---

[4]Ibid.
[5]The Carnegie Foundation for the Advancement of Teaching, National Survey of Undergraduates, 1984.
[6]Chuck V. Loring, "A Time for Action—A Message from the President," *National Interfraternity Conference Annual Report 1988*, Indianapolis, Indiana, 1988.

and universities intensify their efforts to make their campuses hospitable to all groups, Greek organizations must take an active role in ensuring that their values and behaviors contribute to a positive campus life."[7] This should be the guiding principle for all groups on the campus.

Looking at the larger picture, we conclude that while subgroups on campus are important, they are not sufficient. As the vice chancellor of a western university put it: "There is a great deal of 'orbital energy' among the many subgroups, a magnetism that tugs at these groups, pulling them away from any common agenda." In today's world students must connect with the institution as a whole, and we were encouraged to discover that chief administrators on campus say that strengthening community is a top priority for them; only 13 percent of the presidents we surveyed feel that "community can be sustained only in small groups or units."[8] The need, on campus—and in society—is for something more.

Table 13. Presidents Who Say Community Can Be Sustained Only for Small Groups *(Percentage Agreeing)*

All Institutions	Research & Doctorate-Granting	Comprehensive	Liberal Arts	Two-Year
13%	7%	9%	2%	19%

Source: The Carnegie Foundation for the Advancement of Teaching and the American Council on Education, National Survey of College and University Presidents, 1989.

Creating a caring community takes on special significance for older students, who often march to a different drummer. Many hurry on and off the campus as they try to juggle work and family obligations. And we found that presidents are especially concerned about their inability to serve "commuter" students. Inadequate services for commuters was, in fact, rated a problem by about 60 percent of presidents at all four-year institutions. Even at community colleges, where virtually all students commute, about one-third of the presidents defined inadequate service for commuter students as a problem.[9]

Student affairs officers are worried, too. Thirty-six percent of those we surveyed said that "inadequate facilities for commuter students" was a greater problem today than five years ago. Over two-thirds rated "expanded services for nontraditional students" as "very important" for improving campus life.[10] The part-time students are, as one administrator put it, "on the edge of campus life."

---

[7]The Board of Directors, American Council on Education, news release, 4 Sept. 1989.

[8]The Carnegie Foundation for the Advancement of Teaching and the American Council on Education, National Survey of College and University Presidents, 1989.

[9]Ibid.

[10]The American Council on Education and the National Association of Student Personnel Administrators, National Survey of Chief Student Affairs Officers, 1989.

At an urban university in our study, everything closes at 5:00 p.m. and at a rural community college, where almost all students commute, the counseling center is the only office open in the evening—the cafeteria, the bookstore, and the business offices are not. One student commented on this lack of caring when she said, "Here they seem to be worried only about my money."

Table 14. Percentage of Presidents Who Report Service to Commuter Students Is a "Moderate" to "Major" Problem on Their Campus

All Institutions	Research & Doctorate-Granting	Comprehensive	Liberal Arts	Two-Year
45%	58%	56%	60%	32%

Source: The Carnegie Foundation for the Advancement of Teaching and the American Council on Education, National Survey of College and University Presidents, 1989.

We did find that extended office hours, counseling services, and day-care centers have been introduced on many campuses to help commuters. Student affairs staff, in particular, understand just how important it is for students of all ages to receive support, especially students on the margins. These professionals are the people who often put a human face on the institution. Many of the students sense that programs created by student affairs staff—in student unions, in residence halls, and in counseling centers—provide caring outside the classroom. We urge that such services be expanded, and well supported, by every institution.

At California State University, Dominguez Hills, an administrator, describes their program this way: "Our campus is open from eight in the morning to ten at night. We have a lot of support systems for older students to ensure graduation, such as a free learning center with computers for everything from math and physics to English. We also have advisement from the Educational Opportunity office on Saturdays. We've designed the programs to help the students, not to make our employees comfortable." Piedmont Virginia Community College keeps offices open until 7:00 p.m. Administrators also serve on rotation so that one is available until 9:00 p.m. every evening. At the University of Louisville's ACCESS program all major campus services—admissions, registration, financial aid, career planning, and placement—have office hours until 8:00 p.m., and on Saturday morning, too. There is also a lounge and study area available for commuters.

But it's in the classroom where social and intellectual bonding is most likely to occur. For commuter students this is the primary point of campus contact, and community colleges are, we discovered, especially good at building a spirit of community among students. The classroom can be an oasis of social and emotional support in the often hectic lives of older students. At community colleges

we heard students speak with gratitude about professors who gave them sugges-
tions about books or articles to read, who spoke with them after class about ideas
to consider, and even discussed personal plans and life choices.

A young woman student at Montgomery County Community College in
Pennsylvania told a member of our staff: "Before I came, I was told, you will love
MCCC. The professors are terrific. They spend a lot of time with you. That is so
true. You will never find such a family environment as you will find here. The
faculty have been very helpful. I have never been turned away when I went for
advice." Another student at a community college described her instructors as
people "who truly cared."

In reflecting on the impact of community colleges we were reminded that the
spirit of community must be measured, not by the length of time on campus, but
the quality of caring. It's how a student thinks and feels about a place that matters
most, and even students who come to campus just several hours a week will feel
part of a community if there is a supportive climate in the classroom, if they are
treated with dignity by registrars and financial aid officers and the like, and if the
office hours are arranged to serve the needs of students, not the system.

Finally, in a caring community, students should make a connection between
what they learn and how they live. A college is a humane enterprise and it is more
than mere sentiment to suggest that its quality depends upon the heads and the
hearts of the individuals in it. The goal of educators should be to help students
see that they are not only autonomous individuals but also members of a larger
community to which they are accountable. Specifically, we urge that all students
be encouraged to complete a community service project as an integral part of the
undergraduate experience.

We are especially concerned that students reach out to others—to children
and to older people to build bridges across the generations. Students also should
be brought in touch with those genuinely in need, and through field experiences,
build relationships that are inter-generational, intercultural, and international,
too. In the end, the campus should be viewed not only as a place of introspection,
but also as a staging ground for action.

At a time when social bonds are tenuous, students during their collegiate years
should discover the reality of their dependence on each other. They must understand what it means to share and understand the benefits of giving. Community
must be built. Thus, a caring community not only enables students to *gain*
knowledge, but helps them channel that knowledge to humane ends.

CHAPTER SIX

A CELEBRATIVE COMMUNITY

Sixth, a college or university is a *celebrative* community, one in which the heritage of the institution is remembered and where rituals affirming both tradition and change are widely shared.

If community in higher education is important—and almost all campus leaders agree that it is—colleges should sustain a keen sense of their own heritage and traditions. Old yearbooks with their depictions of white-glove and black-tie events or May Day ceremonies seem quaint today, and some rituals have lost their meaning. Still, rites, ceremonies, and celebrations unite the campus and give students a sense of belonging to something worthwhile and enduring. Celebrations, if meaningfully designed, sustain the vitality of campuses. The challenge is to instill all rituals and ceremonies with real significance—and fun as well. Such activities—and almost all colleges have their own unique traditions—show how memories can be kept alive and a sense of community can be sustained from year to year. Community must not only be created but recreated continually in institutions of higher education, and ritual has a vital role to play. These celebrations are critical, because from a quarter to a half of the undergraduates are new to a college each fall, and without traditions, continuity is lost.

Freshman orientation has long provided a splendid moment to introduce traditions, but on far too many campuses orientation was trivialized. The president and key academic officers were not involved, and it was left to the student personnel staff, almost exclusively, to help students become full members of the community of learning. But even then the focus was far more on the social than the academic. The good news is that some colleges now have semester-long orientation seminars that highlight the heritage of the college in a richer, fuller sense. Orientation topics include not only a review of rules and regulations, and the hazards of alcohol and drug abuse, but also how and why the college was founded, the purpose of general education, the stories of the heroes of the institution, and the history behind the names on campus buildings.

Special freshman convocations can also highlight the culture of the campus and underscore coming to college as a special rite of passage. Colleges celebrate with students when their academic program is completed. Why not pause at the beginning, too? City College of the City University of New York, with its twenty thousand students, has a New Student Convocation. In this celebrative event, members of the faculty dress in academic garb, and the president talks about City College's academic heritage and honors senior professors who have been outstanding teachers. One recent awardee, in his remarks to new students, made this connection: "What most of you and I have in common," he said, "is that we were the first in our families to go to college. My parents didn't even finish grade school. They weren't even sure that I should go to college because they thought that perhaps I should make my living unloading trucks, next to my father."[1] The faculty and freshmen shared a bond of hope and courage.

Each fall the University of California at Berkeley welcomes students, faculty, and staff with a convocation, replete with refreshments and music. An academic procession wends its way into the Greek Theater. At a different event, the Fall Reception, each new student is greeted by a member of the university's faculty or staff and accompanied through a formal receiving line at the student union, where they meet Berkeley's chancellor. Then the new student is introduced to a senior who becomes his or her host.

Xavier University in New Orleans, which sustains a special feel of community, uses its Founder's Day convocation to celebrate the institution's special mission of serving blacks and other minorities who have been denied educational opportunities. At this campuswide celebration early each fall, outstanding faculty and students are honored, seniors are recognized, new student leaders are inaugurated, and service awards are presented to faculty and staff.[2]

Students at Miami University—and other institutions as well—have a "Little Sibs" weekend to introduce their younger sisters and brothers to the campus. This weekend offers "little sibs" a firsthand opportunity to see what life on campus is like. For the students, the role of guide is a chance to renew their own ties to their community and culture. Siblings at Miami get to see and learn about the school's

---

[1] The Carnegie Foundation for the Advancement of Teaching, Campus Visits, 1989.
[2] We are indebted to George D. Kuh, John H. Schuh, and Elizabeth J. Whitt and Associates for permission to use these examples taken from a book to be published in 1991 by Jossey-Bass, tentatively titled *Involving Colleges: Encouraging Student Learning and Personal Development Through Out-of-Class Experiences.*

popular traditions such as the Miami bike race, alumni weekend, avoiding "stepping on the seal" (or you will fail your next exam), kissing in the Upham Arches, and the Western College "Shore to Slimy Shore Boat Race," in which teams design and race paper boats. Traditions like these are passed on to students in a number of ways—from their alumni parents, during tours of the campus, and at orientation and other freshman activities. These traditions all affirm the excitement and the variety of opportunities available for every student, and encourage their participation in the larger life of the college.[3]

Beyond fall orientation, colleges and universities can create on campus a climate of continuous bonding. At Evergreen State College, for example, faculty host potlucks in their homes, and retreats are held at The Farmhouse (a small lodge) at the Organic Farm. At the end of each academic year Evergreen celebrates Super Saturday. This event was initiated by a former Dean of Students and is a chance to thank everyone for another year. Super Saturday has grown to include a street fair, entertainment on three stages, two beer gardens, barbecues, and a "Friends of the Library" book sale, and it attracts nearly twenty-five thousand people. It not only brings the campus together, but also provides a unique opportunity to build goodwill between the college and the larger community.[4]

Another form of celebration can be less tangible, it's something "in the air." The intellectual accomplishments of the institution, for example, can offer this kind of atmosphere, and on several campuses we visited, students expressed pride in their school's "academic reputation," calling it the inspiration that holds the place together. Here's how one student put it: "Our departments are ranked high. The faculty win so many awards. This is such an amazing place. Everything here is part of the university. There is a community feeling, a sense of pride." Students from a southern university, also, proud of the intellectual quality of the institution, compared themselves favorably to the large public university close by, declaring themselves to be more serious students.

Colleges sometimes also celebrate their buildings. "Old Mains" often have an honorable history, and occasionally humorous legends worth telling and retelling. Buildings are often named to celebrate individuals important in the folklore of the institution. Their stories should be told. Special landmarks and beautiful spots on the campus also give distinctiveness to the institution. Knowing more about these legacies and landmarks adds to the sense of belonging students feel— they enhance a community.

---

[3]Ibid.
[4]Ibid.

Reverence for the beauty of Indiana University at Bloomington helps unite the campus and even though Herman B. Wells retired from the presidency of Indiana almost thirty years ago, stories still are told about how he would send architects back to their drawing boards to save a tree. Such stories, often told with zest and affection, underscore how the physical setting can be a source of informal celebration.

Commencements and alumni weekends surely can have a distinctive flair. At Montgomery County Community College in Pennsylvania, students know each spring that their degrees will be granted in a tent ceremony. The practice began when the college was still in its infancy, in the early 1970s, because there was no building on campus large enough to allow more than four hundred people to gather at once. Now, even though more accommodating facilities are available, the tradition of commencement in a tent behind College Hall persists.

At Princeton University alumni return en masse each spring to march in a parade with graduating seniors. Known as the "Parade," the procession is led by members of the 25th-year reunion class, followed by the oldest alumni, known as the "Old Guard." Strung out behind the "Old Guard" are classes of more recent vintage, in descending order, with the seniors bringing up the rear. Carrying class banners and dressed in colorful costumes and special blazers to distinguish each class, the alumni and their families and the seniors—some ten thousand strong— march through the campus to Clarke Field. The ceremony binds the youngest graduates to the generations preceding them.

Perhaps no campus tradition is more celebrative than sports, and certainly there is much to be said for the role of athletics in higher education. On the playing field, students have been taught discipline and fair play, and athletics has contributed greatly to the spirit of community on campus as well, powerfully uniting students, faculty, and alumni behind a common passion. But over the last century in America, intercollegiate athletics has developed a life of its own, one that has often distorted values, focusing not on the enrichment of student life, but on money.

Almost a hundred years ago, Woodrow Wilson, as president of Princeton University, lamented the negative influence of football: "As far as colleges go, the sideshows have swallowed up the circus, and we in the main tent do not know what is going on."[5] The situation today, at many of our best-known institutions, is very much worse, so that whatever these colleges or universities gain from

---

[5]Woodrow Wilson, "What Is a College For?" in *The Papers of Woodrow Wilson*, vol. 19, ed. Arthur S. Link (Princeton: Princeton University Press, 1975), p. 344. (The article originally appeared in *Scribner's Magazine*, 46 [1909], pp. 570-77.)

sports in the way of community and enrichment of students is overshadowed by what they lose in terms of the integrity and central mission of higher education.

Intercollegiate athletics must enrich the academic mission, not negate it, and we found, in our study, places where sports do still serve the students, not the other way around. We found institutions where sports are put in the proper perspective and where the predominant attitude toward athletics among the students is one of playfulness. For example, at Earlham College, students proudly deemphasize sports, and approach them with a jovial, fun-filled attitude. Here, where sports teams are called "The Fighting Quakers," the athletic director has even forfeited games because team members were consumed by academic projects.

We compare this playful attitude and sense of perspective to the big-time sports, where athletics means staggering amounts of money, multi-million dollar television contracts, and unbelievably aggressive recruitment of students, who become pawns in an unseemly saga as their agents guide them not through their academic programs, but (realistically for only a few) toward professional football and basketball teams. In this environment, the pressure is great for administrators and faculty alike to bend the academic rules to the breaking point. What should be playful, even if disciplined, becomes deadly serious and damaging to the fundamental purpose of the institution.

While it may be unrealistic to expect colleges and universities with a tradition of big-time sports to deemphasize athletics, still, it is reasonable to call for a return to the middle ground. When celebration becomes hype and hysteria, and when it leads to dishonesty and to the establishment of a double academic standard, when it no longer truly serves the students, then the time has come for an institution to reexamine its priorities and build its tradition on integrity, not abuse.

The celebrative community uses ceremony and ritual to recall the past, to affirm tradition and build larger loyalties on campus. But as colleges and universities become more richly inclusive, as the student body becomes more and more diverse, campuses should find ways to celebrate, not just tradition, but change and innovation as well.

We mentioned earlier the P-rade at Princeton. It's worth noting how the dynamics of that event are affected when the class that first opened its ranks to women marches along the parade route. There is cheering, dancing, and enthusiastic celebration of a significant change in the history of the university. In that same spirit colleges and universities should schedule special events throughout the year that highlight the rich contributions of the racial and ethnic groups on campus. Martin Luther King, Jr., Day, for example, should be honored and times also should be put aside to feature Hispanic, Asian, and Native American cultures. We urge, too, that the influence of women, nationally and within the institution, be a part of the celebrative community.

At Northern Arizona University, Honor Weeks 1989 was the scene for a host of distinguished speakers such as Wilma Mankiller, principal chief of Cherokee Nation of Oklahoma. The speakers all brought perspectives from culturally diverse populations. The event sent a special message that such speakers are not brought in just for Martin Luther King Day or *Cinco de Mayo.* Rather, it demonstrated that culturally diverse perspectives are an essential part of what everyone in the community needs to know.

Foreign students on campus also should be brought more significantly into the celebrative campus community. They provide colleges and universities with unique opportunities to create connections between students of dramatically different backgrounds, broadening the experience and learning of all. Too often, however, foreign students are isolated. Though they come together themselves for formal talks, discussions, and celebrations, with few exceptions students in the larger community remain uninformed by their contributions.

We are convinced that far more can and should be done, administratively, to tap this intellectual and cultural wealth of the international community on campus. Campuswide events—formal talks as well as festivities with food, music, and dance—should routinely take place every year so that large numbers of students could benefit from the presence of these students who come from all over the world. Further, international students should be viewed as a rich educational resource and be asked, from time to time, to give special lectures in classes, featured as a unique resource on the campus.

Older students, also, bring a wealth of experience to the campus community, but often remain detached from the mainstream of campus life. Again, community colleges, we found, frequently demonstrate a great commitment to older students, and plan events with their needs and contributions in mind. But for the most part, the experience that older students bring with them to campus is left unexplored and unappreciated. When older students are only tolerated instead of meaningfully included, an important part of the mission of higher education fails. Colleges and universities should, we believe, make a special effort to celebrate the diversity older students add to campus life, scheduling events and talks in which these students' perspectives and special needs are highlighted, and thereby teaching younger students to regard them with respect.

While leaving space for privacy and individual interests, we believe that a university at its best encourages people to share rituals and traditions that connect them to the campus community and that improve the civic culture and diversity of the institution. The academic mission and the integrity of the higher learning institution, as well as the diversity of people who make up the community, should inform all celebrations on campus, formal and informal, academic and athletic.

EPILOGUE

COMPACT FOR COMMUNITY

A ringing call for the renewal of community in higher learning may, at first, seem quixotic. Not only has cultural coherence faded, but the very notion of commonalities seems strikingly inapplicable to the vigorous diversity of contemporary life. Within the academy itself, the fragmentation of knowledge, narrow departmentalism, and an intense vocationalism are, as we have acknowledged, the strongest characteristics of collegiate education.

Still, we believe the undergraduate experience can, by bringing together the separate parts, create something greater than the sum, and offer the prospect that the channels of our common life will be renewed and deepened.

Students come to college to follow their own special aptitudes and interests. They are eager to get credentials and get a job, become productive, self-reliant human beings and, with new knowledge, continue to learn after college days are over. Serving the educational needs of each student must remain a top priority in higher education, but private concerns, while important, are insufficient.

Perhaps we can draw an analogy from a different field. Paul Goldberger, architecture critic for *The New York Times*, observed that while city life has always been characterized by a struggle between the private and public sectors, there was once general respect for buildings and spaces "of the public realm." In New York City, for example, this meant Central Park, Grand Central Terminal, the New York Public Library, the road, park, and tunnel systems. In recent years, however, commitment to the public realm diminished or, as Goldberger put it, commitment "to the very idea . . . that the city is a collective, shared place, a place that is in the most literal sense common ground."[1]

As the inspiration of shared spaces lost appeal—with people retreating increasingly into their own private worlds—many seemed to feel that the public domain in cities could not be reclaimed. Still, a city simply cannot function

---

[1]Paul Goldberger, "Why Design Can't Transform Cities," *The New York Times Magazine*, 25 June 1989, p. 1.

physically without an infrastructure—roadways, pipes and tunnels for water and waste, basic public services—nor can it survive spiritually without the spaces and places that sustain its intellectual, social, and artistic life.

So it is with higher education. The nation and the world need educated men and women who not only pursue their own personal interests but also are prepared to fulfill their social and civic obligations. And it is during the college years, perhaps more than at any other time, that these essential qualities of mind and character are refined.

The academic and social divisions that characterize the modern campus create a special need for common purposes to give meaning to the enterprise. And while higher education has a wide range of priorities to pursue, we are convinced that all parts of campus life can relate to one another and contribute to a sense of wholeness.

It is of special significance, we believe, that higher learning institutions, even the big, complex ones, continue to use the familiar rhetoric of "community" to describe campus life and even use the metaphor of "family." Especially significant, 97 percent of the college and university presidents we surveyed said they "strongly believe in the importance of community." Almost all the presidents agreed that "community is appropriate for my campus" and also support the proposition that "administrators should make a greater effort to strengthen common purposes and shared experiences."[2]

We proceed then with the conviction that if a balance can be struck between individual interests and shared concerns, a strong learning community will result. We believe the six principles highlighted in this report—purposefulness, openness, justice, discipline, caring, and celebration—can form the foundation on which a vital community of learning can be built. Now, more than ever, colleges and universities should be guided by a larger vision.

Building community in higher education calls for leadership at the highest level. The president sets the tone of the institution and, in large measure, determines the priorities to be pursued. The president, as chief *administrator*, is engaged in the day-to-day details of management. But the task of the president as *leader* is to transcend details, present a larger, more inspired vision and remind the community of those essential qualities that guide the institution.

But how can the principles proposed in this report be converted into practice? As a first step, the president may wish to convene a campuswide forum, or use

---

[2]The Carnegie Foundation for the Advancement of Teaching and the American Council on Education, National Survey of College and University Presidents, 1989.

existing forums such as the faculty senate or student assembly, to discuss the six principles and the idea of adopting them, more formally, as a campus *compact*. And we urge that trustees, early on, be brought into the discussion. The entire board could be engaged in a consideration of the principles of community and also ratify them as the framework to be used in shaping policy and practice.

Table 15. Presidents' Views on the Role of Community *(Percentage Responding "Agree")*

All Institutions	Research & Doctorate-Granting	Comprehensive	Liberal Arts	Two-Year
Administrators should make a greater effort to strengthen common purposes and shared experiences				
97%	96%	100%	99%	95%
I strongly believe in the importance of "community"				
96%	97%	99%	100%	93%
The idea of "community" is no longer appropriate for an institution such as this				
4%	0%	4%	0%	7%

Source: The Carnegie Foundation for the Advancement of Teaching and the American Council on Education, National Survey of College and University Presidents, 1989.

To adopt the principles as a campus compact would signal the seriousness with which the enduring values of the institution were understood and embraced. All members of the community would be reminded of their importance and, as a compact, the principles could be referred to, with authority, and passed on from one student generation to another.

The compact could be used by the president in working with his or her administrative team. Consider the possibility of a fall retreat in which key officials meet together for several days to discuss the six dimensions of community and use them as a way to assess the institution. For example, a report card might be prepared, one that evaluates current college performance against each principle and includes an action plan to improve campus life in those areas where the institution is judged deficient.

We also could imagine using the compact in orienting incoming students to the college and we could imagine, as well, a semester-long series of events in which one principle—a *just* community, for example—would be the subject of guest lecturers, faculty symposia, and student forums. Then another principle could be explored.

Further, with the six principles to guide the conversation, faculty and administrators could meet on common ground when academic policies are considered. Student personnel officers also might find the principles useful in resolving matters affecting student life. And could student, faculty, and administrative leaders use the principles to guide day-to-day decisions—from inviting speakers or entertainment groups, to planning courses, to academic evaluations and even hiring personnel?

They could be used also by administrators as a litmus test to evaluate the appropriateness of new student organizations—or to measure the worthiness of existing ones. A fraternity, for example, might be asked to assess the value of its programs by using purposefulness, openness, justice, discipline, caring, and celebration as the yardsticks of assessment.

Looking beyond the campus, accreditation bodies might use the compact in their assessment of the quality of a college or university. Instead of evaluating the institution on the basis of administrative functions—instructional, library, student services and the rest—could the accreditation team apply the six principles to critique both academic and nonacademic actions?

Again, the president clearly has a crucial role to play in reminding all constituencies that the campus is being guided by high standards, not ad hoc arrangements. While affirming principles surely will not resolve all differences of opinion, it would, we believe, help lift the level of discourse and provide an appropriate framework within which campus decisions might be made.

But leadership means far more than inspired direction from the top. It also means assuring that decision making at all levels will be based on high standards that are widely shared. And it is our hope that the guidelines discussed in this report might provide the thread of a durable new compact, one in which students and faculty come together as scholars-citizens to create an organic community whose members are not only intellectually engaged, but also committed to civility on campus.

In the end, building a vital community is a challenge confronting not just higher learning, but the whole society. In our hard-edged competitive world, more humane, more integrative purposes must be defined. And perhaps it is not too much to hope that as colleges and universities affirm a new vision of community on campus, they may also promote the common good in the neighborhood, the nation, and the world.

APPENDIX A

NATIONAL SURVEY OF COLLEGE AND UNIVERSITY PRESIDENTS, 1989

Table A-1. Campus Life Issues of Greatest Concern (Percentage of Presidents Listing Each Response)

All Institutions	Research & Doctorate-Granting	Comprehensive	Liberal Arts	Two-Year
Substance abuse (primarily alcohol)				
45%	51%	54%	50%	37%
Student apathy				
30%	12%	20%	23%	43%
Campus security and crime				
25%	31%	30%	19%	24%
Inadequate facilities				
18%	19%	10%	16%	22%
Interracial/intercultural relations				
13%	32%	21%	14%	5%
Adequacy of services and programming for commuter/nontraditional students				
11%	6%	4%	8%	18%
AIDS education and issues of human sexuality				
9%	8%	7%	7%	11%
Incivility, disrespect by students				
9%	5%	3%	9%	14%
Inadequate advising				
8%	4%	6%	0%	13%
Lack of student leadership				
8%	2%	9%	9%	8%
Student stress/dysfunction				
7%	10%	2%	13%	6%

Table A-1. (continued)

All Institutions	Research & Doctorate-Granting	Comprehensive	Liberal Arts	Two-Year
Academic dishonesty, student values				
7%	8%	10%	10%	5%
General lack of sense of campus community				
7%	8%	7%	11%	5%
Quality of residential life				
6%	8%	5%	12%	3%
Vandalism				
6%	2%	8%	6%	6%
Recruitment/retention of minorities				
5%	9%	2%	5%	6%
Greek organizations				
5%	7%	7%	12%	0%
College costs/aid availability				
4%	11%	6%	2%	2%
Regulation of alcohol use, on and off campus				
4%	4%	5%	7%	2%
Lack of appreciation for differences				
3%	11%	6%	3%	0%
Budgetary constraints				
3%	9%	3%	3%	2%
Retention				
3%	1%	7%	2%	2%
Sexual harassment				
2%	2%	3%	4%	0%
Faculty-student interaction				
2%	2%	2%	3%	2%
Other				
60%	39%	65%	54%	65%

Source: The Carnegie Foundation for the Advancement of Teaching and the American Council on Education, National Survey of College and University Presidents, 1989.

Table A-2. Extent of Problems Reported by Presidents (Percentage Giving Each Response)

	All Institutions	Research & Doctorate-Granting	Comprehensive	Liberal Arts	Two-Year
Few students participate in campus events					
MAJOR	14%	11%	11%	14%	15%
4	33%	20%	29%	30%	39%
MODERATE	29%	21%	38%	26%	28%
2	16%	36%	19%	22%	10%
NOT A PROBLEM	10%	15%	5%	11%	11%
Inadequate facilities for campus gatherings					
MAJOR	13%	15%	8%	16%	14%
4	20%	27%	20%	23%	17%
MODERATE	22%	18%	24%	21%	22%
2	19%	27%	24%	21%	15%
NOT A PROBLEM	28%	16%	27%	22%	34%
Alcohol abuse					
MAJOR	11%	17%	15%	12%	7%
4	22%	47%	29%	24%	14%
MODERATE	34%	18%	40%	39%	32%
2	20%	17%	11%	22%	24%
NOT A PROBLEM	15%	3%	8%	5%	25%
Overcrowded or outdated residence halls					
MAJOR	9%	11%	10%	15%	3%
4	9%	19%	11%	15%	2%
MODERATE	18%	21%	22%	22%	12%
2	14%	29%	20%	15%	6%
NOT A PROBLEM	54%	23%	40%	35%	80%
Inadequate facilities for commuter students					
MAJOR	7%	10%	8%	7%	6%
4	14%	19%	17%	15%	12%
MODERATE	28%	31%	35%	41%	18%
2	22%	23%	24%	23%	20%
NOT A PROBLEM	32%	19%	20%	17%	47%

Table A-2. *(continued)*

	All Institutions	Research & Doctorate-Granting	Comprehensive	Liberal Arts	Two-Year
Inadequate services for commuter students					
MAJOR	5%	7%	7%	6%	3%
4	12%	11%	17%	13%	10%
MODERATE	28%	40%	32%	41%	19%
2	25%	27%	33%	26%	21%
NOT A PROBLEM	32%	18%	13%	17%	50%
Excessive noise and disruptiveness in campus residences					
MAJOR	4%	3%	2%	6%	3%
4	16%	17%	16%	20%	13%
MODERATE	29%	39%	41%	39%	15%
2	23%	38%	29%	27%	15%
NOT A PROBLEM	30%	6%	15%	11%	56%
Thefts					
MAJOR	3%	2%	2%	3%	4%
4	10%	16%	7%	9%	11%
MODERATE	34%	45%	48%	26%	29%
2	42%	34%	41%	47%	41%
NOT A PROBLEM	14%	3%	5%	18%	18%
Drug/substance abuse					
MAJOR	3%	3%	5%	2%	3%
4	7%	13%	8%	9%	4%
MODERATE	35%	30%	33%	28%	40%
2	40%	49%	45%	51%	31%
NOT A PROBLEM	17%	8%	11%	13%	24%
Poor academic advising					
MAJOR	2%	9%	2%	2%	2%
4	12%	26%	20%	7%	8%
MODERATE	29%	37%	32%	28%	26%
2	36%	28%	31%	40%	39%
NOT A PROBLEM	23%	3%	18%	26%	27%

Table A-2. *(continued)*

	All Institutions	Research & Doctorate-Granting	Comprehensive	Liberal Arts	Two-Year
Inadequate security					
MAJOR	2%	2%	2%	2%	2%
4	8%	9%	6%	8%	8%
MODERATE	28%	23%	26%	31%	29%
2	32%	51%	33%	43%	24%
NOT A PROBLEM	33%	18%	36%	18%	40%
Racial tensions/hostilities					
MAJOR	2%	6%	3%	1%	1%
4	5%	16%	4%	10%	1%
MODERATE	17%	46%	13%	17%	13%
2	39%	29%	43%	41%	39%
NOT A PROBLEM	40%	5%	39%	34%	50%
Greek life problems					
MAJOR	2%	5%	1%	5%	1%
4	5%	14%	9%	8%	1%
MODERATE	12%	35%	24%	12%	1%
2	10%	29%	15%	14%	1%
NOT A PROBLEM	74%	20%	54%	64%	101%
Vandalism and destruction of property					
MAJOR	1%	0%	2%	1%	2%
4	8%	9%	5%	11%	7%
MODERATE	27%	47%	37%	24%	20%
2	46%	35%	52%	49%	44%
NOT A PROBLEM	20%	9%	7%	18%	30%
Crude and offensive behavior at sports events					
MAJOR	1%	3%	2%	1%	1%
4	5%	13%	3%	6%	3%
MODERATE	9%	17%	13%	11%	5%
2	31%	39%	43%	36%	20%
NOT A PROBLEM	57%	30%	41%	49%	74%

Table A-2. *(continued)*

	All Institutions	Research & Doctorate-Granting	Comprehensive	Liberal Arts	Two-Year
Sexual harassment					
MAJOR	1%	2%	1%	1%	1%
4	4%	13%	3%	5%	3%
MODERATE	23%	47%	28%	24%	16%
2	46%	36%	55%	46%	43%
NOT A PROBLEM	29%	4%	17%	27%	40%
Violations of honor codes or rules of academic integrity					
MAJOR	1%	1%	1%	1%	1%
4	4%	15%	1%	5%	4%
MODERATE	21%	31%	23%	30%	14%
2	43%	43%	58%	43%	37%
NOT A PROBLEM	34%	13%	21%	24%	48%
Incidents involving physical violence					
MAJOR	1%	1%	2%	2%	1%
4	4%	5%	4%	5%	4%
MODERATE	13%	25%	14%	8%	13%
2	38%	55%	46%	45%	27%
NOT A PROBLEM	46%	17%	37%	43%	58%
Disruptive behavior by nonstudents					
MAJOR	1%	1%	3%	1%	1%
4	4%	7%	4%	5%	4%
MODERATE	13%	18%	13%	11%	12%
2	29%	37%	38%	38%	19%
NOT A PROBLEM	56%	40%	44%	47%	68%
Rape/sexual assault					
MAJOR	1%	1%	2%	1%	1%
4	4%	17%	2%	5%	3%
MODERATE	9%	32%	12%	13%	2%
2	34%	35%	51%	38%	24%
NOT A PROBLEM	55%	17%	36%	46%	74%

Table A-2. *(continued)*

	All Institutions	Research & Doctorate-Granting	Comprehensive	Liberal Arts	Two-Year
Suicides and suicide attempts					
MAJOR	1%	3%	1%	1%	2%
4	3%	11%	3%	3%	2%
MODERATE	14%	29%	25%	19%	4%
2	40%	43%	47%	46%	33%
NOT A PROBLEM	44%	17%	27%	33%	62%
Racial intimidation/harassment					
MAJOR	1%	2%	3%	1%	1%
4	3%	9%	3%	4%	2%
MODERATE	12%	37%	12%	10%	10%
2	36%	44%	39%	42%	31%
NOT A PROBLEM	50%	10%	45%	47%	60%
Lack of civility when disputes arise					
MAJOR	1%	2%	1%	3%	1%
4	3%	4%	3%	4%	3%
MODERATE	8%	20%	7%	7%	7%
2	37%	48%	45%	43%	29%
NOT A PROBLEM	53%	29%	47%	46%	63%
Excessive drinking at sports events					
MAJOR	1%	6%	1%	1%	1%
4	3%	13%	2%	3%	2%
MODERATE	5%	14%	9%	5%	2%
2	20%	30%	32%	17%	14%
NOT A PROBLEM	73%	39%	59%	77%	84%
Hazing incidents					
MAJOR	1%	2%	1%	1%	1%
4	2%	4%	2%	6%	1%
MODERATE	8%	18%	14%	9%	2%
2	16%	52%	27%	20%	3%
NOT A PROBLEM	76%	26%	59%	67%	97%

Table A-2. *(continued)*

	All Institutions	Research & Doctorate-Granting	Comprehensive	Liberal Arts	Two-Year
Disruptive behavior at commencement or convocation ceremonies					
MAJOR	1%	2%	1%	1%	1%
4	1%	3%	1%	3%	1%
MODERATE	5%	14%	9%	1%	3%
2	14%	20%	16%	14%	12%
NOT A PROBLEM	82%	64%	76%	84%	87%
Incidents involving guns and other weapons					
MAJOR	1%	1%	1%	1%	1%
4	1%	1%	1%	1%	2%
MODERATE	4%	6%	7%	3%	3%
2	20%	36%	25%	17%	17%
NOT A PROBLEM	77%	60%	70%	82%	80%
Disruptive protest demonstrations					
MAJOR	1%	1%	1%	1%	1%
4	1%	3%	1%	1%	1%
MODERATE	1%	8%	1%	1%	1%
2	8%	31%	13%	7%	3%
NOT A PROBLEM	91%	60%	88%	92%	98%
Other					
MAJOR	21%	31%	70%	14%	11%
4	11%	31%	1%	1%	12%
MODERATE	18%	29%	1%	1%	23%
2	2%	12%	1%	1%	1%
NOT A PROBLEM	52%	1%	31%	87%	56%

Source: The Carnegie Foundation for the Advancement of Teaching and the American Council on Education, National Survey of College and University Presidents, 1989.

Table A-3. Campus Life Issues in Context (Percentage of Presidents Giving Each Response)

	All Institutions	Research & Doctorate-Granting	Comprehensive	Liberal Arts	Two-Year
Campus life problems are made more difficult by conditions in the larger society					
YES	72%	85%	82%	86%	59%
NO	22%	8%	16%	7%	34%
UNCERTAIN	6%	7%	3%	7%	7%
The quality of campus life is of greater concern today, versus a few years ago					
YES	52%	58%	46%	58%	52%
NO	38%	36%	42%	37%	36%
UNCERTAIN	10%	6%	12%	5%	11%
Campus life problems are made more difficult by changes in the composition of the student body					
YES	38%	36%	31%	44%	39%
NO	57%	57%	63%	51%	57%
UNCERTAIN	5%	7%	7%	5%	5%
Campus life problems are made more difficult by conditions in the surrounding community					
YES	35%	53%	43%	32%	29%
NO	58%	44%	52%	61%	61%
UNCERTAIN	7%	3%	5%	8%	9%
Campus life problems are made more difficult by your campus's enrollment size					
YES	27%	29%	20%	24%	31%
NO	69%	65%	75%	70%	66%
UNCERTAIN	4%	6%	5%	6%	3%

Source: The Carnegie Foundation for the Advancement of Teaching and the American Council on Education, National Survey of College and University Presidents, 1989.

Table A-4. Presidents' Views on Improving Campus Life (Percentage Giving Each Response)

	All Institutions	Research & Doctorate-Granting	Comprehensive	Liberal Arts	Two-Year
Greater effort to build a stronger overall sense of community					
VERY IMPORTANT	71%	87%	74%	79%	64%
SOMEWHAT IMPORTANT	27%	12%	26%	20%	34%
NOT IMPORTANT	1%	2%	0%	1%	2%
More interaction between students and faculty					
VERY IMPORTANT	64%	76%	61%	65%	63%
SOMEWHAT IMPORTANT	34%	24%	38%	29%	35%
NOT IMPORTANT	3%	0%	1%	5%	2%
Better campus communications					
VERY IMPORTANT	60%	58%	53%	47%	69%
SOMEWHAT IMPORTANT	38%	39%	43%	48%	30%
NOT IMPORTANT	3%	3%	4%	5%	1%
More events that affirm the institution's mission, objectives, and values					
VERY IMPORTANT	60%	71%	67%	65%	52%
SOMEWHAT IMPORTANT	37%	27%	30%	29%	45%
NOT IMPORTANT	4%	2%	3%	7%	3%
More events that bring large numbers of students, faculty, and staff together					
VERY IMPORTANT	59%	49%	55%	62%	61%
SOMEWHAT IMPORTANT	35%	47%	43%	32%	30%
NOT IMPORTANT	7%	4%	2%	6%	9%
Closer links between classroom and out-of-class activities					
VERY IMPORTANT	56%	64%	48%	72%	51%
SOMEWHAT IMPORTANT	40%	31%	51%	26%	43%
NOT IMPORTANT	4%	5%	1%	2%	6%
Expanded services for nontraditional students					
VERY IMPORTANT	50%	37%	55%	32%	57%
SOMEWHAT IMPORTANT	39%	53%	39%	48%	34%
NOT IMPORTANT	11%	11%	5%	20%	9%

Table A-4. *(continued)*

	All Institutions	Research & Doctorate-Granting	Comprehensive	Liberal Arts	Two-Year
Greater understanding and awareness of racial/ethnic diversity					
VERY IMPORTANT	49%	82%	62%	51%	36%
SOMEWHAT IMPORTANT	40%	18%	34%	38%	47%
NOT IMPORTANT	11%	0%	4%	11%	17%
More leadership opportunities for students					
VERY IMPORTANT	47%	35%	49%	40%	51%
SOMEWHAT IMPORTANT	47%	49%	49%	49%	44%
NOT IMPORTANT	7%	16%	1%	11%	6%
Better orientation programs					
VERY IMPORTANT	46%	36%	40%	34%	55%
SOMEWHAT IMPORTANT	49%	57%	53%	60%	42%
NOT IMPORTANT	5%	7%	7%	6%	3%
More aggressive programs to prevent alcohol and drug abuse					
VERY IMPORTANT	45%	60%	52%	44%	40%
SOMEWHAT IMPORTANT	44%	29%	35%	51%	48%
NOT IMPORTANT	10%	11%	13%	5%	11%
More explicit expectations for student behavior and responsibilities					
VERY IMPORTANT	39%	33%	36%	40%	42%
SOMEWHAT IMPORTANT	50%	57%	51%	51%	49%
NOT IMPORTANT	10%	9%	14%	10%	9%
Greater incentives for alcohol-free events					
VERY IMPORTANT	39%	51%	50%	33%	34%
SOMEWHAT IMPORTANT	36%	32%	37%	36%	37%
NOT IMPORTANT	25%	17%	14%	31%	29%
More collaborative learning among students					
VERY IMPORTANT	33%	22%	35%	25%	37%
SOMEWHAT IMPORTANT	58%	64%	61%	67%	50%
NOT IMPORTANT	10%	14%	4%	7%	13%

Table A-4. *(continued)*

	All Institutions	Research & Doctorate-Granting	Comprehensive	Liberal Arts	Two-Year
Workshops on conflict resolution					
VERY IMPORTANT	23%	15%	19%	18%	28%
SOMEWHAT IMPORTANT	46%	63%	55%	49%	38%
NOT IMPORTANT	31%	22%	26%	33%	34%
New or revised statements on civility and respect for others					
VERY IMPORTANT	23%	20%	24%	23%	24%
SOMEWHAT IMPORTANT	44%	66%	43%	43%	42%
NOT IMPORTANT	33%	14%	33%	34%	35%
Better enforcement of rules governing student behavior					
VERY IMPORTANT	21%	19%	22%	19%	22%
SOMEWHAT IMPORTANT	55%	66%	64%	59%	48%
NOT IMPORTANT	24%	15%	14%	22%	31%
Better procedures for handling complaints and grievances					
VERY IMPORTANT	21%	20%	23%	15%	24%
SOMEWHAT IMPORTANT	52%	59%	57%	62%	43%
NOT IMPORTANT	27%	21%	20%	23%	33%
Strengthened campus police force and security					
VERY IMPORTANT	20%	16%	26%	16%	19%
SOMEWHAT IMPORTANT	55%	57%	48%	58%	56%
NOT IMPORTANT	26%	27%	26%	26%	25%
Other					
VERY IMPORTANT	46%	85%	0%	0%	50%
SOMEWHAT IMPORTANT	4%	15%	0%	0%	0%
NOT IMPORTANT	50%	0%	100%	100%	50%

Source: The Carnegie Foundation for the Advancement of Teaching and the American Council on Education, National Survey of College and University Presidents, 1989.

Table A-5. Most Positive Developments to Address Campus Life Issues (Percentage of Presidents Listing Each Response)

All Institutions	Research & Doctorate-Granting	Comprehensive	Liberal Arts	Two-Year
Active student government/greater student involvement				
26%	12%	19%	15%	42%
Better campus communications				
19%	20%	18%	11%	23%
Increased awareness/commitment to improve campus life				
12%	19%	16%	13%	8%
New or expanded student activities programming				
12%	10%	13%	10%	13%
Able, effective student affairs personnel				
10%	9%	16%	8%	8%
Construction of student center or other campus facility for social gatherings				
9%	4%	7%	8%	10%
New/improved counseling program				
9%	3%	4%	9%	13%
Development/redesign of orientation program or course				
8%	7%	2%	14%	8%
Formal project/group commissioned to monitor quality of campus life				
7%	9%	3%	12%	5%
Improved administration or coordination of student services				
6%	10%	15%	2%	3%
Creation of alcohol/substance abuse program				
6%	9%	5%	10%	3%
Specific board/committee created				
6%	2%	9%	4%	5%
New student affairs personnel or senior administrator concerned with student life				
5%	8%	2%	6%	5%
Planned forums or other scheduled community events on campus life issues				
5%	4%	2%	6%	8%
Long-range planning				
5%	3%	5%	15%	0%
Specific policy/program created				
4%	5%	4%	9%	0%

Table A-5. *(continued)*

All Institutions	Research & Doctorate-Granting	Comprehensive	Liberal Arts	Two-Year
Leadership development program				
4%	2%	5%	2%	5%
Existing committee structure				
4%	0%	2%	0%	8%
Renovation or construction of student housing				
3%	10%	2%	4%	3%
New policies, programs, or personnel in residence halls				
3%	8%	3%	6%	0%
Committee on the status of minorities and/or campus diversity				
3%	6%	5%	2%	3%
Attention to hiring and retention of minority students and faculty				
3%	4%	0%	1%	5%
New policies or programs affecting Greek organizations				
2%	2%	2%	4%	0%
New student organization formed				
2%	1%	2%	1%	3%
Presidential leadership				
1%	6%	0%	1%	0%
Enforcement of policies/practices				
1%	0%	4%	0%	0%
Greater effort to build community				
1%	0%	2%	3%	0%
Other				
25%	26%	32%	25%	21%

Source: The Carnegie Foundation for the Advancement of Teaching and the American Council on Education, National Survey of College and University Presidents, 1989.

Table A-6. Most Important Actions to Improve Campus Life (Percentage of Presidents Listing Each Response)

All Institutions	Research & Doctorate-Granting	Comprehensive	Liberal Arts	Two-Year
Be visible and involved in campus events				
39%	34%	32%	40%	45%
Be accessible to students, faculty and staff				
27%	23%	33%	21%	26%
Act as role model to communicate campus values and standards				
23%	24%	28%	29%	16%
Provide adequate facilities/staff for campus programs				
19%	9%	18%	22%	21%
Advocate for programs that improve campus life				
17%	31%	7%	19%	18%
Listen to and stay familiar with student and faculty concerns				
17%	9%	16%	24%	16%
Affirm institutional mission, objectives and values				
13%	16%	22%	14%	5%
Provide strong leadership				
12%	22%	9%	17%	8%
Support student services/affairs staff				
12%	12%	13%	15%	11%
Cultivate a sense of community				
12%	9%	19%	13%	8%
Enhance campus communication among students/faculty/staff/administrators				
11%	13%	8%	6%	16%
Hire qualified and innovative staff to address these issues				
8%	12%	7%	3%	11%
Support student government and/or other student organizations				
8%	5%	7%	4%	11%
Acknowledge quality of campus life as a priority				
7%	4%	6%	2%	11%
Encourage, reward faculty-student interaction				
6%	7%	7%	3%	8%
Enforce existing rules and regulations; discipline violators				
5%	8%	10%	9%	0%
Set institutional goals and provide funds to meet them				
4%	3%	4%	1%	5%

Table A-6. *(continued)*

All Institutions	Research & Doctorate-Granting	Comprehensive	Liberal Arts	Two-Year
Encourage campus participation				
4%	2%	3%	4%	5%
Be proactive in identifying and addressing campus concerns				
3%	1%	0%	9%	3%
Ensure open discussion of campus issues				
2%	4%	2%	3%	0%
Be open to divergent views				
2%	0%	0%	2%	3%
Be knowledgeable of campus services				
1%	0%	0%	2%	0%
Be actively involved in faculty and staff hiring				
1%	0%	0%	0%	3%
Other				
48%	52%	48%	38%	53%

Source: The Carnegie Foundation for the Advancement of Teaching and the American Council on Education, National Survey of College and University Presidents, 1989.

Table A-7. Presidents' Views on the Role of Community (Percentage Giving Each Response)

	All Institutions	Research & Doctorate-Granting	Comprehensive	Liberal Arts	Two-Year
Administrators should make a greater effort to strengthen common purposes and shared experiences at their institutions.					
AGREE	97%	96%	100%	99%	95%
DISAGREE	3%	4%	0%	1%	5%
I strongly believe in the importance of "community" for an institution such as this.					
AGREE	96%	97%	99%	100%	93%
DISAGREE	4%	3%	1%	0%	7%
"Community" is appropriate for my campus.					
YES	91%	92%	95%	97%	86%
NO	1%	2%	0%	0%	2%
PARTLY	8%	6%	5%	3%	12%
"Community" can be sustained only for small groups or units, not for this institution as a whole.					
AGREE	13%	7%	9%	2%	19%
DISAGREE	87%	93%	91%	98%	81%
The idea of "community" is no longer appropriate for an institution such as this.					
AGREE	4%	0%	4%	0%	7%
DISAGREE	96%	100%	96%	100%	93%

Source: The Carnegie Foundation for the Advancement of Teaching and the American Council on Education, National Survey of College and University Presidents, 1989.

NATIONAL SURVEY OF CHIEF STUDENT AFFAIRS OFFICERS, 1989

Table B-1. Institutional Characteristics (Percentage Giving Each Response)

	All Institutions	Research & Doctorate-Granting	Comprehensive	Liberal Arts	Two-Year
Institution is:					
Rural/small city	54%	31%	39%	64%	61%
Suburban	22%	17%	27%	20%	21%
Urban	24%	52%	33%	16%	18%
Primarily residential	33%	48%	34%	71%	14%
Primarily commuter	57%	31%	45%	16%	85%
Evenly divided	10%	21%	22%	13%	1%

Source: The American Council on Education and the National Association of Student Personnel Administrators, National Survey of Chief Student Affairs Officers, 1989.

Table B-2. Student Characteristics (Percentage Giving Each Response)

	All Institutions	Research & Doctorate-Granting	Comprehensive	Liberal Arts	Two-Year
Percentage of all undergraduates:					
Over age 25					
LESS THAN 10 PERCENT	20%	26%	22%	43%	8%
10-24 PERCENT	21%	38%	32%	27%	11%
25-49 PERCENT	25%	26%	25%	21%	26%
50-74 PERCENT	29%	9%	20%	4%	47%
75 PERCENT OR MORE	5%	1%	1%	5%	7%

Table B-2. *(continued)*

	All Institutions	Research & Doctorate-Granting	Comprehensive	Liberal Arts	Two-Year
Part-time students					
LESS THAN 10 PERCENT	21%	30%	21%	41%	10%
10-24 PERCENT	23%	44%	36%	32%	9%
25-49 PERCENT	19%	20%	27%	20%	15%
50-74 PERCENT	30%	6%	15%	5%	53%
75 PERCENT OR MORE	7%	0%	1%	2%	13%
In residence halls					
LESS THAN 10 PERCENT	41%	6%	26%	7%	77%
10-24 PERCENT	11%	27%	15%	8%	7%
25-49 PERCENT	14%	35%	22%	12%	6%
50 PERCENT OR MORE	34%	31%	37%	74%	10%
In fraternity/sorority housing					
LESS THAN 1 PERCENT	75%	15%	67%	65%	98%
1-9 PERCENT	13%	54%	22%	8%	2%
10 PERCENT OR MORE	12%	31%	11%	28%	0%
Leave during or after first year					
LESS THAN 1 PERCENT	1%	2%	3%	2%	0%
1-9 PERCENT	10%	12%	6%	23%	5%
10-24 PERCENT	41%	57%	63%	49%	21%
25-49 PERCENT	41%	28%	22%	24%	62%
50 PERCENT OR MORE	7%	2%	6%	2%	12%
Black					
LESS THAN 5 PERCENT	46%	46%	38%	59%	44%
5-15 PERCENT	39%	53%	47%	37%	35%
MORE THAN 15 PERCENT	15%	1%	16%	4%	21%
Hispanic					
LESS THAN 1 PERCENT	15%	6%	11%	15%	19%
1-9 PERCENT	75%	89%	74%	81%	70%
10 PERCENT OR MORE	10%	5%	15%	4%	11%

Table B-2. *(continued)*

	All Institutions	Research & Doctorate-Granting	Comprehensive	Liberal Arts	Two-Year
Asian American					
LESS THAN 1 PERCENT	18%	8%	15%	19%	22%
1-9 PERCENT	79%	77%	83%	79%	77%
10 PERCENT OR MORE	3%	15%	2%	2%	1%
American Indian					
LESS THAN 1 PERCENT	42%	49%	45%	58%	32%
1-9 PERCENT	57%	51%	55%	42%	65%
10 PERCENT OR MORE	1%	0%	0%	0%	3%

Source: The American Council on Education and the National Association of Student Personnel Administrators, National Survey of Chief Student Affairs Officers, 1989.

Table B-3. Changes in Student Affairs Budget (Percentage Giving Each Repsonse)

	All Institutions	Research & Doctorate-Granting	Comprehensive	Liberal Arts	Two-Year
Budget changes over the past five years:					
Increases exceeding inflation	20%	27%	24%	32%	12%
Increases matching inflation	34%	43%	38%	26%	33%
Little or no change	33%	14%	24%	22%	46%
Budget cuts or reversions	13%	16%	14%	20%	9%

Source: The American Council on Education and the National Association of Student Personnel Administrators, National Survey of Chief Student Affairs Officers, 1989.

Table B-4. Rating of Quality of Campus Life (Percentage Giving Each Response)

	All Institutions	Research & Doctorate-Granting	Comprehensive	Liberal Arts	Two-Year
Campus life today is:					
Excellent	12%	20%	16%	14%	7%
Good	69%	65%	66%	73%	69%
Fair	19%	14%	17%	12%	23%
Poor	1%	1%	1%	1%	1%
Compared with five years ago:					
Better	58%	69%	69%	73%	45%
Largely the same	32%	23%	23%	21%	43%
Not as good	10%	8%	8%	7%	12%

Source: The American Council on Education and the National Association of Student Personnel Administrators, National Survey of Chief Student Affairs Officers, 1989.

Table B-5. Five-Year Change in Problems of Campus Life (Percentage Giving Each Response)

	All Institutions	Research & Doctorate-Granting	Comprehensive	Liberal Arts	Two-Year
Inadequate facilities for campus gatherings					
GREATER PROBLEM	42%	37%	41%	48%	40%
ABOUT THE SAME	30%	36%	29%	26%	32%
LESS OF A PROBLEM	11%	15%	12%	13%	8%
NOT A PROBLEM	17%	13%	19%	13%	19%
Inadequate facilities for commuter students					
GREATER PROBLEM	36%	29%	31%	40%	37%
ABOUT THE SAME	32%	45%	38%	40%	23%
LESS OF A PROBLEM	10%	9%	11%	9%	11%
NOT A PROBLEM	22%	17%	19%	12%	29%
Alcohol abuse					
GREATER PROBLEM	32%	50%	39%	40%	22%
ABOUT THE SAME	41%	34%	50%	36%	40%
LESS OF A PROBLEM	14%	14%	7%	18%	15%
NOT A PROBLEM	13%	3%	4%	6%	23%
Few students participate in campus events					
GREATER PROBLEM	29%	11%	26%	27%	35%
ABOUT THE SAME	47%	60%	45%	41%	48%
LESS OF A PROBLEM	15%	16%	23%	21%	7%
NOT A PROBLEM	9%	14%	6%	10%	10%
Inadequate services for commuter students					
GREATER PROBLEM	28%	24%	26%	38%	24%
ABOUT THE SAME	36%	49%	41%	35%	32%
LESS OF A PROBLEM	13%	11%	15%	13%	12%
NOT A PROBLEM	24%	16%	18%	15%	32%
Drug/substance abuse					
GREATER PROBLEM	25%	21%	33%	17%	25%
ABOUT THE SAME	45%	56%	51%	52%	37%
LESS OF A PROBLEM	14%	19%	12%	14%	14%
NOT A PROBLEM	16%	4%	4%	16%	25%

Table B-5. *(continued)*

	All Institutions	Research & Doctorate-Granting	Comprehensive	Liberal Arts	Two-Year
Overcrowded or outdated residence halls					
GREATER PROBLEM	25%	23%	32%	43%	9%
ABOUT THE SAME	23%	36%	12%	24%	26%
LESS OF A PROBLEM	14%	24%	24%	17%	3%
NOT A PROBLEM	38%	17%	32%	15%	62%
Thefts					
GREATER PROBLEM	22%	33%	27%	25%	17%
ABOUT THE SAME	56%	56%	56%	58%	55%
LESS OF A PROBLEM	9%	10%	11%	12%	7%
NOT A PROBLEM	13%	1%	6%	5%	21%
Violations of honor codes or rules of academic integrity					
GREATER PROBLEM	19%	22%	17%	29%	14%
ABOUT THE SAME	49%	74%	57%	53%	40%
LESS OF A PROBLEM	5%	1%	9%	5%	5%
NOT A PROBLEM	27%	3%	18%	13%	41%
Incidents involving physical violence					
GREATER PROBLEM	18%	34%	24%	21%	12%
ABOUT THE SAME	43%	52%	49%	32%	43%
LESS OF A PROBLEM	9%	11%	12%	16%	3%
NOT A PROBLEM	30%	3%	14%	31%	42%
Suicides and suicide attempts					
GREATER PROBLEM	17%	34%	28%	19%	8%
ABOUT THE SAME	44%	55%	47%	54%	37%
LESS OF A PROBLEM	9%	4%	9%	11%	8%
NOT A PROBLEM	30%	7%	16%	16%	47%
Inadequate security					
GREATER PROBLEM	17%	14%	17%	26%	14%
ABOUT THE SAME	35%	50%	29%	26%	40%
LESS OF A PROBLEM	18%	24%	27%	25%	8%
NOT A PROBLEM	30%	11%	27%	23%	38%

Table B-5. *(continued)*

	All Institutions	Research & Doctorate-Granting	Comprehensive	Liberal Arts	Two-Year
Vandalism and destruction of property					
GREATER PROBLEM	16%	20%	16%	17%	16%
ABOUT THE SAME	45%	53%	49%	39%	44%
LESS OF A PROBLEM	19%	25%	25%	30%	11%
NOT A PROBLEM	20%	2%	11%	14%	30%
Excessive noise and disruptiveness in campus residences					
GREATER PROBLEM	16%	9%	17%	27%	11%
ABOUT THE SAME	41%	70%	45%	50%	26%
LESS OF A PROBLEM	19%	17%	27%	19%	15%
NOT A PROBLEM	24%	4%	12%	4%	48%
Racial tensions/hostilities					
GREATER PROBLEM	16%	32%	17%	21%	11%
ABOUT THE SAME	35%	52%	45%	35%	27%
LESS OF A PROBLEM	15%	11%	11%	16%	18%
NOT A PROBLEM	34%	6%	27%	28%	44%
Disruptive behavior by nonstudents					
GREATER PROBLEM	16%	18%	19%	19%	14%
ABOUT THE SAME	30%	43%	30%	37%	25%
LESS OF A PROBLEM	8%	13%	13%	9%	5%
NOT A PROBLEM	45%	26%	37%	36%	57%
Poor academic advising					
GREATER PROBLEM	15%	22%	18%	12%	14%
ABOUT THE SAME	37%	53%	38%	44%	31%
LESS OF A PROBLEM	28%	20%	31%	28%	27%
NOT A PROBLEM	20%	5%	14%	15%	27%
Lack of civility when disputes arise					
GREATER PROBLEM	15%	23%	17%	25%	8%
ABOUT THE SAME	36%	55%	43%	36%	30%
LESS OF A PROBLEM	8%	6%	14%	9%	6%
NOT A PROBLEM	40%	16%	26%	30%	55%

Table B-5. *(continued)*

	All Institutions	Research & Doctorate-Granting	Comprehensive	Liberal Arts	Two-Year
Sexual harassment					
GREATER PROBLEM	14%	32%	17%	11%	12%
ABOUT THE SAME	50%	62%	57%	59%	42%
LESS OF A PROBLEM	9%	5%	11%	5%	10%
NOT A PROBLEM	26%	2%	15%	25%	36%
Racial intimidation/harassment					
GREATER PROBLEM	11%	24%	11%	13%	8%
ABOUT THE SAME	35%	57%	43%	38%	27%
LESS OF A PROBLEM	13%	13%	12%	15%	13%
NOT A PROBLEM	40%	7%	34%	34%	52%
Crude and offensive behavior at sports events					
GREATER PROBLEM	11%	13%	11%	14%	9%
ABOUT THE SAME	26%	49%	29%	33%	18%
LESS OF A PROBLEM	17%	19%	20%	19%	14%
NOT A PROBLEM	46%	19%	40%	34%	59%
Rape/sexual assault					
GREATER PROBLEM	10%	23%	15%	15%	4%
ABOUT THE SAME	40%	67%	53%	54%	22%
LESS OF A PROBLEM	10%	6%	12%	8%	11%
NOT A PROBLEM	40%	3%	20%	23%	63%
Incidents involving guns and other weapons					
GREATER PROBLEM	8%	7%	17%	7%	5%
ABOUT THE SAME	26%	52%	28%	29%	19%
LESS OF A PROBLEM	16%	13%	23%	9%	17%
NOT A PROBLEM	50%	28%	32%	55%	59%
Greek life problems					
GREATER PROBLEM	8%	28%	12%	10%	0%
ABOUT THE SAME	21%	41%	34%	23%	5%
LESS OF A PROBLEM	10%	25%	15%	11%	3%
NOT A PROBLEM	61%	6%	39%	55%	91%

Table B-5. *(continued)*

	All Institutions	Research & Doctorate-Granting	Comprehensive	Liberal Arts	Two-Year
Excessive drinking at sports events					
GREATER PROBLEM	5%	8%	6%	3%	4%
ABOUT THE SAME	19%	36%	22%	14%	17%
LESS OF A PROBLEM	17%	31%	23%	24%	9%
NOT A PROBLEM	59%	26%	50%	59%	70%
Disruptive behavior at commencement or convocation ceremonies					
GREATER PROBLEM	3%	9%	3%	6%	1%
ABOUT THE SAME	19%	25%	20%	23%	16%
LESS OF A PROBLEM	14%	33%	13%	11%	12%
NOT A PROBLEM	64%	33%	63%	60%	71%
Hazing incidents					
GREATER PROBLEM	3%	10%	4%	5%	0%
ABOUT THE SAME	18%	38%	29%	22%	6%
LESS OF A PROBLEM	21%	37%	35%	32%	5%
NOT A PROBLEM	58%	15%	33%	42%	89%
Disruptive protest demonstrations					
GREATER PROBLEM	1%	10%	1%	1%	0%
ABOUT THE SAME	13%	22%	13%	19%	9%
LESS OF A PROBLEM	15%	26%	24%	14%	8%
NOT A PROBLEM	71%	42%	61%	66%	83%
Other					
GREATER PROBLEM	63%	37%	69%	0%	0%
ABOUT THE SAME	37%	63%	31%	0%	0%
LESS OF A PROBLEM	0%	0%	0%	0%	0%
NOT A PROBLEM	0%	0%	0%	0%	0%

Source: The American Council on Education and the National Association of Student Personnel Administrators, National Survey of Chief Student Affairs Officers, 1989.

Table B-6. Five-year Change in Campus Crime (Percentage Giving Each Response)

	All Institutions	Research & Doctorate-Granting	Comprehensive	Liberal Arts	Two-Year
Number of reported crimes on campus					
INCREASE	26%	43%	35%	32%	16%
NO CHANGE	50%	31%	40%	45%	59%
DECREASE	15%	21%	16%	12%	15%
DON'T KNOW	9%	4%	9%	11%	10%
Severity of crimes on campus					
INCREASE	14%	20%	16%	14%	11%
NO CHANGE	63%	60%	60%	61%	65%
DECREASE	16%	16%	19%	21%	13%
DON'T KNOW	7%	4%	5%	3%	1%
Number of reported crimes in surrounding community					
INCREASE	50%	59%	54%	42%	49%
NO CHANGE	28%	19%	23%	30%	32%
DECREASE	3%	4%	4%	5%	1%
DON'T KNOW	19%	18%	19%	23%	17%
Severity of crimes in surrounding community					
INCREASE	41%	56%	46%	30%	41%
NO CHANGE	39%	23%	32%	46%	43%
DECREASE	3%	3%	4%	4%	3%
DON'T KNOW	17%	19%	18%	20%	14%

Source: The American Council on Education and the National Association of Student Personnel Administrators, National Survey of Chief Student Affairs Officers, 1989.

Table B-7. Five-Year Change in Violation of Institutional Rules (Percentage Giving Each Response)

	All Institutions	Research & Doctorate-Granting	Comprehensive	Liberal Arts	Two-Year
Campus residence halls:					
Number of violations					
INCREASE	26%	31%	27%	32%	18%
NO CHANGE	52%	59%	43%	43%	67%
DECREASE	19%	10%	29%	24%	10%
DON'T KNOW	2%	0%	1%	1%	5%
Severity of violations					
INCREASE	12%	15%	13%	16%	5%
NO CHANGE	67%	74%	65%	61%	73%
DECREASE	20%	11%	21%	22%	22%
DON'T KNOW	1%	0%	1%	1%	0%
Fraternity/sorority system:					
Number of violations					
INCREASE	17%	42%	13%	18%	5%
NO CHANGE	58%	42%	59%	49%	76%
DECREASE	18%	16%	19%	25%	9%
DON'T KNOW	7%	0%	9%	8%	10%
Severity of violations					
INCREASE	10%	20%	9%	10%	5%
NO CHANGE	65%	66%	66%	47%	80%
DECREASE	18%	14%	17%	33%	10%
DON'T KNOW	7%	0%	8%	10%	5%
Other campus settings:					
Number of violations					
INCREASE	13%	16%	17%	12%	11%
NO CHANGE	67%	72%	59%	63%	73%
DECREASE	14%	6%	19%	18%	11%
DON'T KNOW	6%	5%	5%	7%	5%
Severity of violations					
INCREASE	10%	13%	14%	11%	7%
NO CHANGE	68%	75%	66%	62%	71%
DECREASE	14%	8%	13%	16%	16%
DON'T KNOW	7%	3%	8%	11%	6%

Source: The American Council on Education and the National Association of Student Personnel Administrators, National Survey of Chief Student Affairs Officers, 1989.

Table B-8. Racial/Ethnic Incidents and Regulations of Student Conduct (Percentage Giving Each Response)

	All Institutions	Research & Doctorate-Granting	Comprehensive	Liberal Arts	Two-Year
Racial/ethnic incidents this year					
None	78%	50%	73%	76%	87%
One	12%	26%	16%	14%	6%
More than one	10%	24%	11%	9%	7%
Five-year change in racial/ethnic incidents					
Increase	15%	30%	15%	18%	12%
No change	73%	61%	76%	69%	74%
Decrease	12%	9%	9%	12%	14%
Five-year change in regulation of student conduct					
More explicit	54%	63%	55%	66%	48%
About the same	45%	37%	45%	31%	52%
Less explicit	1%	0%	0%	3%	0%
More systematic enforcement	54%	61%	65%	68%	40%
About the same	44%	38%	34%	27%	59%
Less systematic enforcement	2%	1%	1%	5%	1%
Campus has written policy on bigotry, racial harassment or intimidation					
Yes	60%	69%	61%	58%	59%
Is developing one	11%	18%	15%	14%	7%
No	29%	13%	24%	28%	34%

Source: The American Council on Education and the National Association of Student Personnel Administrators, National Survey of Chief Student Affairs Officers, 1989.

Table B-9. Changes in Student Orientation Programs (Percentage Giving Each Response)

	All Institutions	Research & Doctorate-Granting	Comprehensive	Liberal Arts	Two-Year
Program changes over the last five years:					
More time spent in orientation	59%	58%	62%	58%	58%
About the same	35%	40%	34%	31%	36%
Less now	6%	2%	4%	11%	6%
Broader coverage of issues	79%	86%	78%	84%	76%
About the same	19%	12%	21%	14%	21%
Narrower coverage of issues	3%	2%	1%	2%	4%

Source: The American Council on Education and the National Association of Student Personnel Administrators, National Survey of Chief Student Affairs Officers, 1989.

Table B-10. Five-Year Change in Concern About Campus Life (Percentage Giving Each Response)

	All Institutions	Research & Doctorate-Granting	Comprehensive	Liberal Arts	Two-Year
Concerns expressed by:					
Parents					
INCREASED CONCERN	45%	64%	66%	54%	26%
NO CHANGE	47%	30%	31%	39%	61%
DECREASED CONCERN	3%	2%	0%	2%	5%
DON'T KNOW	6%	3%	2%	4%	9%
Community representatives					
INCREASED CONCERN	41%	42%	58%	28%	39%
NO CHANGE	47%	51%	32%	46%	54%
DECREASED CONCERN	3%	2%	3%	4%	3%
DON'T KNOW	9%	4%	8%	21%	5%
Legislators					
INCREASED CONCERN	33%	43%	37%	20%	36%
NO CHANGE	48%	44%	46%	46%	50%
DECREASED CONCERN	2%	3%	1%	0%	4%
DON'T KNOW	16%	9%	16%	34%	10%

Table B-10. *(continued)*

	All Institutions	Research & Doctorate-Granting	Comprehensive	Liberal Arts	Two-Year
Alumni/ae					
INCREASED CONCERN	25%	39%	40%	32%	11%
NO CHANGE	62%	52%	51%	53%	74%
DECREASED CONCERN	3%	2%	1%	4%	3%
DON'T KNOW	11%	7%	7%	11%	13%
Donors					
INCREASED CONCERN	22%	32%	27%	35%	11%
NO CHANGE	56%	54%	52%	34%	70%
DECREASED CONCERN	1%	3%	1%	0%	1%
DON'T KNOW	20%	11%	20%	30%	18%

Source: The American Council on Education and the National Association of Student Personnel Administrators, National Survey of Chief Student Affairs Officers, 1989.

Table B-11. Views on Improving Campus Life (Percentage Giving Each Response)

	All Institutions	Research & Doctorate-Granting	Comprehensive	Liberal Arts	Two-Year
Greater effort to build a stronger overall sense of community					
VERY IMPORTANT	77%	81%	74%	92%	72%
SOMEWHAT IMPORTANT	21%	18%	23%	8%	27%
NOT IMPORTANT	1%	0%	3%	1%	1%
DON'T KNOW	0%	1%	0%	0%	0%
More interaction between students and faculty					
VERY IMPORTANT	75%	82%	74%	76%	74%
SOMEWHAT IMPORTANT	23%	16%	25%	23%	22%
NOT IMPORTANT	2%	1%	1%	0%	4%
DON'T KNOW	0%	0%	0%	0%	0%
Expanded services for nontraditional students					
VERY IMPORTANT	68%	66%	61%	61%	76%
SOMEWHAT IMPORTANT	27%	29%	33%	38%	19%
NOT IMPORTANT	4%	4%	6%	1%	5%
DON'T KNOW	0%	0%	0%	0%	0%

Table B-11. (continued)

	All Institutions	Research & Doctorate-Granting	Comprehensive	Liberal Arts	Two-Year
More events that affirm the institution's mission, objectives and values					
VERY IMPORTANT	67%	57%	72%	73%	63%
SOMEWHAT IMPORTANT	30%	40%	24%	24%	33%
NOT IMPORTANT	3%	3%	3%	3%	4%
DON'T KNOW	0%	1%	0%	0%	0%
Closer links between classroom and out-of-class activities					
VERY IMPORTANT	66%	69%	67%	71%	64%
SOMEWHAT IMPORTANT	27%	28%	29%	27%	25%
NOT IMPORTANT	7%	3%	2%	3%	11%
DON'T KNOW	0%	0%	1%	0%	0%
More collaborative learning among students					
VERY IMPORTANT	61%	49%	64%	59%	63%
SOMEWHAT IMPORTANT	34%	44%	28%	34%	36%
NOT IMPORTANT	4%	6%	9%	5%	1%
DON'T KNOW	1%	1%	0%	2%	0%
More leadership opportunities for students					
VERY IMPORTANT	60%	89%	66%	62%	52%
SOMEWHAT IMPORTANT	32%	11%	26%	34%	37%
NOT IMPORTANT	7%	0%	6%	2%	11%
DON'T KNOW	1%	0%	1%	2%	0%
Greater incentives for alcohol-free events					
VERY IMPORTANT	59%	63%	61%	62%	56%
SOMEWHAT IMPORTANT	34%	33%	37%	32%	34%
NOT IMPORTANT	6%	4%	2%	6%	9%
DON'T KNOW	1%	0%	0%	0%	1%
More events that bring large numbers of students, faculty and staff together					
VERY IMPORTANT	57%	41%	57%	62%	58%
SOMEWHAT IMPORTANT	36%	51%	38%	30%	35%
NOT IMPORTANT	7%	7%	4%	8%	7%
DON'T KNOW	0%	1%	0%	0%	0%

Table B-11. (continued)

	All Institutions	Research & Doctorate-Granting	Comprehensive	Liberal Arts	Two-Year
More aggressive programs to prevent alcohol and drug abuse					
VERY IMPORTANT	54%	41%	47%	44%	64%
SOMEWHAT IMPORTANT	36%	45%	45%	42%	27%
NOT IMPORTANT	10%	14%	8%	12%	9%
DON'T KNOW	0%	0%	0%	1%	0%
Workshops on conflict resolution					
VERY IMPORTANT	49%	50%	56%	55%	43%
SOMEWHAT IMPORTANT	35%	39%	36%	31%	35%
NOT IMPORTANT	15%	11%	8%	13%	19%
DON'T KNOW	1%	0%	0%	2%	2%
More explicit expectations for student behavior and responsibilities					
VERY IMPORTANT	44%	41%	50%	53%	37%
SOMEWHAT IMPORTANT	46%	49%	43%	36%	51%
NOT IMPORTANT	10%	10%	6%	9%	12%
DON'T KNOW	1%	0%	0%	3%	0%
Better orientation programs					
VERY IMPORTANT	38%	45%	38%	35%	39%
SOMEWHAT IMPORTANT	52%	45%	50%	55%	52%
NOT IMPORTANT	8%	7%	7%	4%	9%
DON'T KNOW	2%	3%	5%	5%	0%
Better campus communications					
VERY IMPORTANT	37%	38%	40%	38%	35%
SOMEWHAT IMPORTANT	47%	57%	47%	49%	44%
NOT IMPORTANT	15%	6%	12%	10%	20%
DON'T KNOW	1%	0%	1%	3%	0%
New or revised statements on civility and respect for others					
VERY IMPORTANT	33%	38%	39%	37%	28%
SOMEWHAT IMPORTANT	46%	50%	46%	46%	45%
NOT IMPORTANT	18%	13%	14%	13%	23%
DON'T KNOW	3%	0%	1%	4%	5%

Table B-11. (continued)

	All Institutions	Research & Doctorate-Granting	Comprehensive	Liberal Arts	Two-Year
Better enforcement of rules governing student behavior					
VERY IMPORTANT	32%	28%	32%	30%	33%
SOMEWHAT IMPORTANT	51%	54%	51%	59%	47%
NOT IMPORTANT	17%	17%	17%	11%	19%
DON'T KNOW	1%	0%	0%	0%	1%
Greater understanding and awareness of racial/ethnic diversity					
VERY IMPORTANT	27%	25%	31%	38%	21%
SOMEWHAT IMPORTANT	53%	58%	56%	53%	52%
NOT IMPORTANT	19%	17%	12%	8%	27%
DON'T KNOW	0%	0%	1%	1%	0%
Strengthened campus police and security					
VERY IMPORTANT	27%	21%	28%	39%	22%
SOMEWHAT IMPORTANT	46%	54%	47%	42%	45%
NOT IMPORTANT	26%	23%	24%	17%	31%
DON'T KNOW	1%	1%	1%	2%	1%
Better procedures for handling complaints and grievances					
VERY IMPORTANT	25%	30%	22%	30%	24%
SOMEWHAT IMPORTANT	52%	56%	55%	54%	49%
NOT IMPORTANT	20%	14%	19%	14%	25%
DON'T KNOW	2%	0%	4%	3%	1%
Other					
VERY IMPORTANT	100%	100%	100%	100%	100%
SOMEWHAT IMPORTANT	0%	0%	0%	0%	0%
NOT IMPORTANT	0%	0%	0%	0%	0%
DON'T KNOW	0%	0%	0%	0%	0%

Source: The American Council on Education and the National Association of Student Personnel Administrators, National Survey of Chief Student Affairs Officers, 1989.

Table B-12. "One Change" Student Affairs Officers Say They Would Make to Improve Campus Life (Percentage Listing Each Response)

All Institutions	Research & Doctorate-Granting	Comprehensive	Liberal Arts	Two-Year
Build or improve residences, student union or other campus facilities				
24%	16%	16%	21%	33%
Improve faculty/staff/student interaction				
16%	24%	14%	9%	19%
Increase funds for Student Affairs				
12%	3%	15%	15%	9%
Build sense of community for all				
5%	6%	3%	8%	4%
Build or improve recreation center				
5%	3%	7%	4%	6%
Improve student involvement				
5%	3%	4%	4%	8%
Improve ethics, values, standards, respect for authority				
5%	3%	3%	6%	5%
Reduce alcohol/drug consumption				
4%	7%	7%	5%	2%
Improve relations/increase diversity/retention—racial, religious				
4%	3%	10%	3%	2%
Required program (orientation/course) for freshmen; mentoring				
2%	9%	3%	0%	2%
Improve academic advising				
2%	2%	5%	2%	0%
Give Student Affairs greater voice				
2%	2%	0%	3%	2%
More support and interest by president				
2%	2%	0%	2%	4%
Build or improve athletic facilities				
2%	1%	4%	0%	2%
More focus on activities for older students and off-campus students				
2%	0%	0%	3%	2%
Stress concern for "whole student"				
1%	5%	0%	3%	0%

Table B-12. (continued)

All Institutions	Research & Doctorate-Granting	Comprehensive	Liberal Arts	Two-Year
Reduce effects of and change Greek system				
1%	3%	2%	3%	0%
More student housing/assistance				
1%	2%	2%	2%	0%
Strengthen security				
1%	2%	0%	3%	0%
Improve faculty retention				
1%	0%	0%	3%	0%
More social activities				
1%	0%	0%	0%	2%
Less territoriality				
0%	2%	0%	0%	0%
Parking				
0%	2%	0%	0%	0%
Eliminate deferred maintenance in residence halls				
0%	2%	0%	0%	0%
More emphasis on teaching; less on research				
0%	2%	0%	0%	0%
Fill out fewer questionnaires				
0%	0%	2%	0%	0%
Increase campus population				
0%	0%	2%	0%	0%
Increase library hours				
0%	0%	2%	0%	0%
Stricter conduct code for faculty				
0%	0%	0%	1%	0%
Emphasis on student leadership				
0%	0%	0%	0%	0%
Increase night life off campus for students				
0%	0%	0%	0%	0%

Note: The open-ended question read: "If you could make one change at your institution to improve the quality of campus life, what change would you make?"

Source: The American Council on Education and the National Association of Student Personnel Administrators, National Survey of Chief Student Affairs Officers, 1989.

TECHNICAL NOTES

The Carnegie Foundation for the Advancement of Teaching and the American Council on Education jointly conducted the National Survey of College and University Presidents. The National Survey of Chief Student Affairs Officers was administered by the American Council on Education and the National Association of Student Personnel Administrators. Both of these surveys on the quality of campus life were completed in 1989.

The institutional population from which the study's sample was drawn is a modification of that found in The Carnegie Foundation for the Advancement of Teaching's *A Classification of Institutions of Higher Learning*, 1987 edition. This list of institutions was chosen because it provided a degree of differentiation for universities and for liberal arts colleges. Furthermore, the classification system proposed by the U.S. Department of Education in the early 1980s that paralleled to some degree the Carnegie system was never updated.

The Carnegie list was matched with data from the most recent institutional data from the Department of Education, the 1987-88 Institutional Characteristics File. Institutions on the Carnegie file that did not appear on the Department of Education's file were traced to learn if they had changed their name, merged with other institutions, changed accreditation status, or closed.

It was assumed that the primary thrust of the survey was to look at life on campus as it is experienced by most undergraduate students. It was therefore decided to eliminate graduate-only institutions, specialized institutions (such as schools of religion and theology, medicine, law, teacher education, engineering and technology, business and management, art, music and design), and institutions of less than 300 enrollment as reported on the Department of Education's 1987-88 computer tape of institutional characteristics.

These procedures netted a population of 2,540 institutions. From this total, 19 institutions were eliminated because they were to participate in the site visit portion of the survey. Their willingness to undergo the close scrutiny of the visitors was deemed to be a sufficient contribution to the study. Two additional institutions were found to have been closed. Thus, the survey's population consists of a total of 2,519 colleges and universities with undergraduate programs and with total enrollments of 300 or more students.

For sampling purposes, it was decided to adjust the Carnegie classification categories somewhat. Consequently, the four categories of major universities (Research Universities I and II, and Doctorate-granting Universities and Colleges I and II) were consolidated into two strata, research universities and doctorate-granting universities. The two categories of Comprehensive Universities and Colleges were combined into one. However, the two liberal arts college categories remain separate, and all the two-year institutions remained in a single stratum.

Responses were received from 382 institutions in the National Survey of College and University Presidents (including 105 research and doctorate-granting institutions, 76 comprehensive institutions, 112 liberal arts institutions and 89 two-year colleges) representing a 76 percent response rate. In the National Survey of Chief Student Affairs Officers, 355 institutions responded (including 95 research and doctorate-granting institutions, 82 comprehensive institutions, 102 liberal arts institutions, and 76 two-year colleges), resulting in a 71 percent response rate. All data is weighted. *Some figures in the tables may not add up to 100 percent due to rounding.*

A few questions on the survey instruments were constructed to elicit an open-ended response. For example, presidents were asked, "During 1988-89, what three campus-life issues on your campus have given you the greatest concern?" The responses to these questions were grouped and coded by the survey administrators.

A third survey, The Carnegie Foundation for the Advancement of Teaching's 1989 National Survey of Faculty, is mentioned periodically. This questionnaire was mailed to 10,000 faculty at two-year and four-year institutions. Responses were received from 5,450.

CARNEGIE CLASSIFICATIONS

The 1987 Carnegie Classification includes all colleges and universities in the United States listed in the 1985-86 *Higher Education General Information Survey of Institutional Characteristics*. It groups institutions into categories on the basis of the level of degree offered—ranging from prebaccalaureate to the doctorate—and the comprehensiveness of their missions. The categories are as follows:

Research Universities I: These institutions offer a full range of baccalaureate programs, are committed to graduate education through the doctorate degree, and give high priority to research. They receive annually at least $33.5 million in federal support and awarded at least 50 Ph.D. degrees each year.

Research Universities II: These institutions offer a full range of baccalaureate programs, are committed to graduate education through the doctorate degree, and give high priority to research. They receive annually at least $12.5 million in federal support and awarded at least 50 Ph.D. degrees each year.

Doctorate-granting Universities I: In addition to offering a full range of baccalaureate programs, the mission of these institutions includes a commitment to graduate education through the doctorate degree. They award at least 40 Ph.D. degrees annually in five or more academic disciplines.

Doctorate-granting Universities II: In addition to offering a full range of baccalaureate programs, the mission of these institutions includes a commitment to graduate education through the doctorate degree. They award annually 20 or more Ph.D. degrees in at least one discipline or 10 or more Ph.D. degrees in three or more disciplines.

Comprehensive Universities and Colleges I: These institutions offer baccalaureate programs and, with few exceptions, graduate education through the master's degree. More than half of their baccalaureate degrees are awarded in two or more occupational or professional disciplines such as engineering or business administration. All of the institutions in this group enroll at least 2,500 students.

Comprehensive Universities and Colleges II: These institutions award more than half of their baccalaureate degrees in two or more occupational or professional disciplines, such as engineering or business administration, and many also offer graduate education through the master's degree. All of the institutions in this group enroll between 1,500 and 2,500 students.

Liberal Arts Colleges I: These highly selective institutions are primarily undergraduate colleges that award more than half of their baccalaureate degrees in art and science fields.

Liberal Arts Colleges II: These institutions are primarily undergraduate colleges that are less selective and award more than half of their degrees in liberal arts fields. This category also includes a group of colleges that award less than half of their degrees in liberal arts fields but, with fewer than 1,500 students, are too small to be considered comprehensive.

Two-Year Community, Junior, and Technical Colleges: These institutions offer certificate or degree programs through the Associate of Arts level and, with few exceptions, offer no baccalaureate degrees.

DISCUSSION GUIDE

FOREWORD AND PROLOGUE

1. How would you describe the overall health of the community on your campus? What factors contribute to its health? What factors detract from its health?

2. How is tradition defined on your campus? In what way(s), if any, do campus traditions contribute to the health of community on your campus? Detract from the health of your campus?

3. What social forces contribute to the health of community on your campus? Detract from the health of community on your campus?

4. How has the fabric of community on your campus changed, if at all, in recent years? Over the course of decades? The 1980s? The 1990s? The 2000s?

5. In what way(s), if at all, have the expectations of students coming to your campus changed over the years in relation to campus community? Administrators? Faculty members?

6. In what way(s), if at all, does your campus think about the fabric of its community as an extension of its Christian mission?

CHAPTER ONE

1. How do you define purpose? Your colleagues? Your students? What points of overlap, if any, exist between how those groups define purpose? What gaps, if any, exist?

2. In relation to your particular campus, how, if at all, is purpose communicated? Cultivated? Reinforced?

3. In relation to your particular campus, who, if anyone, is responsible for leading efforts to define purpose? Communicate it? Cultivate it? Reinforce it?

4. What distinctive qualities of purpose define your campus? In comparison to your peer institutions? Aspirant institutions?

5. In your estimation, do any of those qualities reinforce one another? Contradict one another?

6. What role do you implicitly and/or explicitly play in defining those qualities? Communicating those qualities? Reinforcing those qualities?

CHAPTER TWO

1. How is openness defined on your campus? How did you learn that definition? Is that definition clear?

2. How do students on your campus define openness? How do they learn that definition? Is that definition clear to them?

3. What responsibility or responsibilities do individual members on your campus have in relation to the cultivation of openness? Members of that community as a whole?

4. What limits, if any, exist to openness on your campus? If there are limits, how are perceptions of them communicated? Cultivated? Reinforced?

5. By their nature, are theological commitments and openness complementary to one another? Contradictory to one another?

6. At the present time, what topics provide the greatest opportunity to cultivate the spirit of openness on your campus? Challenge that spirit?

CHAPTER THREE

1. How do you define justice? In what way(s) is your definition different from and/or in harmony with other definitions on campus?

2. In recent years, has your definition, if at all, changed? In recent years, have other definitions changed?

3. In what way(s), if any, are those definitions of justice drawn from the Christian mission of the campus? Detract from the Christian mission of the campus?

4. Do any particular topics being discussed on campus demand more than other topics that a definition of justice be part of the discussion? If so, can the definition(s) of justice operative on campus sustain interaction with those topics?

5. Are curricular and cocurricular educators offered sufficient professional development opportunities in relation to how they understand justice?

6. Do all groups that make up your campus community experience the same definition of justice? If so, how? If not, why not?

CHAPTER FOUR

1. What characteristics define how discipline is understood on your campus? In what ways, if any, do those characteristics differ among students? Faculty members? Administrators?

2. In what way(s) do those characteristics compare with the Christian mission of your campus? Do they complement it? Diverge from it?

3. How do new members of your community learn those characteristics? Who leads those efforts for students? Faculty members? Administrators?

4. What, if any, are the greatest challenges to the spirit of discipline on your campus among students? Faculty members? Administrators?

5. How does one know when that process goes well? How does one know when that process has gone awry? When that process has gone awry, what means are available to rectify the situation? For students? Faculty members? Administrators?

CHAPTER FIVE

1. How do you define care? How does your definition of care compare with the one(s) defined by your colleagues?

2. Does your campus communicate (implicitly and/or explicitly) an understanding of care? If so, how, if at all, is it derived from the Christian mission of your campus?

3. What responsibility, if any, do you have to care for your colleagues? Your students? What, if any, are the limits of that responsibility to care?

4. In relation to your students, what, if any, are the most common reasons one may be called to exercise a measure of care?

5. In relation to your colleagues, what, if any, are the most common reasons one may be called to exercise a measure of care?

CHAPTER SIX

1. In an academic context, what does it mean for a community to be celebrative? A Christian academic context?

2. Does your community possess a common understanding of what efforts, achievements, and so on are worthy of celebration? By students? Faculty members? Administrators?

3. If your campus does possess a common understanding of what efforts, achievements, and so on are worthy of celebration, who on campus identifies them? Initiates relevant forms of celebration?

4. What internal forces, if any, hinder your campus from being a celebrative community? What, if anything, can be done to address those forces?

5. What external forces, if any, hinder your campus from being a celebrative community? What, if anything, can be done to address those forces?

6. What efforts, achievements, and so on, if any, need to be added to the ones your community recognizes as worthy of celebration?

EPILOGUE

1. In what way(s), if at all, should new members of the community (students, administrators, faculty members, etc.) be expected to learn about the fabric of community that defines your campus? Contribute to it? Not detract from it?

2. What educational programs contribute to that learning process? Who, if anyone, is charged with leading that process?

3. Looking to the future, what do you perceive to be the greatest opportunities in terms of the fabric of community on your campus? In what way(s), if at all, is your campus preparing to capitalize on those opportunities?

4. Looking to the future, what do you perceive to be the greatest threats to the fabric of community on your campus? In what way(s), if at all, is your campus preparing to address those threats?

5. What responsibility, if any, do more long-standing members of your campus (e.g., students who are juniors and seniors, associate and full professors, administrators with greater numbers of years of service) have in relation to the cultivation of the fabric of community?

6. Is the fabric of community part of your campus's strategic plan? If so, in what way(s)?

7. If not, do you think the fabric of community should be part of your campus's strategic plan? If so, in what way(s)?

CONTRIBUTORS

Randall Basinger is the provost at Messiah College. In 1983 he joined the faculty of Messiah College as a professor of philosophy. He has served as dean of curriculum and has been the provost of Messiah College since 2005. Randall coauthored *Philosophy and Miracle: The Contemporary Debate* (with David Basinger) and coedited *Predestination and Free Will* (with David Basinger). He has written articles for various publications, including *Christian Scholar's Review* and *Religious Studies.*

Stephen T. Beers is the vice president for student development and associate professor of higher education at John Brown University. Previously he served at Taylor University and Northwestern College (Iowa). Steve has served as the president of the Association of Christians in Student Development and as the chair of the Student Development Commission for the Council for Christians Colleges and Universities. He is the editor of *The Soul of the Christian University* and coeditor of *Funding the Future* and *Making A Difference.* Steve continues to write and speak on issues pertaining to Christian higher education.

David Brooks became an op-ed columnist for the *New York Times* in September 2003, where his work appears every Tuesday and Friday. He is currently a commentator on PBS *NewsHour*, NPR's *All Things Considered*, and NBC's *Meet the Press.* He is the author of *The Road to Character, The Social Animal: The Hidden Sources of Love, Character, and Achievement, Bobos in Paradise: The New Upper Class and How They Got There*, and *On Paradise Drive: How We Live Now (and Always Have) in the Future Tense.* David also teaches at Yale University and is a member of the American Academy of Arts and Sciences.

Paul O. Chelsen began his career in student development twenty-six years ago as a residence director at Coe College and then at North Central College (Illinois), respectively. As the assistant director of student development at the University of Illinois, Chicago, Paul facilitated leadership programming and advised student government. Next, he served as the director of residence life and housing at Wheaton College (Illinois) before being appointed as the vice president for student development at Wheaton with responsibility over athletics, graduate student life, residence life, student care, student engagement, and student publications.

Margaret Diddams is provost and professor of psychology at Wheaton College, where she has oversight of the Academic Affairs Division and serves on the senior administrative cabinet. As an industrial/organizational psychologist her areas of scholarship and practice are transformational leadership development, team building, the meaning of work, healthy vacations, and statistical analysis. Her scholarship can be found in *Leadership Quarterly*, *Academy of Management Review*, and the *Journal of Psychology and Theology*. She considers it a joy and privilege to work with the faculty, staff, and students of Wheaton College.

Edward Ericson III serves as the vice president for academic affairs at John Brown University, where he supervises undergraduate, degree completion, and graduate programs as well as the library, registrar, academic support services, distance learning, and institutional research. Ericson came to JBU in 1994 as an instructor of history, specializing in diplomatic and military history, and is known for his use of historical simulations as learning tools. He has since served as head of the History/Political Science Department, chair of the Division of Social and Behavior Studies, associate dean of Undergraduate Studies, and the dean of Undergraduate Studies. Prior to coming to JBU, he was an instructor of history at Calvin College. Ericson has served in a number of prominent national roles with the National Conference of Academic Deans, the American Academic Leadership Institute, the Council of Independent Colleges, and the Council of Christian Colleges and Universities.

Kris Hansen-Kieffer is the vice provost/dean of students at Messiah College. Kris is currently also an assistant professor of exercise science and has previously held the position of director of academic advising. She has coached volleyball and worked as a residence director at other institutions. Kris has chaired the Master's in Higher Education committee at Messiah College and has also consulted and presented on assessment. She led her team in hosting the Association for Christians in Student Development conference at Messiah College in 2010 and recently served as the organization's president. Her research and publications focus on assessment, wellness, and healthy body image for women.

Brad Lau has served as vice president for student life at George Fox University since 2000. He oversees a wide range of programs including residence life, health and counseling, spiritual life, intercultural life, campus safety, intercollegiate athletics, campus recreation, and student leadership. Prior to coming to George Fox, Brad served in various administrative roles at institutions in Pennsylvania, Kansas, Colorado, and Virginia. Further, Brad has served as president of the Association for Christians in Student Development and as chair of the Student Development Commission for the Council for Christian Colleges and Universities. He contributes to a variety of publications, including *Christian Higher Education* and *Christian Scholar's Review.*

Drew Moser is dean of student engagement and associate professor of higher education and student development at Taylor University in Upland, Indiana. He is the lead editor of *Scholarship Reconsidered: Priorities of the Professoriate*, expanded edition (Jossey-Bass, 2016), and coauthor *of Ready or Not: Leaning into Life in Our Twenties* (NavPress, 2018). He serves as the scholarship chair on the executive committee of the Association for Christians in Student Development, a guest mentor for the EDGE Mentoring Network, an affiliate consultant for CREDO, and is a board member of Lemonade International. He lives in Upland, Indiana, with his wife and five children. Follow his work at www.drewmoser.com.

Doretha O'Quinn is the provost and vice president for academic affairs at Vanguard University and an ordained minister in the International Church of the Foursquare Gospel. Previously, she served as an administrator and as a faculty member at Biola University, Point Loma Nazarene University, and Azusa Pacific University. She has also served as a K-12 principal and teacher. She is the author of *Silent Voices, Powerful Messages* and is a contributing author to *Mothers Are Leaders, Our Voices: Issues Facing Black Women in America, Alone in Marriage, Women in Ministry Leadership*, and educational journals such as *Urban Education* and *Women in Ministry.* Her international travel involves leadership development of government officials, NGO leaders, and expatriates in East, West, and South Africa, Indonesia, China, Martinique, and other countries around the world.

Todd C. Ream is professor of higher education at Taylor University, senior fellow with the Lumen Research Institute, and publisher for *Christian Scholar's Review.* Previously he served on college and university campuses in residence life, student support services, honors programs, and as a chief student development officer. He is the author and editor of numerous books and contributes to a wide variety of publications, including *About Campus, Christianity Today, First Things, Gastronomica, Inside Higher Ed, Modern Theology, New Blackfriars, Notre Dame Magazine, The Review of Higher Education*, and *Teachers College Record.* He is presently working on a series of books concerning Theodore M. Hesburgh, CSC.

Linda Samek is the provost and chief academic officer at George Fox University, where she has been a faculty member and an administrator for fourteen years. Prior to this role as provost, she was dean of the College of Education and a teacher educator specializing in mathematics education and middle grades teacher preparation. Linda's most recent publication is the edited volume *Imagine a Place: Stories from Middle Grades Educators*. Through work with teachers and activists in several developing countries, Linda has learned that cultural humility is an essential skill across all facets of life. She also finds that humility is critical for her work as a senior administrator.

Mark L. Sargent is the provost and dean of the faculty at Westmont College in California. Previously, he served as provost at Gordon College and Spring Arbor University. A former Fulbright scholar at the University of Utrecht in the Netherlands, he has taught or consulted in over twenty-five countries. Sargent was awarded the National Chief Academic Officers Award from the Council of Independent Colleges and the Whitehill Award in Early American History for his research. He has served in several roles for the Council of Christian Colleges and Universities.

Edee Schulze serves as the vice president for student life at Westmont College with prior experience at Bethel University (Minnesota) and Wheaton College (Illinois). For over thirty years, she has been passionate about creating environments where students can thrive as whole persons. Schulze has been an active leader in several national organizations, including the Association for Christians in Student Development and the Council for Christian Colleges and Universities.

Beck A. Taylor is the president of Whitworth University. He came to Whitworth after serving as dean and professor of economics for the Brock School of Business at Samford University and as associate dean for research and faculty development for the Hankamer School of Business at Baylor University, where he was also the W. H. Smith Professor of Economics. In his first year as Whitworth's president, Taylor led the development of Whitworth's ten-year vision and strategic plan, Whitworth 2021: Courage at the Crossroads, which details plans to continue to elevate Whitworth among the leading Christian universities in the country.

Tim Young is the vice president for student affairs at Vanguard University. Since 2012 Young has provided strategic leadership for various campus operations, including facilities operations, auxiliary services, campus public safety, environmental health and safety, and campus construction and planning. Previously, he served at Vanguard in residence life and as a school counselor in a variety of districts in Southern California. He is also the founder and president of the Joshua Foundation, an organization focused on the support of Christian mentoring ministries and the implementation of spiritual formation groups designed to develop Christian leaders.

INDEX